The <u>Stolen</u> Pinkerton Reports of the Colonel Albert J. Fountain Murder Investigation

First Edition

David G. Thomas, Editor

Mesilla Valley History Series, Vol 6

Copyright © 2020 by Doc45 Publishing

All Rights Reserved

This book, or parts thereof, may not be reproduced in any form, including information storage and retrieval systems, without explicit permission from Doc45 Publishing, except for brief quotations included in articles and reviews.

Doc45 Publishing, P. O. Box 5044, Las Cruces, N. M. 88003
books@doc45.com

To obtain books, visit:
doc45.com

YouTube Channel
youtube.com/c/Doc45Publications

Cover artwork by Dusan Arsenic.

ISBN 978-0-9828709-6-9

DOC45 PUBLISHING

Dedicated To

Friends of Pat Garrett

friendsofpatgarrett.com

Mesilla Valley History Series

La Posta – From the Founding of Mesilla, to Corn Exchange Hotel, to Billy the Kid Museum, to Famous Landmark – by David G. Thomas

Giovanni Maria de Agostini, Wonder of The Century – The Astonishing World Traveler Who Was A Hermit – by David G. Thomas

Screen with a Voice – A History of Moving Pictures in Las Cruces, New Mexico – by David G. Thomas

Billy the Kid's Grave – A History of the Wild West's Most Famous Death Marker – by David G. Thomas

Killing Garrett, The Wild West's Most Famous Lawman – Murder or Self-Defense? – by David G. Thomas

The Stolen Pinkerton Reports of Colonel Albert J. Fountain Investigation — David G. Thomas, Editor

Mesilla Valley Reprints

When New Mexico Was Young – by Harry H. Bailey

Doc 45

Buenas noches boys,
A social call no doubt –
Do we talk it over,
Or do we shoot it out?

I'm Doc 45,
Toughest man alive.
Hand over those golden bills
Or I'll dose you up with dirty leaden pills.

Contents

Table of Contents

Acknowledgments	vi
Preface	vii
1. Introduction	1
2. Fraser Assigned	29
3. Fraser Investigates	41
4. Status And Recommendations	109
5. Sayers Investigates	117
6. The Trial	173
Appendix A – Albert J. Fountain Affidavit	177
Notes	179
Index	181

List of Images

1.	Colonel Albert J. Fountain	viii
2.	Mariana (Contreras Pérez de Onate) Fountain, Colonel Fountain's Wife	2
3.	Henry J. Fountain, Maria de Jesus Pérez, and Tomas Pérez	3
4.	David M. Sutherland's House in La Luz	4
5.	Oliver Milton Lee's Dog Canyon Ranch House	4
6.	Oliver Milton Lee	5
7.	James R. "Jim" Gililland	6
8.	Map of Routes Taken by the Fountain Posses	8
9.	Chalk Hill Site Where the Fountains Were Ambushed	10
10.	Satellite Image of Chalk Hill	10
11.	Ruins of Luna's Well	11
12.	Patrick Floyd Jarvis Garrett	12
13.	John Conklin Fraser, Pinkerton Operative	12
14.	"Duplicate" Copy of Operative Fraser's First Reports	14
15.	Katherine Stoes	16
16.	Attorney Albert B. Fall	16
17.	Ely E. "Slick" Miller	18
18.	Dona Ana Courthouse Officials	20
19.	New Mexico Territorial Penitentiary	20
20.	Ruins of Eduard W. Brown's Ranch House	22
21.	John "Jack" W. Maxwell	24
22.	Major William Henry H. Llewellyn	24
23.	Attorney Simon B. Newcomb	24
24.	Judge John Robert McFie	24
25.	Charles C. Perry	26
26.	Susan Ellen McSween Barber	26
27.	Major Eugene Van Patten	28
28.	Hillsboro at the Time of the Fountain Murder Trial	174

Acknowledgments

I thank Karl Laumbach, Human Systems Research, Inc. (HSR), for showing me to the Chalk Hill site where Colonel Fountain and Henry were ambushed, and discussing numerous still-baffling aspects of the case with me. I thank Dan Aranda, Dan Crow, and Lucinda Allshouse for proofing the manuscript and making corrections and suggestions.

Special thanks to the many who provided source materials and invaluable help in my research efforts: Dennis Daily and Elizabeth Villa, Library Archives & Special Collections, NMSU; Evan Davies, Institute of Historical Survey Foundation; Karl Laumbach, Human Systems Research, Inc.; Gail Packard and Dena Hunt, State Archives of New Mexico; Gerry Veara, White Sands Missile Range Museum Archives; Abbie H. Weiser, and Anne M. Allis, C. L. Sonnichsen Special Collections, UTEP; Whitney Hamm, Special Collections, MSSU; Loretta Deaver, Manuscript Division, Library of Congress; John LeMay and Janice Dunnahoo, Historical Society For Southeast New Mexico (HSSNM).

Preface

The abduction and apparent murder of Colonel Albert J. and Henry Fountain on February 1, 1896, shocked and outraged the citizens of New Mexico. It was not the killing of Colonel Fountain, a Union Civil War veteran and a prominent New Mexico attorney, which roused the physical disgust of the citizenry – after all, it was not unknown for distinguished men to be killed. It was the cold-blooded murder of his eight-year-old son which provoked the public outcry and revulsion.

The evidence indicated that although Colonel Albert J. Fountain was killed during the ambush, his son was taken alive, and only killed the next day.

The public was left without answers to the questions:

- Who ambushed and killed Colonel Fountain?
- Who was willing to kill his young son in cold-blood after holding him captive for twenty-four hours?

The case was never solved. Two men were eventually tried for and acquitted of the crime (see Chapter 6 for a discussion of the trial).

The case file for the crime contains almost no information. There are no trial transcripts or witness testimonies. The only reports that exist today of the investigation of the case are these Pinkerton Reports, which were commissioned by the Territorial Governor, and then stolen from his office four months after the murders. These Reports, now recovered, are published here.

These Reports are important historical documents, not only for what they reveal about the Fountain murders, but also as a fascinating window into how the most famous professional detective agency in the United States in the 1890s – the Pinkerton Detective Agency – went about investigating a murder, at a time when scientific forensic evidence was virtually non-existent.

The two Pinkerton Operatives sent to investigate the crime were John Conklin Fraser and William C. Sayers, the Agency's most competent detectives. Their investigative methods revolved around taking witness and suspect statements, and then working to verify what they were told, a process that remains at the heart of criminal investigation today.

As of the date of this writing, the Dona Ana County Sheriff's Office has reclassified the murders as an Active Case.

The text of the Reports presented here is based on the copy of the Reports in the Katherine D. Stoes Papers, Archives and Special Collections, New Mexico State University, supplemented by material from the Arrell Gibson Collection, Archives and Special Collections, Missouri Southern State University. I have modernized the punctuation and paragraphing of the Reports.

Colonel Albert J. Fountain. Undated photo. Courtesy Archives and Special Collections, NMSU.

Chapter 1 | Introduction

The Fountain Murders

Colonel Albert J. Fountain and his son Henry disappeared and were apparently killed February 1, 1896. Colonel Fountain was a Union Civil War veteran, an eminent New Mexico lawyer, and the staff attorney and lead investigator for the Southeastern New Mexico Stock Growers' Association. He had been aggressively pursuing a campaign against rustlers in Southern New Mexico.

The Association was formed March 12, 1894. The mission of the Association was to track down and convict livestock thieves in Lincoln, Socorro, Dona Ana, and Chaves, Counties.[1] At the July 7, 1894, meeting of the Association, Colonel Fountain reported to the membership that:

"...progress had been made in detecting and breaking up a well-organized and most dangerous gang of cattle thieves operating in Southern New Mexico on a large scale."

"Large numbers of the stolen cattle have been traced from the place of theft to the place of sale, and sufficient evidence obtained of these illegal transactions to secure the indictment and conviction of the guilty parties."

"a large number of prosecutions... have been instituted and others will follow. It was shown that the number of cattle known to have been stolen by the parties accused to exceed two thousand head." [2]

In recognition of his efforts, the Association tendered a vote of thanks:

"...to Col. A. J. Fountain, the association attorney, for the zeal and ability manifested by him in protecting the interests of the association in the successful prosecution of cattle thieves." [3]

The Association held its first annual meeting March 2, 1895. In the annual report to the members, the Association reported triumphantly that Colonel Fountain had secured convictions for 15 livestock thieves. Called out in the report were six "notorious" cases:

- "Slick" Miller, convicted at Roswell, received a term of ten years (convicted on 11 counts of larceny)
- Aberan (Abram) Miller, convicted at Roswell, received a term of ten years
- Juan Bernal, convicted at Lincoln, received a term of nine years
- Henry Brown, convicted at Socorro, received a term of five years
- "Doc" Evans, convicted at Roswell, received a term of two years
- George Craig, convicted at Lincoln, received a term of one year [4]

A seventh person, Ed (Eduard) Brown, who Colonel Fountain had indicted successfully, had *"gone on the run"* while out on bond.[5]

Both "Slick" Miller and Ed Brown appear prominently in the Pinkerton Reports.

Mariana (Contreras Pérez de Onate) Fountain, Colonel Fountain's wife. Painting. Courtesy Archives and Special Collections, NMSU.

Henry J. Fountain, Maria de Jesus Pérez (Mariana's mother), and Tomas Pérez (left to right). Undated photo. Henry is wearing a "waist," just as he was when he was abducted (see page 51). Courtesy Archives and Special Collections, NMSU.

David M. Sutherland house in La Luz where Colonel Fountain and Henry spent their last night (January 31, 1896) before disappearing. 2007 photo.

Oliver Milton Lee's Dog Canyon Ranch house, circa 1936. Courtesy Archives and Special Collections, NMSU.

Oliver Milton Lee. It is said that Lee always carried a side-arm, even after his election to the New Mexico Senate. Undated photo. Courtesy Center for Southwest Research and Special Collections, UNM.

James R. "Jim" Gililland, shortly before he died August 8, 1946. Courtesy Center for Southwest Research and Special Collections, UNM.

The Association reported also that it was responsible for:

"...the new brand law passed by the last legislature, which revises and alters the entire system of brands and marks in the territory. It prohibits the recording of more than one brand in the future by any man, company, or corporation... in fact, it carries into effect the 'one man, one brand' idea." [6]

By early January, 1896, Colonel Fountain had the evidence needed to indict another batch of men for rustling. On January 12, he and his eight-year-old son Henry left for the county courthouse in Lincoln, New Mexico, to place his evidence before a grand jury.[7]

Colonel Fountain was well aware that he had a risky job, that the men he was pursuing were capable of extreme violence. He had received many examples of this since taking the Association job:

"I was anonymously notified that if I attempted to prosecute these parties I would be killed. Of course I paid no attention to these threats." (See full letter on page 38) [8]

It was this self-evident danger that had induced Colonel Fountain's wife Mariana to convince Colonel Fountain to take his son with him on his trip to Lincoln. She believed that the presence of her youngest son would prevent any violence directed at Colonel Fountain.[9]

On January 21, Colonel Fountain secured indictments against 23 men for "larceny of cattle" and "brand defacing." Among the men indicted were two who will appear repeatedly in the Pinkerton Reports: Oliver Milton Lee and William McNew. Lee was indicted for brand defacing; McNew for larceny of cattle.[10]

On the last day of the court session, as Colonel Fountain stepped out of the front door of the courthouse, a man who he did not recognize came up to him and handed him a folded sheet of paper. When Colonel Fountain unfolded the paper, he read:

"If you drop this [to the ground], Fountain, we will be your friends. If you go on with it you will never reach home alive." [11]

This kind of note, known as a "coffin notice," was common at the time in management-labor disputes in the mining industry.

Ignoring the note and its lethal implications, Colonel Fountain started immediately for his home in Las Cruces. That day, January 28, he made about 50 miles, spending the night at Blazer's Mill, a site famous for the killing of "Buckshot" Roberts during the infamous Lincoln County Wars. He discussed his grand jury appearance in Lincoln with the mill's owner, Doctor Joseph F. Blazer. Blazer later testified in court that:

"[Fountain said] he had secured indictments against a gang of cattle thieves, and he had enough evidence to convict and send them to the penitentiary, if they did not succeed in making away either with him or his witnesses." [12]

Colonel Fountain also told Doctor Blazer that he had been followed all day by two men on horseback. The men had stayed just far enough away to be unrecognizable.[13]

The second night Colonel Fountain and Henry stayed with William P. Shields at his home near the town of Tularosa.[14] The third night they stayed with a friend in the small village of La Luz.[15]

Chapter 1

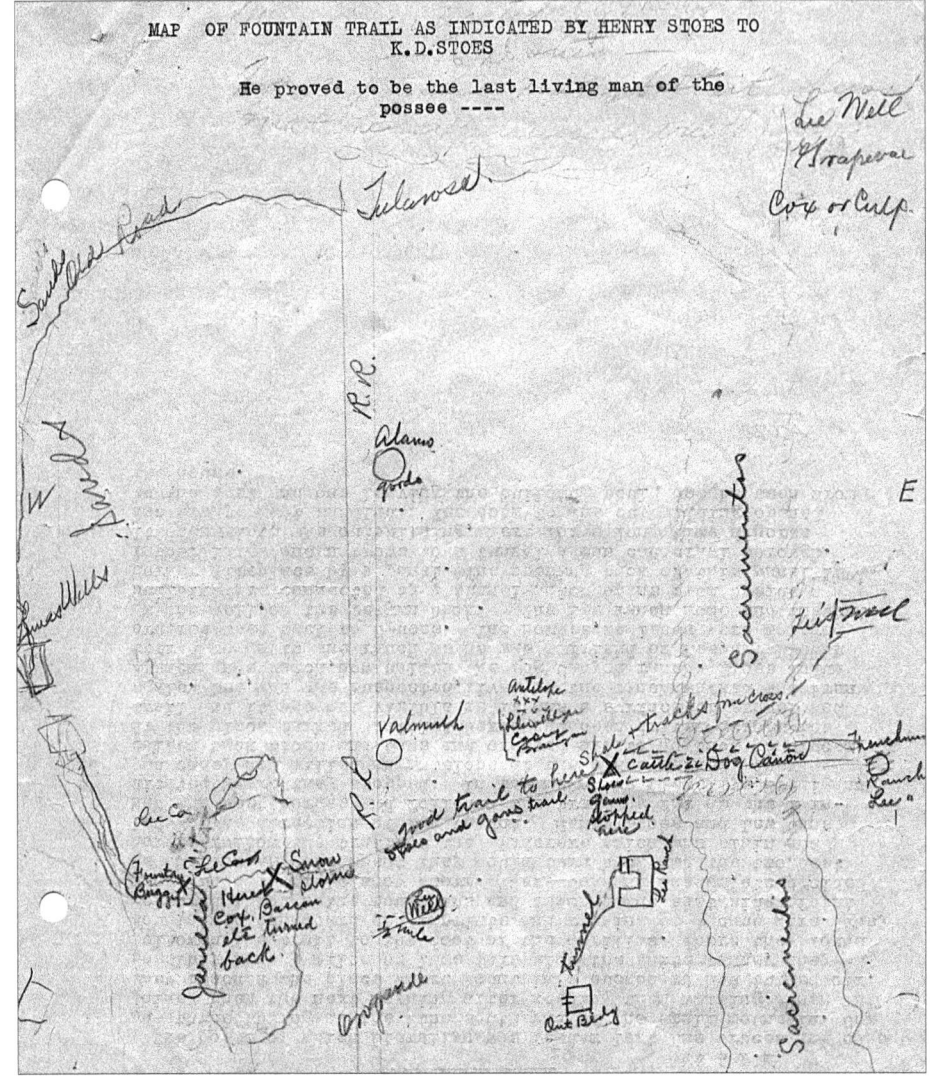

Map of the routes taken by the Fountain posses as described by posse member Henry Stoes to his wife Katherine D. Stoes. The map shows:

(a) The road from Tularosa that Fountain was travelling when he disappeared;
(b) The spot where Fountain's buggy was found;
(c) The trail of horse tracks from the buggy toward Oliver Lee's Dog Canyon Ranch;
(d) The spot – marked by an "X" – where Lee's cattle were driven over the tracks;
(e) Lee's Dog Canyon Ranch house, showing the tunnel dug from the residence to an outbuilding;
(f) Wildy Well – marked as "Lee Well;"
(g) The towns of Alamogordo, Valmont (Camp City), and Orogrande;

Courtesy Archives and Special Collections, NMSU.

On leaving La Luz, several people observed that Colonel Fountain and his son were being shadowed, this time by three men on horses, one riding a white horse. One of these witnesses, Saturnino Barela, a mail carrier, felt compelled to stop Colonel Fountain and warn him:

> "...I told him about the men whom I had seen.... Col. Fountain asked me if I knew the horsemen. I told him I did not." [16]

The next day, just past the spot where he had last observed Colonel Fountain, Barela noticed that Fountain's buggy tracks left the road, heading south. Worried, because of what he had seen the day before, he followed the buggy tracks far enough to determine that foul play was likely.[17]

Barela raced to Las Cruces and reported what he had found.[18] Fountain's family was already upset because he had been expected home the previous evening.[19]

Fountain's two oldest sons, father-in-law, and several friends immediately rode out to look for Colonel Fountain and Henry. A little later, a more official posse, which included the county sheriff, left to join the search.[20]

Both posses found evidence that Colonel Fountain had been murdered, and that Henry had been taken alive, and killed later.

The Crime Scenes

A short distance beyond where postman Barela had ventured the previous day, the searchers found where Colonel Fountain's buggy had been ambushed, as testified to by Major Eugene Van Patten:

> "I found several human tracks and prints of knees behind a bush and several empty shells." [21]

Also found at the site was "a pool of blood:"

> "It was 7 or 8 inches deep and twice or three times as large as a spittoon." [22]

The buggy tracks and blood evidence suggested that Colonel Fountain was shot while trying to flee. Blood from his wound(s) collected in his overcoat. When the running horses made a sudden left turn, Colonel Fountain's body was flung out of the buggy, and the blood spurted from the overcoat, making a large splatter. [23]

From the apparent ambush site, tracks trailed about a mile south to where the buggy was found (see map page 8).[24] The buggy had been searched by the ambushers:

> "The valise and boxes had been opened and their contents were either missing or scattered around. The little hat of Henry's had been left behind inside the valise. A bottle of liquor had been broken. The tracks of three men were plainly visible in the sand at and around the [buggy]...." [25]

A complete list of what was missing from the buggy is given on page 72.

The visible evidence suggested that after abandoning the ransacked buggy, the ambushers took Colonel Fountain's horses and rode southwest.[26] About five miles distant, the searchers found the *"charred remnants of a campfire."* [27]

The old road from Tularosa trailing down the west side of Chalk Hill. Colonel Albert J. Fountain and Henry were ambushed at this location, as they descended the hill in their buggy. The abandoned road is badly eroded today. Located on the White Sands Missile Range. 2019 photo.

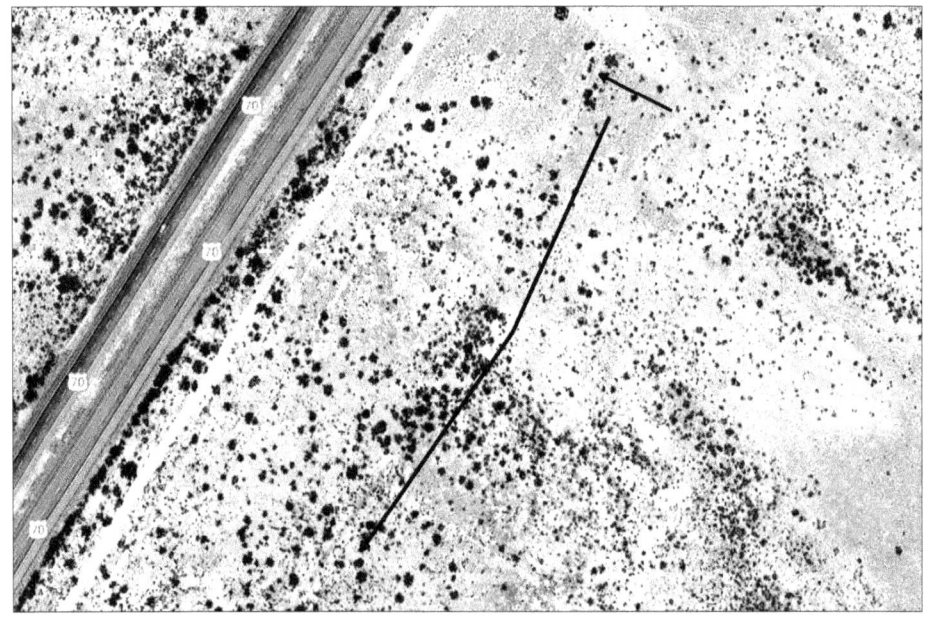

Satellite image of Chalk Hill. The short arrow indicates the location where the Fountains were ambushed. The long arrow indicates the still visible environmental disturbances of the old Tularosa-Las Cruces road.

Marks on the ground at the campfire suggested that Colonel Fountain's body had been carried there wrapped in a blanket, and that Henry was still alive: [28]

"There were 3 or 4 child's tracks, all made by the right shoe." [29]

One of the searchers thought the tracks had been faked by someone who *"had taken the child's shoe in his hand or on a stick and made impressions with it."* [30]

From the campfire site, the searchers followed the tracks to a point where they split. One set of horse tracks led to Wildy Well, a livestock watering-well powered by a steam engine, which was owned by Oliver Milton Lee, one of the men who would be indicted eventually for the murder of Colonel Fountain and Henry. The other sets of tracks led toward Lee's Dog Canyon ranch.[31]

A few miles distant from Lee's ranch, the searchers encountered a problem:

"A herd of cattle, driven by a man, crossed the trail and obliterated it." [32]

The man was one of Lee's ranch hands. His action appeared to be intentional. The obliteration of the tracks destroyed all hope of tracking the apparent killers any further and thereby producing evidence of their identity.

The Investigation

The apparent killing of Colonel Fountain – and especially his little son – shocked the citizens of New Mexico. The Governor of the Territory, William T. Thornton, immediately involved himself in the investigation. With the support of most of the prominent men of Dona Ana County, Governor Thornton hired Patrick Floyd Jarvis Garrett to investigate the crime.[33] Pat Garrett was still the most famous Western lawman, even fourteen years after he killed Billy the Kid.

Ruins of Luna's Well. The house consisted of three adobe rooms with the well at the back door. A horse hitched to a pole drew the water by means of a windlass. It was located about four miles west of White Sands. At the time of the Reports, Pedro Luna owned the well. The charge for water was 25 cents per head for livestock and extra for canteens and water kegs. Courtesy Archives and Special Collections, NMSU.

Patrick Floyd Jarvis Garrett. Undated photo. Courtesy Center for Southwest Research and Special Collections, UNM.

John Conklin Fraser, Pinkerton National Detective Agency operative, sent to Las Cruces March 5, 1896, to investigate the disappearance of Colonel Albert J. Fountain and Henry. Undated photo. Courtesy Library of Congress.

Garrett was living in Uvalde, Texas, at the time he was hired. He initially was paid as a private detective. Later he was made sheriff of Dona Ana County. The story of Garrett's hiring, move to Las Cruces, investigation of the Fountain disappearances, and two terms as county sheriff is told in my book, *"Killing Pat Garrett, The Wild West's Most Famous Lawman – Murder Or Self-Defense?"* [34] It will not be repeated here.

As a backup plan, Governor Thornton hired the Pinkerton National Detective Agency to investigate the Fountain case. The Agency sent one its best operatives to Las Cruces, John Conklin Fraser. Fraser was later replaced by Operative William C. Sayers.[35]

The Reports in the chapters that follow were sent to both the Agency office in Denver, Colorado, and to Governor Thornton. Each Report details one day's investigation by the Operative. Each report is signed "S," as per the practice of the Agency, to keep the real identity of the Operative hidden.

Pinkerton Reports Stolen

The first document in the Reports is dated February 27, 1896, when Governor Thornton began corresponding with James McParland, the head of the Denver branch of the Agency. The last Report is dated May 14, 1896, when the Agency "discontinued" the investigation, in the terminology of the Agency.

Why was the Pinkerton investigation discontinued? It was not because the agents discovered who had killed Colonel Fountain and Henry. It was because Governor Thornton ordered the Agency to stop the investigation after he discovered that all of the Reports he had been sent had been stolen.

"The papers... were reports of [an] investigation into the Fountain murders, which had been held with the governor. The papers were stolen from the governor's office, and well-founded suspicion points toward a federal official with a notorious reputation (they are all rather notorious, but this fellow is exceptionally so) as the thief." [36]

It is uncertain who the newspaper was pointing to; probably it was Albert B. Fall, a name that appears often in the Reports.

(It is surprising that Governor Thornton was careless enough to permit the Reports to be stolen, as he had had a previous warning that someone was willing to steal them. On April 15, 1896, one of Operative Fraser's letters *"was taken from his desk by some one interested in protecting these people."* [37])

These Reports do not exist in the Pinkerton National Agency files now residing in the Library of Congress.[38] At some point, they were lost or destroyed by the Agency.

So with Governor Thornton's copy stolen, and the Agency's original copy missing, how is it possible for the Reports to appear in the chapters that follow?

The answer is, what is presented here are the stolen Reports, the Reports taken without permission from Governor Thornton's office.

The first public evidence that at least one version of the Reports had surfaced came in the book *"Tularosa, Last Of The Frontier West,"* by C. L. Sonnichsen. After noting that Governor Thornton had hired the Pinkerton Agency to investigate the case, Sonnichsen wrote:

DUPLICATE.

Denver, Colorado, March 9th, 1896.

Gov. W. T. Thornton,
    Santa Fe, New Mexico.
Dear Sir:-
    Following you will find report of J. C. Fraser on the investigation desired by you.

Monday, March 2nd, 1896.
Today in Denver and enroute,-
    As per instructions from Supt. Jas. McParland, I left Denver at 7 p. m. via the A. T. & S. F. R.R. for Santa Fe, N. M.

La Junta, Colo., Tuesday, March 3rd, 1896
Today enroute,-
    At 1:20 a. m. I arrived at La Junta, being over one hour late, as I could not leave for the south until 9:30 a. m. I went to the depot hotel and retired for the night and at 8 a. m. was called for breakfast. The train for the south was 35 minutes late, so I did not leave La Junta until 10:05 a. m. and arrived at Lamy, N. M. at 11:20 p. m. where I changed cars for Santa Fe. Governor Thornton arrived at Lamy from the South on No. 2 and went into Santa Fe on the same train with me. We were late in leaving Lamy and did not arrive in Santa Fe until 1:10 a. m. I spoke to Gov. Thornton when he left the train at Santa Fe and made an appointment for 9 a. m. at his office.

Wednesday, March 4, 1904.
Today in Santa Fe,-
    I called on the Governor at his office facing the Plaza as per agreement; he was not feeling well, so did not arrive at the office as soon as expected. After his arrival we spent the balance of the forenoon in discussing the case. I learned that Col. A. J. Fountain was last seen on February 1st, 1896, between the hours of 3 and 4 p. m. on the road south of Luna Well and about forty miles north of Las Cruces; he was seen by the mail driver, one Saturnino Barela, who was going towards Lunas Well. Col. Fountain was on his way to Las Cruces, which was his home, from Lincoln by way of Tularosa. Barela, the mail driver, states that he saw three men, two on one side of the road and one on the other just about the time he met Col. Fountain, but they were so far from the road that he could not recognize any of them. All three were mounted. Col. Fountain spoke to Barela and told him that these men had been acting strange and had been following him from Tularosa, but that he could not get near enough to them to see who they were. Gov. Thornton drew a

The "duplicate" copy of Operative Fraser's first Reports. The originals were sent to the Denver office of the Pinkerton National Detective Agency. In May, 1896, all of the Reports that had been sent to Governor Thornton were stolen from his office. The person who stole them is unknown, but at some point they were acquired by Katherine D. Stoes. (Note date typo in the March 4 report.) Courtesy of the Katherine D. Stoes collection, Archives and Special Collections, NMSU.

"[Operative] Fraser knew his business. He made himself known to only a few men at first and moved abut quietly, posing as a salesman of a mining company." [39]

This passage, part of a summary of Fraser's investigative actions in Sonnichsen's book, obviously derives from knowledge of the content of the Reports; Reports believed previously by historians to be unlocatable, probably forever.

When A. M. Gibson was researching his book, *"The Life and Death of Colonel Albert Jennings Fountain,"* he noted Sonnichsen's quoting of the Pinkerton Reports of the Fountain investigation. Unable to locate their source anywhere, he wrote to Sonnichsen for the information. The letter he sent Sonnichsen reads, in part:

"I have just finished your intriguing book – Tularosa."

"Besides admiring your handling of the content, I was impressed by your bibliography. One group of materials especially strike me as unique – The Pinkerton Operative's Reports."

"Can you tell me where these are located and whom one should contact in attempting to gain access to them?" [40]

Sonnichsen responded in a letter, in part:

"I am afraid I can't help you to locate the Pinkerton reports that you inquire about. They should not be made available to the public, I think, for a long time."

"A Las Cruces friend of mine who is now dead got hold of her copy by devious ways. She never told me who had them or how he got them, but he kept them in a drawer with a heavy calibre pistol and felt that he was sitting on dynamite. She felt the same way."

"When it came time for me to use the material, I made a trip to New York and saw the head of the Pinkerton Agency. He gave me permission to use the file, but I sent him a preliminary copy of the manuscript so he could see for himself what I had done." [41]

After a series of passionate entreaties, Sonnichsen agreed to share the Reports with Gibson, who subsequently quoted them in his biography of Fountain. In a letter dated October 16, 1962, Sonnichsen thanked Gibson for the safe return of the Reports:

"Haven't had time till now to tell you that Mr. Pinkerton got back safely. I hope you found him useful." [42]

So, where did Sonnichsen get the Reports? The answer is, from Mrs. Katherine D. Stoes (1874-1957). Katherine was the wife of Henry Stoes, a member of the Fountain search posse. A historian and author, and a life-long resident of Las Cruces, Katherine spent years researching the Fountain disappearances. Although there are numerous indirect indications that she was the source, such as the fact that Sonnichsen identifies his source as female, the provenance is proven by the fact that copies of the original Reports are in Katherine Stoes' papers in the Special Collections Department of NMSU.[43]

The next question: Where did Katherine Stoes get the Reports? This is speculation, but the author believes that they came from Attorney Albert B. Fall, the attorney who defended Oliver Lee and James Gililland in the Fountain Murder Trial. Katherine knew

Katherine Stoes. Undated photo. Archives and Special Collections, NMSU.

Attorney Albert B. Fall. 1905 photo. Courtesy Library of Congress.

Fall well. We know from the fact that they were stolen while the Fountain investigation was active, that the person who took them had a personal interest in the case, and a personal interest in seeing that the Reports were unavailable for use in any trial. (No Pinkerton Operative testified in the subsequent Fountain Murder trial, and no information gleaned by the Operatives was used in the trial.)

A final question: Can we be confident that the Reports presented in this book derive from the copy sent to Governor Thornton? The answer is yes, because the Reports in Stoes Collection are stamped "Duplicate," meaning they are not the originals which were sent to the Agency's Denver office.

Making Garrett Sheriff

When Governor Thornton promised Garrett the position of sheriff of Dona Ana County, he did so knowing that the existing sheriff, Guadalupe Ascarate, a Democrat, had been elected through voter fraud. Investigations following the election turned up evidence of *"stolen ballot boxes, discarded and duplicated ballots, and registration abuses."* [44] Albert Fall, who was the county judge at the time, was in charge of overseeing the election. There was good evidence that Fall had contributed to the fraud, and had perhaps engineered it. The resulting scandal forced Fall to resign as judge, which he did with great bitterness in 1895.[45]

Ascarate's Republican opponent had been Numa Reymond. If Ascarate could be legally removed, it would be Reymond who would replace him. Based on this assumption, the Republicans of Dona Ana County got Reymond to agree that if the courts reversed the election and made him sheriff, he would appoint Garrett as his chief deputy, then resign, making Garrett sheriff.[46]

On March 20, 1896, district court Judge Gideon D. Bantz removed Ascarate and appointed Reymond.[47] But Reymond unexpectedly balked at his side of the deal. With the office in his hands, he refused to resign. He claimed his campaign expenses for his earlier run against Ascarate had cost him thousands of dollars, and he needed to recover the money. In addition, Reymond claimed that he had already promised the chief deputy sheriff position to Oscar Lohman, so he could not appoint Garrett. He did offer to make Garrett a regular deputy, though.[48]

Garrett categorically refused to accept such a proposition.

Rather quickly, a compromise was reached. Reymond resigned and left in a snit to visit his home country of Switzerland, complaining that he had spent over $16,000 seeking the sheriff's seat. Oscar Lohman gave up his claim, and the parties supporting Garrett agreed that Garrett would serve for two months, after which the County Commissioners would meet and pick a sheriff.[49]

This battle is reflected in the Reports, through the attentive eyes of Operative Fraser.

As the end of Garrett's two-month stint approached, the county commissioners made it clear that they would not appoint Garrett to serve out the remainder of Reymond's term. In a stunning legal maneuver, Albert Fall, now supporting Garrett for sheriff, travelled to Santa Fe with Garrett, and got Governor Thornton to remove two of the Republican commissioners and replace them with Democrats. Fall was able to show to Governor Thornton's satisfaction that the surety bonds posted by the two commissioners were invalid.[50]

Ely E. "Slick" Miller. December 4, 1894. Sentenced to 10 years for cattle larceny. His sentence was commuted to time served by Governor Thornton on November 26, 1896. Courtesy 1970-006 New Mexico Department of Corrections Records, State Archives of New Mexico.

With a Democratic majority now on the commission, the commission appointed Garrett sheriff, and he served as appointed sheriff until the term ended in December, 1896, after which, he ran for sheriff and was elected. He was reelected in 1898. (For details on Garrett's two terms as sheriff, see *"Killing Pat Garrett, The Wild West's Most Famous Lawman – Murder Or Self-Defense?"*)

Ely E. "Slick" Miller

"Slick" Miller was, in essence, the pivot of the Pinkerton investigation, around which all of their detective efforts revolved.

In October, 1894, Miller was indicted in Lincoln County for 11 counts of cattle larceny, through the efforts of Colonel Fountain. Miller's lawyer, E. V. Chavez, obtained a change of venue to Chavez County. There, at Roswell, the county seat, Miller was convicted and sentenced to ten years in the New Mexico penitentiary.[51]

Miller's arrest, indictment, and conviction were a surprise to the public. As one Territorial prosecutor later put it:

> *"For ten years... 'Slick' Miller was plastered with indictments for cattle stealing and his shrewdness in evading conviction won for him the sobriquet of 'Slick.'"* [52]

When Colonel Fountain and Henry were killed, Miller saw an opportunity to shorten his penitentiary stay. He sent Governor Thornton a letter detailing a plot to kill Colonel Fountain in 1894. In the plot, he names a number of the members of his ex-gang, known as the Tularosa Gang, but never identifies himself as the leader of the gang. In the letter he states:

> *"After the organization of the Southwestern Stock Association... many of the cattlemen, among whom were Ed Brown, Carr Bros., Bill McNew, were talking among themselves that it would be of no use to try to do business in the County as long as [Fountain and the other Association officers] were allowed to interfere."*

> *"...Their plan of proceeding was as follows; they were to watch for a favorable opportunity and closely observe the locality selected for the execution of the deed. If the scheme as above stated, to take the victims on the road to Socorro should fail, then another place was selected, and from what I have heard recently, Fountain was taken at the very place in February 1896 that was selected by the above named men in 1894."*

The full text of the letter is reproduced on page 36.

The men Miller named became the focus of the Pinkerton investigation, particularly "Ed Brown," whose real name was Eduard M. Brown. The culmination of the Pinkerton investigation was a carefully staged confrontation between Miller and Brown, as detailed in the Reports (see page 164).

Miller's letter and efforts won him the reprieve he sought. On November 26, 1896, his sentence was commuted to time served by Governor Thornton, with the understanding that he would help in the search for the Fountains' murder:

> *"But on regaining his freedom, instead of aiding in the apprehension of the slayers of Fountain, Miller told the officers to 'go to thunder' and he disappeared from his old haunts."* [53]

Back row, left to right: F. A. Kuns, Deputy Clerk; Herbert H. Holt, Reporter; William E. Martin, Interpreter. Front row, left to right: Simon B. Newcomb, District Attorney; Colonel Albert J. Fountain, attorney; John R. McFie, District Judge; A. L. Christy, Clerk. Photo taken May 30, 1891, in front of the Dona Ana Courthouse. Courtesy Archives and Special Collections, NMSU.

New Mexico Territorial Penitentiary. Undated photo.

On June 6 or 7, 1901, a man named W. M. Rose died in El Paso of paralysis. The local newspaper noted that Rose was a stranger in town. When Rose's pockets were searched, documents were found that identified Rose as Ely E. Miller.[54]

The newspaper, recounting his death, noted:

"[Before his sentencing] Miller was well fixed, but [he] had to spend all he possessed trying to keep out of the penitentiary." [55]

Cast of Characters

Here are brief biographies of the most important persons appearing the Reports. Many of the individuals mentioned are too obscure today to find identifying information..

Ascarate, Guadalupe. Sheriff of Dona Ana County at the time Colonel Fountain and Henry's disappeared. Removed from office by Judge Bantz due to evidence of voter fraud (probably engineered by Albert B. Fall).

Alvarado, Santos. Mail carrier from Luna's Well to La Luz.

Baca, Elfego. Attorney, junior member Feeman & Baca. Deputy Socorro sheriff and county clerk at the time of the Reports. Indicted for attempted murder of W. E. Martin on April 14, 1896, but acquitted. Died August 27, 1945.

Baca, Librado C. de. Brother of Elfego Baca. Deputy sheriff, later sheriff of Luna County.

Baird, James. Rancher. Member of the search party that looked for Colonel Fountain and Henry.

Banner, E. E. Deputy U.S. Marshal at the time of the Reports, later deputy under Pat Garrett.

Bantz, Judge Gideon D. Succeeded Albert Fall as Dona Ana County Judge when Fall resigned. Bantz left office in February, 1898. Died August 7, 1898.

Barber, Susan Ellen McSween. Widow of Alexander A. McSween, killed during the Lincoln County War. Later married George B. Barber. At the time of the Reports, she was divorced from Barber and owned the Three Rivers Ranch (later bought by Albert Fall). Due to that ranch ownership, she was known as the "Cattle Queen of New Mexico." The Reports repeat the calumny against her circulated by McSween's enemies during the Lincoln County War that she was not sexually faithful to McSween.

Barela, Saturnino. Mail carrier between Las Cruces and Luna's Well. Last person to see Colonel Fountain and Henry alive.

Bascom, Frederick H. Las Cruces merchant. Member of the search party that looked for Colonel Fountain and Henry. Died July 20, 1912.

Bergmann, Colonel Edward H. (Bergamer in the Reports). Supervisor of the New Mexico penitentiary. Union Civil War veteran.

Blazer, Doctor, Joseph F. Owner of Blazer's Mill, site of the famous shootout between Andrew "Buckshot" Roberts and the Regulators (which included Billy the Kid) during the Lincoln County War.

Blevin, Alfred (Bleven in the Reports). Employee of the Texas and Pacific Railroad. He claimed to have seen Lee, McNew, and Gililland at Lee's ranch the day the Colonel Fountain disappeared, providing the three men with an alibi. He testified for the defense in the Fountain Murder Trial.

Boxwell. Cover name for Operative William C. Sayers.

Branigan, Thomas (Brannigan in the Reports). Resident of Las Cruces, chief of scouts for the Mescalero Apache tribe for 18 years.

Brown, Dick. Brother of Eduard Brown.

Brown, Eduard W. (Ed. Brown in the Reports). Ranch owner and cowhand working for Colonel Mothersill. Later foreman of the Detroit & Rio Grande Live Stock Company. In May, 1896, Brown volunteered for military service to fight in the Spanish American War and served in Company G of the New Mexico Volunteer Cavalry. Killed by a lightening strike in 1902.

Bursum, H. O. Sheriff of Socorro County.

Carr, William "Bill" "Goodeye." Spanish nickname: Tuerto (one-eyed). Blind in one eye. Indicted for killing Colonel Fountain and Henry, charges dropped. Believed by Garrett to be one of the men who followed Colonel Fountain and Henry from Lincoln.

Chatfield, Frank. In February, 1894, C. F. Hilton, who was unarmed, was shot and killed by James Smith. Chatfield was a member of Smith's party, and reportedly drew a gun on Hilton's companions, preventing them from defending Hilton.

Ruins of the Eduard W. Brown's ranch house, located in Lava Gap, west of Capitol Peak, north of Silvertop, in the Northern San Andres Mountains. Now on the White Sands Missile Range. Undated photo. Courtesy of WSMR Museum Archives.

Chavez, E. V. Eduard W. Brown's attorney. Also represented Slick Miller at his larceny trial.

Christy, Albert L. (Christie in the Reports). Las Cruces attorney and member of the New Mexico Territorial Assembly. He died suddenly December 25, 1896, of typhoid fever. He was 35.

Coe, George. Participant in the Lincoln County War. Good friend of Billy the Kid.

Cox, William W. Cattleman. Owner of the San Augustine Ranch, located on the east side of the Organ Mountains.

Cree, James E. Englishman, owner of the large Angus V. V. Cattle Ranch, near Fort Stanton. In September, 1885, Garrett was hired as the general manager of the V. V. ranch. He served as manager until April, 1886.

Crosson, Doctor Francis. Physician and chemist of Santa Fe, formerly assistant chemist Bellevue hospital, N. Y. He testified for the prosecution in the Fountain Murder Trial.

Cruickshank, Charles Glanville (Crookshanks in the Reports). Physician based in San Marcial, died October 12, 1904.

Ellis, Albert. Las Cruces barber, strong ally of Albert B. Fall and Oliver M. Lee.

Evans, Doc. Real name Aquillo L. Evans. Indicted for cattle larceny with Slick Miller.

Fall, Albert B. Las Cruces attorney, head of the Democratic Party of New Mexico. Just prior to Colonel Fountain and Henry's disappearance, he was the Dona Ana County judge. He resigned when accused of election fraud.

Fitchett, Dan (Fitchet in the Reports). He testified for the defense in the Fountain murder trial. In 1909, Fitchett was a Texas Mounted Officer. He killed Isidro Rubio after Rubio fired on the officer when he tried to arrest Rubio. Fitchett was acquitted.

Fountain, Albert J. Oldest son of Colonel Fountain.

Fountain, Jack. Son of Colonel Fountain.

Fraser, John Conklin. Pinkerton Operative based in the Denver Office.

Freeman, Judge Andreius A. Senior law partner of Elfego Baca.

Freudenthal, Julius. At the time of the Reports, owner of the L. B. Freudenthal dry goods store at Las Cruces. He held the government contract for the mail delivery between Las Cruces and Tularosa/La Luz. Saturnino Barela and Santos Alvarado were his employees. In July, 1896, Julius Freudenthal skipped town owing thousands of dollars to his creditors.

Garrett, Patrick Floyd Jarvis. Became Dona Ana County sheriff when Sheriff Guadalupe Ascarate was removed for voter fraud by Judge Bantz. Numa Reymond then agreed, reluctantly, to appoint Garrett his deputy and resign, making Garrett sheriff for the remainder of Reymond's term. Garrett was elected Dona Ana sheriff November 6, 1896, and again November 8, 1898.

Gililland, James "Jim" (Gilliland in the Reports). One of two men indicted and tried for the murder of Henry Fountain. Acquitted.

Graham, Frank. One of the Grahams of the Tewkesbury-Graham feud.

John "Jack" W. Maxwell. Signed $2,000 contract with Garrett and Perry. Undated painting. Courtesy Karl Laumbach.

Major William Henry H. Llewellyn. Undated photo. Courtesy Center for Southwest Research and Special Collections, UNM.

Simon B. Newcomb. Undated photo. Courtesy Center for Southwest Research and Special Collections, UNM.

Judge John Robert McFie. Undated photo. Courtesy Center for Southwest Research and Special Collections, UNM.

Griego, Maximiano (Maxammeano Greago in Reports). At the time of the Reports, Griego had just had his conviction for the murder of Juan Prieto reversed on appeal by Judge Bantz. Judge Freeman was his attorney. Griego was retried for the murder in January, 1897, and acquitted.

Guerra, Alvino. Stage driver and mail carrier from Luna's Well to La Luz.

Herrera, Luis. Mistakenly indicted by Garrett for the Fountain killings. His white horse was found wondering loose near where Fountain's buggy was found. He was able to provide an alibi and so prove that he was not involved in the killings.

Hill, Frank. Cowhand for Detroit & Rio Grande Live Stock Company, nephew of Frank Graham.

James, Emerald. Unknown.

Lee, Oliver Milton. Cattleman, owner of the Dog Canyon Ranch, indicted for and acquitted of murdering Henry Fountain.

Llewellyn, Major William Henry H. Attorney. Member of the search party that looked for Colonel Fountain and Henry. He testified at the Fountain Murder Trial for the prosecution. Was elected to the Territorial Assembly in 1896.

Llewellyn, Morgan. Son of Major W. H. H. Lewellyn.

Lohman, Oscar. Owner of a meat market in Las Cruces.

Luna, Pedro. Owner of Luna's Well.

Maxwell, John "Jack" W. Claimed to have been at Lee's Dog Canyon ranch on the day Colonel Fountain and Henry disappeared. On March 26, 1896, he signed a contract with Garrett and Sheriff C. C. Perry which promised him $2,000 if his testimony led to the conviction of Lee and Gililland for the Fountain murders (see page 175). He testified for the prosecution at the Fountain Murder Trial.

McCowan, Duncan. Miner and mine owner.

McCowan, Mrs. Duncan. Wife of Duncan McCowan. Ran a rooming house in Organ, New Mexico. Her ads in the local newspaper advertised *"pure water, pure air, no dust."*

McFie, Judge John Robert. Proceeded Albert Fall as Dona Ana County Judge. Union Civil War veteran.

McNew, William. Cattleman and rancher. Indicted for the murder of Colonel Fountain and Henry. Charged dropped. Owned a ranch near Orogrande.

McParland, James. Superintendent of Pinkerton's Denver Office, and of the Pinkerton's Western Division.

Meadows, James "John" P. Deputy under Garrett. Friend of Billy the Kid.

Morgan, Joe. Ally of Albert Fall. U.S. Marshal and Dona Ana County deputy sheriff at the time of Colonel Fountain's disappearance. He testified for defense at the Fountain Murder Trial. Fall's brother-in-law.

Mothersill, Colonel Phillip. General manager Detroit & Rio Grande Live Stock Company at Eagle, New Mexico. He sold the ranch in January, 1898.

Newcomb, Simon B. Attorney. Ex-judge of Dona Ana County. Died May 23, 1901.

Charles C. Perry. February 19, 1891, Austin, Texas. Courtesy Historical Society For Southeast New Mexico.

Susan Ellen McSween Barber. Undated photo. Courtesy Center for Southwest Research and Special Collections, UNM.

Pellman, Frank W. Owner of Pellman's Well, located two miles west of White Sands on the road between La Luz and Las Cruces. Father-in-law of Eduard Brown.

Perry, Charles C. Chavez County Sheriff. He worked with Garrett investigating the Fountain case, and co-signed with Garrett the contract to pay Maxwell for his testimony. Removed from office July 24, 1896, by Governor Thornton for embezelling $8,000 in county and city funds. He fled to South Africa and was never brought to justice. In 1870, he killed, at the mouth of the Penasco River, one of the last living wild bison in New Mexico. The skull was found in 1895 with "Perry, 1870" carved in it.

Rey, Antonio. Employee of Pedro Luna; lived at Luna's well.

Reymond, Numa (Raymond in the Reports). Wealthy Las Cruces merchant. Was cheated out of the sheriff position in 1894 due to election fraud. Appointed sheriff to replace Guadalupe Ascarate by Judge Bantz; Reymond then appointed Garrett his chief deputy and resigned.

Riley, John. Ally of Lawrence Murphy during the Lincoln County War. At the time of the Reports, owner of large ranches in New Mexico and Colorado.

Russell, Baldy, real name William Mitchell. Baldy believed his father was unjustly hung in Texas in 1875. Thirteen years later, Baldy killed James Truitt, the man he held responsible for his father's death. Baldy was identified and arrested for the murder in 1910. Died October, 1928.

Scott, Green. Unknown.

Shields, William "Billy" P. Colonel Fountain and Henry spent their second-to-last night alive at this man's house.

Smith, J. F. "Bud." Susan McSween Barber's ex-foreman. Jack Maxwell worked for him at one time. He testified for the defense in the Fountain Murder Trial. Died March, 1903.

Sutherland, David M. Attorney, living at La Luz. Colonel Fountain and Henry spent their last night alive at Sutherland's house in La Luz.

Taylor, Mrs. Eva D. Resident of La Luz.

Tewkesbury-Graham Feud, also known as the Tonto Basin War. The most famous Arizona feud. The Tewkesburys were sheepmen. The Grahams were cattlemen. The two families lived on opposite sides of Cherry Creek. By the end of the five-year feud, according to contemporary newspaper sources, 14 men on the Tewkesbury side and 27 on the Graham's side had been killed. Included in the dead were four Graham brothers and five Tewkesbury brothers. In August, 1887, in one of the early battles between the two sides, Thomas Tucker was shot and wounded by a Tewkesbury.

Thornton, William T. Governor of New Mexico, 1893 to 1897.

Tucker, Jack. Brother of Tom Tucker.

Tucker, Thomas "Tom." Fought on the Graham side in Tewkesbury War. In August, 1887, Tucker was shot in the back by James Tewkesbury. Two men in Tucker's party and three horses were killed in the resulting gunfight.

Van Patten, Major Eugene. Member of the search party that looked for Colonel Fountain and Henry. He testified for the prosecution in the Fountain Murder Trial.

Williams, Ben. Investigator for Colonel Fountain. Territorial Cattle Inspector, and Las Cruces sheriff constable. On August 14, 1895, Williams and Joe Morgan got into an argument on the streets of Las Cruces which escalated into a shootout. Williams was hit in the left arm and crippled for life. Morgan was also hit in the arm, with no permanent damage.

Williams, Lee. Unknown.

Yoast, Hiram A. (Yost in Reports). Cowhand for Detroit & Rio Grande Live Stock Company, Tom Tucker's first cousin.

Yoast, Jonathan B. (Yost in the Reports). Brother of Hiram Yoast.

Major Eugene Van Patten. Undated photo. Courtesy Center for Southwest Research and Special Collections, UNM.

Chapter 2 | Fraser Assigned

New Mexico Governor Thornton contacted the Denver Office of the Pinkerton National Detective Agency some time prior to February 27, 1896, asking about hiring an Operative to investigate the Fountain disappearance and apparent murder. The head of the Denver Office was James McParland. The two men agreed to terms, and on March 2, Operative John Conklin Fraser was assigned to the case. The Pinkerton Reports of the Fountain Case begin with the letter shown below, a formal authorization by Governor Thornton to initiate the investigation.

TERRITORY OF NEW MEXICO
OFFICE OF THE EXECUTIVE
Santa Fe, N.Mex., Feb. 27, 1896

James McParland, Esq.
Denver, Colorado

Dear Sir:-

Your favor was received and I telegraphed you yesterday that the terms were satisfactory, and to await reception of ticket. I am compelled to leave Santa Fe to-night and cannot be back before Tuesday next. It is necessary for me to have a full conference with the party you send down and to fully instruct him before he goes upon the ground; it will therefore not be necessary for him to reach Santa Fe before my return. If he does not receive the ticket, let him come anyway. He can start from Denver Monday and reach here by the time I have returned.

Yours very truly,
W. T. Thornton,
Governor New Mexico Territory

Denver, Colorado, February 28, 1896
Hon. W. T. Thornton,
Gov. New Mexico, Santa Fe, New Mexico.

Dear Sir:-

This afternoon I received the following message from Mr. Frey, Gen'l Manager of the A. T. & S. F. R. R [the Atchison, Topeka and Santa Fe Railroad]:

> "Please call on our Agent J. P. Hall for transportation to Las Cruces and on Agent at latter point for return pass."

Now after deliberating on the matter in question, I concluded that it would expedite matters a great deal to send Mr. J. C. [John Conklin] Fraser, my assistant here, on the ground and have him make a through open investigation. Such an investigation generally develops who the parties are that may have instigated or actually committed the crime; then we can place a practical cowboy Opt. [Operative] such as Opt. Boxwell [William C. Sayers] to work secretly unknown to any person except yourself. If I should send Boxwell, he would have to make this investigation anyhow and thereby spoil his usefulness to work secretly. An open investigation sometimes develops such facts that it is not necessary to place a man to work secretly; anyhow, it expedites matters and gets at certain things in a short time that an Opt. working secretly would not develop for quite a while.

Now, as Mr. Fraser could not travel on transportation issued to Boxwell, I telegraphed Mr. Frey as follows:-

"Relative to the transportation forwarded to me for W. S. Boxwell on account of Gov. Thornton of N.M. from Denver to Las Cruces, I wish you would substitute the name of J. C. Fraser as Boxwell is not able to go. I wish to send Fraser to-night."

"Jas. McParland"

I presumed that the transportation was issued on your account and therefore framed my telegram to that effect. If transportation doesn't arrive this evening I will telegraph you a night message.

Yours truly,
James McParland,
Supt.

Denver, Colo., March 2, 1896
The Hon. W. T. Thornton
Gov. New Mexico
Santa Fe, New Mexico.

Dear Sir:-

This will introduce to you Mr. J. C. Fraser, my assistant, whom I have detailed to make an open investigation on the matter on which we have corresponded. You can confer freely with Mr. Fraser.

Yours Truly,
James McParland,
Supt.

[First Report by Fraser]

Monday, March 2nd, 1896

Today in Denver and enroute,-

As per instructions from Supt. Jas. McParland, I left Denver at 7 p. m. via the A. T. & S. F. R.R. for Santa Fe, N. M.

Tuesday, March 3rd, 1896
La Junta, Colo.

Today enroute,-

At 1:20 a. m. I arrived at La Junta, being over one hour late, as I could not leave for the south until 9:30 a.m. I went to the depot hotel and retired for the night and at 8 a. m. was called for breakfast. The train for the south was 35 minutes late, so I did not leave La Junta until 10:05 a. m. and arrived at Lamy, N. M., at 11:20 p. m., where I changed cars for Santa Fe.

Governor Thornton arrived at Lamy from the South on No. 2 and went into Santa Fe on the same train with me. We were late in leaving Lamy and did not arrive in Santa Fe until 1:10 a. m. I spoke to Gov. Thornton when he left the train at Santa Fe and made an appointment for 9 a. m. at his office.

Wednesday, March 4, 1896

Today in Santa Fe,-

I called on the Governor at his office facing the Plaza as per agreement; he was not feeling well, so did not arrive at the office as soon as expected. After his arrival we spent the balance of the forenoon in discussing the case. I learned that Col. A. J. Fountain was last seen on February 1st, 1896, between the hours of 3 and 4 p. m., on the road south of Luna's Well and about forty miles north of Las Cruces; he was seen by the mail driver, one Saturnino Barela, who was going towards Luna's Well. Col. Fountain was on his way to Las Cruces. [Barela] saw three men, two on one side of the road and one on the other just about the time he met Col. Fountain, but they were so far from the road that he could not recognize any of them.

All three were mounted. Col. Fountain spoke to Barela and told him that these men had been acting strange and had been following him from Tularosa, but that he could not get near enough to them to see who they were. Gov. Thornton drew a diagram of the road followed by Col. Fountain from Tularosa showing where the buckboard was found off from the main road about twelve [miles] from where his buckboard left that road. The colonel was driving a team of horses hitched to the buckboard, [which were] found, with the exception of one [horse]. [The] buckboard and the harness was also found with the exception of one bridle and two straps. The bedding carried by the colonel was also gone.

All three horses belonging to the Colonel have since been found. I was also informed that Col. Fountain had disappeared once before in very mysterious manner for fifteen days and then showed up again. He is said to be of sensational disposition, but in this case there was every reason to believe that he and son, seven or eight years of age, were both dead.

He had many enemies, owing to his position as attorney for stock growers association; he had always been a bitter prosecutor of cattle thieves and was a fearless man. Governor Thornton gave me the copy of a letter from Col. Fountain to one James E. Cree, a member of the stock growers association who lives at or near Fort Stanton, N. M., also recent letter from Mr. Cree to himself. I enclose both with this report. The copy of Col. Fountain's letter for file and the one from Mr. Cree to be copied for file and then the original to be mailed to Gov. Thornton.

I have today written to Gov. Thornton to find out, if possible, who the prominent member of the Stock Growers Association [that] he mentions in this letter to Mr. Cree as *"not acting in good faith in the matter of the Tularosa gang."* This letter to M. Cree shows as far back as Oct. 1895 Col. Fountain had become aware of threats against his life. The parties who are suspected of this crime are, Oliver Lee, William McNew, James Gilliland or Jack Tucker, all cattlemen.

The men for me to meet at Las Cruces who are interested in this case are Major W. H. H. Llewellyn, S. B. Newcomb, and A. L. Christie [Christy]; all these men are Masons and are interested in running this matter down. The blood found near Chalk Hill, close to where the mail driver met Col. Fountain and his boy, has been examined by a doctor at Santa Fe and he says it is blood, but does not say that it is human blood. It was at this same place that the nickel and dime were found, also a piece of shirting said to be a piece of the boys shirt.

Governor Thornton then told me about a woman making affidavit that she saw three men cross the road near La Luz on Sunday morning about day break; they were coming from the direction of the white sands [White Sands] and she was going towards Tularosa on the buckboard with the Mexican mail driver. This woman, Mrs. [Eva] Taylor, claims to have identified two of these men as two of the suspected parties,

Oliver Lee and William McNew, and gave a description of the third man. Now, if this woman's statement is true then the point would seem to be a strong one. The men mentioned as being suspected in this case are said to be hard men. Some of the horses are said to have been traced to near Oliver Lee's home ranch which is off the Tularosa road a long distance and in Dog Canyon. Lee has another ranch near the Jarillas [Wildy Well] which is a few miles from where the buck board was found.

Gov. Thornton was not feeling well, having caught a bad cold on his last trip, so at 12:30 p. m. we adjourned for dinner to meet again at his office at 2 p. m., but when he came to the office he was feeling worse and had to go home; he gave me letters to Major Llewellyn, Mr. Christie, and District Attorney Young. The latter is not to be trusted but I will call on him and learn what I can.

Mr. Van Patten was also mentioned as a man whom I could perhaps obtain some information from as he was deeply interested in running this mystery down. Pat Garrett was also mentioned as a man whom I could rely on and who was now out looking for the bodies. I was also informed by Gov. Thornton that S. B. Newcomb, the attorney, and one of the men whom I was to confer [with] at Las Cruces was in town on business and that I could find him at the Palace Hotel.

I then left the governor and went in search of Mr. Newcomb but did not find him until 5:30 p.m. I had an hour's talk with him, but learned nothing new owing to the fact that all of his papers were in Las Cruces. I saw he was busy, so left him to meet again at Las Cruces in a few days when he expects to be home. After supper I called on the governor at home and had some further talk on the matter, but nothing new was developed during this conversation.

At 10:10 p.m. I left Santa Fe for Las Cruces and was on the road all night. Nothing of importance occurred to report.

TERRITORY OF NEW MEXICO
OFFICE OF THE EXECUTIVE
Santa Fe, N.Mex., March 6

James McParland, Esq.
Denver, Colo.

Dear Sir:-

I have just returned home and find your favor of the 26th ult. You neglected to send me the guarantee which you refer to as being enclosed in your letter. I saw Mr. Fraser and sent him upon his work. I offered to pay him in advance for his services, but he declined to accept anything. I hold myself personally responsible for his expenses until he is discharged. You will please forward the guarantee to me which you mention and oblige.

Yours very truly,
W. T. Thornton

TERRITORY OF NEW MEXICO
OFFICE OF THE EXECUTIVE
Santa Fe, N. Mex., March 6, 1896.

Mr. John C. Fraser,
Las Cruces, N.M.

Dear Sir:-

There is a man confined in the Territorial prison in this city convicted of stealing cattle in 1894 whose name is Eli [Ely] or "Slick" Miller, who used to belong to the "gang" suspected of having killed Col. Fountain and his little son. Enclosed I send you this man's statement of a conspiracy to kill Fountain in 1894. I particularly desire that this name should be kept secret. The statement may give you some information which will be valuable. I feel very certain that the man, Ed. [Eduard W.] Brown, is one of the parties who left Socorro a few days before the killing, and that he took a part in it, and afterwards returned through the San Andreas mountains, possibly leaving the bodies at the point designated in this statement, and was the man seen in the cottonwood groves near Rincon a day or two after the murder.

Another matter that may be of some importance to you, I learn to-day from a friend who was at the Ruidoso Post Office in the County of Lincoln; while there, he heard the postmaster and a cattleman, who he thinks was from Penyasco [Peñasco], talking. They said the cattleman had stayed all night at the Lee ranch on Sunday and Monday following the murder [February 2 and 3], and that Lee, McNew, and Chatfield were present; that they were very nervous, and watched him particularly; sent him to a room to bed about nine o'clock and in going out of the room kept their faces towards him and carried guns, and instead of staying in the house, went out and slept both nights in the brush, and seemed to be constantly on the watch. It will be no trouble for you to learn from the postmaster who this cattleman is. [The man is Jack Maxwell.]

Dr. Crosson having been sick, I have not yet been able to get him to examine the material clipped from the horse to see if there is any blood contained in the material. I will notify you as soon as this analysis is made. Please keep this statement secret and return it to me when you have finished it. [The "material" is horse hair soaked in blood. The investigators believe the blood is from Colonel Fountain and the horse was used to transport the body.]

Yours respectfully,
W. T. Thornton

[Statement of Slick Miller]

Speaking the other day about this Fountain mystery, a man seemingly well acquainted with the citizens of Lincoln County, their doings and their tendencies, but more particularly with the stockmen and the localities of that County, made the following statement:

"After the organization of the Southwestern Stock Association in March, 1894, of which W. C. McDonald was President, James Cree, Secy., and Albert Fountain, Atty., many of the cattlemen, among whom were Ed Brown, Carr Bros., Bill McNew, were talking among themselves that it would be of no use to try to do business in the County as long as those fellows (meaning McDonald, Cree, and Fountain) were allowed to interfere."

"I know all this from the fact that I was thoroughly acquainted with all of them; slept with the man above named [McNew?], and as they had no secrets before me, carried on the conversation in my presence, and afterwards requested me to carry a letter to Spence. Bros. in which the subject they had been talking about should be mentioned to them (Spence Bros)."

"This letter I did not get to deliver, as it must have been sent in some other way, but it reached its destination, for when I arrived at Spence Bros. ranch, Chas. Spence told me of having received that letter that it contained the proposition to waylay and kill Fountain and McDonald; Chas. Spence approved of the scheme and thought it would be an excellent opportunity to get them (Fountain and McDonald) while on their way to Socorro; they were expected to go there from Lincoln."

"He also informed me that Ed Brown had stated to him, he (Brown) had hired a man to do his (Brown's) required part of the business. Charles Spence, however, objected to this, and said he would never trust such important work to hired men, but would do his share himself. He was sure also that Bob Gray would do his part, and that Carr would get together three or four parties more, which would bring up the number to eight or nine; Charles Spence thought that Chas. Bruton (or Burton) might be induced to join them, but he was not sure."

"Some days after this talk with Chas. Spence, I had a long and confidential talk with E. [Ed] W. Brown on the very same subject. Brown informed me that the thing had been properly arranged, and named the whole party who would participate in the murder. Their names were as follows, to-wit: Bob Gray, Charles Spence, Ed Brown, Billy McNew, Charles Bruton, Jack Tucker, Carr (also called goodeye) and Bill Sykes, a fellow to come from Old Mexico; there was another fellow named Powder Bill; he, (Powder Bill) had been hired, by whom I cannot distinctly remember, but I know he was to get $750 and one horse for the job. The horse Powder Bill was to get was pointed out to me; I knew it well, it was a bay horse and belonged to Chas. Spence."

"I enjoyed the fullest confidence of nearly all of the party. Spence and Brown were using all of their endeavors to get me to join them in the plot. They offered me in the beginning $500 and two horses and afterwards raised that offer to $2,000 and when finding that I obstinately refused to take a hand in any killing, I was threatened and told, that as I knew the whole plot, I had to take an active part in the undertaking, or they would make me leave the country. It was Ed Brown who talked to me in particular in this respect, and gave me the advice to leave. Although I was fully aware, that at that time, they had the murder pretty thoroughly planned and laid out and the respective duties assigned to each and every member of the conspiracy, still I did not believe they were going to carry their intentions into effect at that time."

"Their plan of proceeding was as follows; they were to watch for a favorable opportunity and closely observe the locality selected for the execution of the deed. If the scheme as above stated, to take the victims on the road to Socorro should fail, then another place was selected, and from what I have heard recently, Fountain was taken at the very place in February 1896 that was selected by the above named men in 1894."

"It was further arranged and agreed upon by all the parties that McNew, Ed Brown, and Carr were to carry the dead bodies or body from the place of the murder to the San Andreas Mts. It was the plan to throw the body or bodies over some of the high ridges, so as to lodge them on shelving or projecting rock, with which the country there is abundantly provided. In that part of the country there is very little stock, and being therefore very little or seldom visited by any one, it was chosen to prevent detection of the crime and the finding of the dead bodies."

"After the killing, the party was to disperse and leave in different directions, obliterate trails and tracks, and make pursuit and trailing a difficult matter. I know that Chas. Spence and Bob Gray were to return by the way of Red Lake to their ranches so as to give the cattle there a chance to obliterate their tracks. The plot failed because of the untimely arrest of Ed Brown, the general scare created by it, and the sudden disappearance of Spence and Gray who left the country. It is my opinion that Jack Tucker and a young fellow by the name of: James Gillan [Gililland] know something, if not a great deal of the Fountain mystery. Tucker is not a brave man, but a braggart, and could easily be induced to talk, with the assistance of a few drinks of whiskey. James is a young fellow who delights in being considered "tough." He does not drink, but if properly approached will not hesitate to tell of his glorious deeds. I am almost certain that these two men had a hand in the affair."

[Miller does not mention that he, not Ed Brown, was the leader of these men and probably the instigator of their plan to murder Colonel Fountain.]

[Fountain letter referenced by Fraser.]
"Office of Southeastern New Mexico Stock Growers' Assn."
"Las Cruces, N. M. Oct. 3, 1895"

"Dear Mr. Cree;-"

"*The New Mexican* received yesterday contained a notice of your arrival at Santa Fe, hence I assume you are now enroute to, or at the ranch and that this will reach you there."

"I have to communicate to you matters of the most grave importance, seriously affecting the interest of all honest stock growers in this country, and especially in the vicinity of Tularosa. I had perhaps better begin at the beginning, and state the facts in detail chronologically."

"In August, I went to Grant County in search of Collins and I found him at work for Lyons on the Gila. My purpose was to have him accompany me to Las Cruces where I intended to use him in aiding [Ben] Williams to ferret out the band of thieves operating in the eastern portion of this county."

"He declined to go to Las Cruces; he admitted he had evaded the officers we sent after him last May, and said the reason was he feared he would be killed it he went to Socorro; he at first denied, but afterwards admitted the receipt of money sent him and gave me a receipt for it; he stated that while at Central he had been informed by his friends that a man well armed had come there and made inquiry for him; that the man said he was an officer from Texas having a warrant for his arrest; that he believed this to be a plot to take him and kill him and for that reason he had concealed himself."

"I do not believe he was telling the truth. I think he made this excuse to avoid appearing at Socorro as a witness against the parties there indicted. I examined him further as to the facts embraced in the statement made by Wilson and as to the discrepancies between his and Wilson's statements, and he admitted that the facts as stated by Wilson were correct, especially as to the division of the money received from Spence, which you will remember Wilson stated was divided equally between Miller, Wilson, and Collins by Bud Merritt at the latter's saloon."

"I made arrangements to communicate with Collins should it be necessary to do so, and returned to Las Cruces, being called back by a telegram that Mrs. Fountaîn's mother was dying. She died the day following my return. In the meantime, I had Williams, Cormack, and others at work in the vicinity of Tularosa and La Luz and soon obtained positive evidence that a man named Dodd was running a butcher shop at Tularosa, and was killing all the cattle that came in his way; a man named Williams, one of the gang, was induced to peach, and through him we learned that Oliver Lee and others of the Fall party were connected with the thieves and this will account for what subsequently occurred."

"Sufficient evidence was obtained to secure the indictment of all the parties by any un-prejudîced grand jury, especially in one case of the killing of a V pitchfork V animal by Dodd, the eye witnesses being at hand to testify as to the stealing and killing."

"We were also able to prove, that in a small valley, over one hundred animals had been killed by these parties. It being impossible to prevent these facts from obtaining publicity, the gang of criminals soon became acquainted with our intentions and became desperate; threats were made against Williams, myself, and all others connected with the proposed prosecutions; this culminated in the shooting of Williams by Fall and Morgan in the streets of Las Cruces."

"I was anonymously notified, that if I attempted to prosecute these parties I would be killed. Of course, I paid no attention to these threats."

"When the Grand Jury convened we found that a large majority were tools of Fall; the Hon. George W. Miles, being the foreman. We had when the Grand Jury met, nine men in jail charged with cattle stealing. Dodd was under arrest awaiting the action of the jury; the witnesses against him were present."

"Instead of investigating these cases, the Grand Jury proceeded to investigate Williams and myself. Fall went before the Grand Jury and swore that the stock association had paid men to assassinate him, and sixteen of his satellites on the Grand Jury did as he wished; there was no investigation of any of the jail cases. Williams was indicted for murder (killing a criminal he was attempting to arrest about a year ago) and some other indictments were found against him in connection with his arrest of Dick Wilson at Clayton (charged by J. H. Riley with horse stealing)."

"I was honored by an indictment charging me with forging a private telegram to myself from Major Tell of El Paso some years ago, saying, *"I will send you papers first mail."* The message from Tell to me was of course genuine; was on our private business, and concerned nobody but ourselves; nevertheless, this ridiculous charge was made by the Grand Jury; the indictment was immediately dismissed by Judge Bantz when it came into court, and he read Mr. Miles a lecture on the subject."

"Failing to intimidate me in this manner, further threats were made of personal violence, but they were treated with contempt. In the meantime, the Grand Jury had refused to hear any evidence against Dodd and returned no-bill against him; Fall moved for his discharge, but I prevailed on the court to place him under recognizance to await the action of the Grand Jury."

"Williams is still in bed seriously wounded. Fall admits he shot him; the Grand Jury reported they could not find time to investigate this shooting. I learn from the inside that the gang we are after are making threats against many of the association members, and especially against yourself. In connection with these matters, I enclose you two letters from Mr. Cormack who is a constable at La Luz; they will explain themselves. Williams being confined to himself was unable to appear before the Grand Jury, but it would have made no difference, as no testimony he could have given would have availed."

"I shall now begin to fight this gang in earnest. I require funds and immediately upon receipt of your check for the quarter beginning September 1st I shall start in person for Tularosa, and begin the work of corralling this entire gang."

"I find that they have no public sentiment to sustain them there or at La Luz. While I entertain no serious apprehension of any attempt on the part of the Tularosa gang to execute their threats against yourself, yet I advise prudence on your part should you be compelled to visit any place where there may be danger of encountering them, and it would be advisable to always travel in company with some person on whom you can rely in an emergency."

"I regret to say that circumstances impel me to the belief that a prominent member of the association is not acting in good faith in the matter of the Tularosa gang, but of this, I will confer with you personally. My family affairs have occasioned me very great anxiety and trouble; the shock of her mother's death greatly affected Mrs. Fountain, and her illness is aggravated by mental trouble arising from her apprehension that my life is in danger."

"I entertain no such apprehension; yet, were I to so believe, I should not be deterred thereby from performing my whole duty. Public opinion here is with us, and the present condition of affairs cannot long exist, nevertheless, I anticipate a hard contest, one perhaps to the death."

"I sincerely trust you found your family quite well on your return. Please convey to them my kindest regards."

"Sincerely yours,"
"A. J. Fountain."

Chapter 3 | Fraser Investigates

Operative Fraser arrived in Las Cruces, March 5, 1896. He sent daily reports to Governor Thornton and his home office until March 26, when he "discontinued" and returned to Denver. At the time he quit the investigation, he expected to be assigned to another case in Europe.

Thursday, March 5, 1896

Today enroute and at Las Cruces,-

I arrived at Las Cruces at 10:05 a.m. and took the bus from the depot to the Rio Grande hotel (the only one in town). After being assigned a room, I started out to find Major Llewellyn, but learned that he was not in town. I then located the law office of A. J. Christie [Christy] and about 3:30 p.m. found him in. I presented my letter from Gov. Thornton and while we were talking Mr. P. H. Curran, another member of the Masonic order, came in and I was introduced to him. Mr. Curran is the jeweler here and is one of the men interested with Major Llewellyn, Mr. Christie, and others in this case.

Mr. Christie expressed his willingness to give me all the information possible and started off by making a pencil sketch of the road to Tularosa showing where Barela, the mail driver, met Mr. Fountain and his son, also showing where the buckboard was found, the location of Oliver Lee's two ranches, and many other points necessary to explain the circumstances in connection with this mysterious case. I expect the best diagram of this road and the points mentioned from Major Llewellyn, who has been over the ground. I learned that the Major had gone to El Paso and would most likely be back tomorrow at noon.

From Mr. Christie I learned that Col. Fountain and his son left Lincoln, N. M. on Wednesday, January 29th, and drove to Dr. Blazer's place [Blazer's Mill], which is 18 miles east of Tularosa. Here they stopped all night and on Thursday, January 30th, he drove to Tularosa and stopped all night with Billy Shields. On Friday he drove on to La Luz and stopped over night, can't say who with, but a man named Sutherland at La Luz can tell you where he stopped.

On Saturday morning he left La Luz and was next seen by Barela, the mail driver, near Chalk Hill. There was another man who saw the Col. at the same time; his name is Fajardo and he is a young man who was with his father and three women folks. They were camped at Chalk Hill. When Barela came along they were just getting ready to move East, so the young man Fajardo rode on horseback along side of the buckboard which was driven by Barela, and his father and the three women folks rode along in the wagon about 1/3 to 1/2 a mile behind. This family and outfit are now living at or near La Luz.

Another circumstance in connection with the case is that of one Joe Morgan, a deputy U.S. marshal, who is said to be closely connected with Ex-Judge A. B. Fell [Fall], Oliver Lee, McNew and other cattle thieves; this man Morgan is said to have gone to Tularosa to make an arrest. He went about the time that court opened at Lincoln and on his arrival at Tularosa he did arrest a woman, but instead of bringing her back himself, he sent another man and he remained at Tularosa until Col. Fountain arrived there on Thursday.

Then, it is said, as soon as Col. Fountain arrived he (Morgan) left the place and went east towards Lincoln, but he must have circled around for he arrived in Las Cruces on Saturday 1st, about 4 p.m., and just about the time the mail driver claims to have seen him 40 miles from Las Cruces; this of course would let Morgan out as one of the actual parties to the murder, but would not prevent him from notifying others of the arrival of the Col.

Morgan is considered a very bad man and goes armed to the teeth, as do several others of the same gang, all of whom are said to be controlled by Ex-Judge A. B. Fall. This man Fell has always been the attorney for these cattle thieves and is said to be tied up with them now. He disliked Col. Fountain very much and seemed to consider him his arch enemy, and Fell told Mr. Christie at one time that he had a notion to resign from the bench (he was judge then) and throw down the gauntlet to Col. Fountain. He was forced to leave the bench and after this he started in to fight Col. Fountain by having him indicted for forging a telegram to himself.

There was nothing to the charge and it was thrown out of court in about fifteen minutes. Gov. Thornton also told me of this same case. Col. Fountain had some 22 indictments against the suspected parties at the time of his disappearance and it is thought that he had notes and papers on some of these cases with him in his grip. I could not learn from either Christie or Curran just what was found belonging to the Col. and just what was missing.

The Fountain family lives here in town [Las Cruces] and are considered very nice people. Mrs. Fountain is said to be Spanish and was somewhat jealous of her husband, but as near as Mr. Christie or Mr. Curran know, there was no trouble between them at the time he went away, and to bear this out, Mr. Christie says that the Col. wrote to Mrs. Fountain saying that they would reach home for Sunday dinner at noon.

He was a man who was very much attached to his children. At the time this affair happened, Col. Fountain's son Tom was working over in the vicinity of Lincoln or at Fort Stanton for Mr. James Cree, and Tom said his father came by there and asked him how he was fixed for money. Tom claimed that he gave his father $250.00 and that besides this amount his father had about $100.00. Tom also says that his father rolled this up in yellow paper and as there was no gum to stick the paper with he took sealing wax (red wax), then placed the package in his pocket.

Now Mr. Christie says that this young man does not handle the truth very carefully and that he never had $250 in his life; still he says that there was yellow paper and red wax found by the searching party. When the buckboard was found, the Col's belt and cartridges were also found under the seat in the buckboard and twelve cartridges were gone; the belt was said to have been full at Tularosa.

I was with Mr. Christie and Mr. Curran up to 6:10 p.m., then left and went to the hotel for supper. After supper I sat and listened to the conversation of Mr. Hatton, proprietor of the hotel, Mr. Gillam, a rancher, and L. W. Lenoir, an ex-lawyer, now interested in mining. I learned from their conversation that none of them liked Col. Fountain personally, but all of then denounced the people who would commit such a crime and especially so providing they killed the boy. All three of them spoke very highly of the action taken by Gov. Thornton in this matter and all seemed to favor Pat Garrett for sheriff, claiming that he would put a stop to these killings.

I spent 50 cents for cigars and drinks with these people and retired at 12 0 'clock.

Yours truly,
"S"

Friday, March 6, 1896

Today in Las Cruces,-

After breakfast I wrote up my reports and then called upon Mr. A. L. Christy (not Christie) at his office. I wanted to get several names and locations mentioned by him correct. I learned that Dist. Atty. Young was at El Paso as was also Ex-Judge A. B. Fall (not Fell.). Major Llewellyn was expected up from El Paso today at noon and Mr. Christy was going to the depot to meet him so I would be able to know him if he got off the train.

At 11:30 a.m., I went to the depot and when the train arrived I mailed my reports; also a letter to Governor Thornton, and at the same time saw Major Llewellyn shake hands with Mr. Christy. I followed the Major to his house and after giving him my letter from the governor we discussed the case until about 1 p.m. As Major Llewellyn has been over the ground he will be able to give me a good drawing of the road, etc.

I came to the hotel for dinner and at 2 p.m. went back to the Major's house and started in to discuss the case, but was interrupted several times by callers. I was informed that the sheriff and deputies all went armed to the teeth and were all under the orders of A. B. Fall, and that every move made by the men interested in running down this matter was closely watched, and that Joe Morgan, the ex-deputy marshal mentioned in my report of yesterday and who is now a deputy sheriff, his commission as U.S. deputy marshal having been taken away, has openly threatened some of the best men in town, claiming that they have been talking too much about this Fountain case.

In addition to a Mexican [Ben Williams] who has been acting as detective for the Stock Growers Association, was arrested and thrown into jail a short time ago for carrying fire arms and a plan was laid by this same gang of deputies to have some Mexican deputies arrest Major Llewellyn and one Bascon [Bascom] for carrying fire arms with the expectation that the Major and Bascon would kill the Mexicans and thus give the white deputies the excuse to kill them, but according to the Major's statement this plan fell through as they went out by a rear door and through a drug store and thus avoided them and left them watching the Pallama Club until it closed.

The Major tells of any number of these cases to show the condition of affairs, and gives the name of a negro barber named [Albert] Ellis as being the right hand man of A. B. Fall. This man Ellis is said to have been a hard character back in Texas where he had committed more than one crime. He is said to be very prominent in dogging the movements of Major Llewellyn and others.

I was also informed by the Major that there were indictments against Oliver Lee and Tom Tucker at El Paso, Texas, for murder and they would no doubt soon be arrested. The sheriff here would not serve warrants on any of these men as he was controlled by the gang, and the district attorney, Mr. Young, was with this gang. While we were talking Judge McFie came in to see the Major and I was introduced to him; I saw that he wanted to see the Major alone, so I left promising to call again.

When I got outside the Major came out and told me that the judge had received a letter through the mail warning him that he was to be killed; this letter was not signed, but the writer said that as the judge had done him a favor while on the bench he warned him.

When I called again on the Major at 4:45 p.m., he told me of this and informed me that owing to the language in the letter and the remark about having done him, the writer, a favor while on the bench, he thought the man wrote the letter was the Negro barber Ellis, for he had loaned him $60 at one time. The Major positively states that these men, to wit: Fall, McNew. Lee, Ellis, Morgan, Tucker, and many others are banded into an oath bond organized body and says that it was not long ago that the judge (A. B. Fall) sent for him through one Mr. Baird and told him (the Major) that they (the Democratic party) want him and Baird with them.

At that time the major had sort of broken away from the [Republican] party as certain things had happened which he did not like. At the time of the conversation Fall was a judge on the bench, and Fall told the Major and Tom Baird that the Democratic party must carry this territory. The Major said that this was impossible, but Fall said it was not as they were banded together like brothers and if any of them got in trouble they could furnish any kind of evidence to clear them. He made this safe offer to the Major and Tom (Jim) Baird in case they got into any trouble. The Major said that this was a surprise to both he and Tom (Jim) Baird and the Major cut it short by saying they would think the matter over, then left; when they got outside he asked Baird what he thought of it, and Baird said *"If that is Democratic politics I don't want any it,"* and the subject was never taken up again.

Only a short time ago Fall tried to kill a man named [Ben] Williams on the street in this town, shot him twice. We have had eleven murders here and no convictions. Oliver Lee, McNew, Tucker, and the balance of the gang are all deputies under the present sheriff and several cold blooded murders are credited up to Oliver Lee and his friends McNew, Tucker and others. All of these killings they claim was done in self defense, but in each case Oliver Lee jumped the ranch of the man he killed.

The Major said he would get up a correct chart and also the statements of himself, Brannigan [Branigan], and others and give the full particulars of what they found in their search for Col. Fountain. He said he thought this should be done as there was no telling what might happen to any of them.

I find everybody very timid about here and for this reason my work is going to be very slow. No one wishes to be connected with me or the case openly, so you can see from this how the feeling stands. I made arrangements with the Major to meet Barela, the mail driver, at Freudenthal's general store at 8 p.m. when the store would be closed. Mr. [Julius] Freudenthal would interpret for me as Barela did not speak English well enough to converse. I was there at the appointed time and was admitted through the side door; I was introduced and found Barela on hand; the Major then left to keep a lookout on the outside for Deputies. The Major also had his son and Mr. Brannigan on the lookout.

The following is a statement of S. [Saturnino] Barela:

"On Saturday February 1st, 1096, I left here (Las Cruces) in the morning at the usual hour, and about 4 p.m. as near as I can tell I saw Col. Fountain and his boy Henry. When I met them they were perhaps two and a half miles east of Chalk Hill coming towards Las Cruces; I was going towards Luna's Well and was perhaps 9 miles this side of Luna's Well; at that time a boy 16 or 17 years of age named Fajardo was riding horse back along side of me; he had joined me at Chalk Hill and was on his way to La Luz; along with him was an old man and two women in a wagon; they had been camped at Chalk Hill or stopped to rest; the wagon was in the rear of us a quarter to half a mile."

"The three men mentioned who were on horse back were about mile ahead of Col. Fountain and the boy coming towards Las Cruces; also the boy Fajardo saw them first and drew my attention to them and said he wondered who they were; I said they were cowboys; they were not nearer to us than a quarter of a mile at any time for they turned from the road when they saw us; we could not identify any of them from that distance, but one rode a white horse and the others dark horses and one wore a black hat and the others light, that is the only description I can give of them."

"When I met Col. Fountain he asked me what the news was at Las Cruces and I said nothing new; then I asked for his son Tom Fountain and he said he was working over at Lincoln and then the Col. asked about his son Jack and I told him he was well and was at Las Cruces. Col. Fountain was very fond of his children."

"He then spoke of the three men ahead of him and asked who they were, but I told him I could not tell as I had not gotten near enough to them as they had turned out from the road before reaching me. I then asked the Col. if they had come through ahead of him and he said yes clear through, but I did not ask him if they had come through from Tularosa or Lincoln. I could see that the Col. was uneasy, and I told him he could turn back to the station (Luna's Well) and stop over night and then come through with me on the next day (Sunday)."

"He thought a while and then said, 'No I guess I will push along,' and started off at a brisk rate. Fajardo was present during this conversation; the Colonel drove a team and led a horse beside the team; he used a buggy not a buckboard. The boy did not speak, did not notice his dress."

"I arrived at the station about 6 p.m. on time. I felt uneasy about the Colonel that night and in the morning I was all hitched and ready to start when Santos Alvarado the other mail driver arrived from the east and left right away. On my way back I watched from where I met the Col. to see if he had turned out from the road and when I found the tracks of his buggy where they had turned out from the road near Chalk Hill I left my buckboard and followed the buggy tracks about 30 or 40 yards. I saw the tracks of other horses and then I feared the worst."

"I went back to my mail and drove to Las Cruces and arrived about 6 p.m. I at once notified the people of what I had seen and of what I feared. I told Mr. Freudenthal and others. No, I could not identify any of these men. I have not been approached by anyone on this subject but a newspaper man, and he wanted my statement for publication in his paper, the **Independent Democrat**."

"The man who takes the mail from me at Luna's Well (Santos Alvardo) says that he saw two or three men riding up and back along the line of the road evidently watching, but not near enough to be able to identify them; this occurred, according to his story, for three or four nights running after the disappearance of Col. Fountain. It will be understood that the mail run from Luna's Wells is made in the night and therefore Alvarado could only see the forms of the men and horses but could not describe them. It is his opinion that these men are watching to see if the bodies are found and he thinks they are buried close by where the Colonel's buggy was found. (This is of course is only his opinion)."

"The young man Fajardo passed me a few days ago coming towards Las Cruces and he told me he was going to Colorado [Rodey], which is near Rincon; this is the young man's home. The man and two women, whose names I did not get, are supposed to be at or near La Luz, but they are said to know no more than Barela or Fajardo."

I pressed Barela as close as possible through my interpreter to give up further information, but he said he had positively given all he knew, I then asked if he would tell providing he had recognized any of these men; he said had he done so he should have told his employer, Mr. Freudenthal, that he had recognized one of these men of more as the case might be and would quit work. This was the substance of Barela's statement and no amount of questioning could change it. I told him of the amount of reward also of how well he would be treated by the Governor, but all to no avail; he said he knew no more and could tell no more. I must say that Barela impressed me as telling the truth all the way through.

After he had gone, Mr. Freudenthal told me that he had known Barela for over twenty years and he was positive that he had told the truth from the start, for when the searching parties went out they found the tracks just as he said and there was no reason to doubt his statement.

At 9:30 P.M. I discontinued for the night.

Yours truly,
"S"

TERRITORY OF NEW M EXICO
OFFICE OF THE EXECUTIVE
Santa Fe., N. Mex., March 7, 1896

John C. Fraser, Esq.
Las Cruces, N. M.

Dear Sir:-

Since writing you, I have received your letter of the 6th inst. I have no knowledge whatever as to who Col. Fountain referred to in his letter to Mr. Cree as being a *"prominent member of the Association who was not acting in good faith,"* but I will by this mail write to Mr. Cree and ask him, and will have him write to you or myself at once.

The letter from the stage driver to Mrs. Taylor, I gave to Pat Garrett, who will show it to you.

Yours very truly,
W. T. Thornton

P. S. The analysis of hair taken from the horse just been completed, and shows blood very plainly.

W. T. T.

Saturday, March 7, 1896

To-day in Las Cruces:-

Continuing on the above I called on Mr. Freudenthal at his store and had a further talk with him about the mail driver Barela, but he again assured me that this man was telling all he knew. I met Major Llewellyn's son Morgan, on the street and he told me that the Major wanted to see me, so I went over to his house and he gave me the map of that part of the country pertaining to this case and I will keep this with me for a guide. We then discussed the case until 1 p.m. The Major informed me that A. B. Fall who is thought to be the leader of this organized band of cattle thieves and assassins had left Las Cruces on Friday about noon, the day before the disappearance of Col. Fountain, for Sunol where he has a mine and a mill both of which are now shut down.

On this same day Major Llewellyn, Jas. A. Baird, and a nephew of Mrs. McCowan met A. B. Fall and Lew Cowan on their way to Sunol from Las Cruces at about 5:30 p.m. At the time they met Fall they (the Major and his party) were in front of Mrs. McCowan's house over at Organ, a mining camp in the Organ mountains about 18 miles from Las Cruces.

Mrs. McCowan's nephew (could not remember name) was at the side of the Major's rig taking out some things that he brought along for his aunt; when Fall drove up he saw him but could not see who he was and he asked in a very excited tone, *"Who is that behind your buggy, who is that man?"* He was very white at the time; the Major and Mr. Baird laughed and said it was Charlie, Mr. McCowan's nephew. After asking a few questions as to where we were, etc. he invited both of us to stop at Sunol any time we were over that way.

Now, continued the major, on Saturday the day of the disappearance of Col. Fountain we are told that Fall remained about the house all day at Sunol until afternoon when he started back with his team, but when he got out a short distance his team balked and he drove back and hitched up a team of mules and started for Las Cruces. Now Fall claims that he got here about 6 p.m. or a little after dark, but this is not so, as he was met by a Mr. [W. W.] Cox on the road from Sunol after half past eight driving like the old Harry, and as one of Mr. Cox's sons had gotten off the wagon to straighten up the load which had shifted and in doing so got his foot under the wheel and was hurt quite badly so they had to stop, and when they did stop Mr. Cox lit a match looked at his watch to see the time and found it was a few minutes after 8:30 p.m.

About this time he says he heard a team coming towards him at a break neck pace and he ran ahead a called to the driver whoever he might be to stop and not run into them.

When the team pulled up Cox found it was Mr. Fall driving a team of mules he spoke to him and told him what the trouble was.

Cox knows Fall very well. Now the distance from Las Cruces to Sunol is about 25 miles and from Chalk Hill to Sunol is about 14 to 16 miles straight across and I am told that you can see the clothes on the line in Cowan's yard from Chalk Hill and can also see people when they are moving about with the naked eye and with a field glass you can tell who they are. Major Llewellyn has sent Mr. Skidmore, the father of Mrs. Lew Cowan, over to see his daughter and find out from her just what Fall did do that day at Sunol, and what time he left there, and Skidmore is expected back to-day or to night.

I met Capt. Branigan who lives with Major Llewellyn and who was with him when he was Indian Agent. Capt. Branigan has had considerable experience in running down the class of criminals they have in this country and was with Major Llewellyn when he went out to search for Col. Fountain. A statement of this trip has been written up by the Major who uses the typewriter and will be signed by all parties who were in this party, this statement will accompany this report.

About 2 p.m., after I had finished dinner, Morgan Llewellyn came to my room with a note from his father requesting me to come over to his place as Major Van Patten, one of the men who was out with Pat Garrett, had arrived. I met Mr. Van Patten and had a long talk with him; he said that they had not found the bodies, but they found where something had been buried and then taken up and he was of the opinion that the bodies had been removed to some distant place by the people who did the killing.

Van Patten also spoke of a peculiar foot print of a man who seemed to have his ankle or knee turned or injured in such a way as to turn his right foot every time he stepped; these tracks were in the sand and were made by a high heel cowboy's boot and this same boot was run down on the outside. While Van Patten was telling this Jas. A. Baird came in and I was introduced to him; he had Van Patten repeat this and then tried to think of anyone over in that country who would fit that foot, but could not do so, but said that he could find out if there was any one, providing the matter was kept quiet.

I then asked Van Patten if he had seen or heard of the three men who were reported by the mail carrier as riding back and forth watching the road and the mail driver; he said they had run the men down and found that they were James R. Gilliland, Dan Fitchet [Fitchett], and one McDougal; all of them belong to the Oliver Lee gang. When Van Patten and his two Mexican's rode up toward them they came on a run for him with rifles ready to use, but when they saw Garrett and the other men, eight in all come up over the hill they drew up and pulled in their horses; they claimed they were looking for cattle.

Now to go back a few years, I wish to state that I am informed by Gov. Thornton and others here that about 1882 one Walter Goode was killed by Oliver Lee, Tom Tucker, and Bill Kellum, known as Cherokee Bill; his body was buried in what is known as the White Sands and were watched for a long time in the same manner as these men have been watching the road in the vicinity of Luna's Wells.

Now I am told by Major Llewellyn that there are requisition papers in the hands of the sheriff here for this same man Jas. R. Gilliland who is wanted for murder in Texas, but none of this searching party seemed to know this.

So far I have been able to keep under cover as I am supposed to be connected with Fraser & Chalmers, the Mining Machinery Co., and I thought owing to the condition of affairs here and the number of spies on the other side of this case that it would be as well to keep under cover as long as possible.

I am told by all who have been on the ground and with whom I have come in contact that I will get no information from any one in the vicinity of where Col. Fountain was last seen as every body is afraid to talk and the only way that information is to be had is through the sources now obtained, friends who communicate through friends only. Major Llewellyn's idea is that there are too many heads and it all should be under the control of one man. He is also very well satisfied and so do all the people here with whom I have come in contact seem to be, that the Negro barber Ellis knows all about this affair; Van Patten is now working on him through a Mexican woman whom he lays up with.

Major Llewellyn says that there was nothing in connection with Col. Fountain's domestic affairs to cause him to disappear, and that there was never any trouble between his wife and himself and that she was never jealous of him; this does not agree with Mr. Christy's statement. Van Patten showed me the nickel and dime found at Chalk Hill and the nickel has stains on it which might have been blood, but they are very dim and the dime has the appearance of being powder burned, on one side only and is still black.

The piece of the boy's shirt waist [a dress for boys, often worn until eight years old or so, see photo page 3] I have not seen, but Van Patten claims positively that it is a piece of the waist he wore the day he left with his father. Van Patten says he was there and helped them get ready to leave; he says the Col. carried two rifles in the rig with him when he left, there was also a small box with the boy's things and a telescope grip with the Colonel's things. Mrs. Fountain they say is flighty and can give no more information than they have; she blames herself for letting the boy go as the Col. did not want to take him.

Now if I am to go over this road it will not do for me to call on Mrs. Fountain or any or her family, or on Dist. Att'y Young or Mr. Fall, but if I am not to go on this trip then I can start in at any time and take their statements. To show how things are being watched by some one, or several, every time one of the citizens who is interested in this affair leaves town on the Tularosa road, they no sooner pass out of town than a shot is fired for each one in the party and the same way when any person or party comes in [to Las Cruces]. These shots are fired only at night and some other signal is supposed to be used in the day time. Fires are also used in the day time.

Mr. Baird and a Government employee of the land office are going over this road in a few days, they expect to leave Wednesday next and I could perhaps arrange to go with them. Pat Garrett and Sheriff Perry of Roswell came in to-night and report no trace; they report the weather terrible on account of the cold wind and sand. Everybody says it is a bad trip. I was at Major Llewellyn's until nearly 7 p.m. and then came to the hotel for supper. Major Llewellyn leaves for Silver City in the morning, but will be back on Monday.

About 9 p.m., Major Llewellyn called at my room and informed me that Mr. Skidmore had returned and reported that his daughter Mrs. Lew Cowan said that A. B. Fall arrived at at her home in Sunol on Friday night and stopped, and on Saturday he complained of not feeling very well and stayed around the house all day up to about 3 p.m., when he hitched up his team and started off, but came back as his horses balked and he changed for a team of mules then drove off; she does not think it was later than 3 or 4 p.m., and if this be the case, then he should have driven where he met Mr. Cox in an hour; but instead of that, he does not reach this part of the road until after 8:30 p.m., if true. I discontinued and retired for the night.

Yours respectfully,
"S"

Sunday, March 8, 1896

To-day in Las Cruces and El Paso, Texas

This a.m. I wrote up my reports and bill for the week. I had a call from Major Llewellyn's son Morgan, who brought me the statements prepared and signed which I mentioned in my previous report. I saw Pat Garrett and C. C. Perry but had no chance to speak to Garrett until about train time when we chanced to be sitting in the hotel alone. He told me that he knew me and knew from the Gov. that I was coming to render him any assistance possible. He told me that he was going to El Paso on the noon train and from El Paso he was going to Santa Fe to consult with the Gov. I told him that I would like to have a talk with him and he said, *"Yes, I want to see you also."* Just at this stage of the conversation some one came up and interrupted the conversation and I had no chance to renew the same as Garrett and Perry had to leave to catch their train.

I went to dinner and when I came from the dining room I found that the bus had not come up from the depot, so I took my overcoat and locking my room went to the depot and was just in time to catch the train. I told Mr. Hatton, Prop. of the Hotel, who was at the depot, that I had made up my mind to run up to El Paso and get some plans and drawings and if he wanted to use my room just to set my things to one side. I did not have time to pay my bill, but he said it would be all right. I did not arrive in El Paso until 2:50 p.m.

Mr. Garrett told me to meet him at the Lindell Hotel. Then he and Perry went off to get some dinner. I did not get a chance to talk to Mr. Garrett until about 9:30 p.m. when we met at his room in the Lindell. He informed me that the Governor had told him of my coming and that the object of my coming was to assist him in this matter.

No trace of the bodies had been found and Mr. Garrett was a little surprised to hear the statement made by Major Van Patten about finding where the bodies had been buried and removed as there was not a word of truth in it. In regard to the three men and a boy who were guarding the road and following the mail carrier there was no truth in that either. Mr. Garrett and Mr. [E. E.] Banner (one of his men) had met two men and a boy; the men were Dan Fetchet [Fitchett] and a man named McDougal; the boy was only about ten or eleven years old and I did not ask his name; the men had no fire arms of any kind and he could not see any signs of a six shooter about either one; they said they were seeking stray cattle or stock.

McDougal said he lived in Arkansas and the stock belonged to him; he asked him what he was going to do with the stock and he said he was going to ship it.

"They knew me," continued Mr. Garrett, *"for I had introduced myself and told them that we were searching for*

the bodies of Col. Fountain and his son. At the time this occurred Major Van Patten was at least four miles away from where this took place and never saw the men and knows nothing except what he heard Banner and myself tell. Van Patten cannot be relied on at all."

In regard to the Mexican who claims that he saw the guards ride the road at night, he saw him himself and he questioned him closely and he told him that he thought he saw someone, he thought there were two horses traveling along the road at a distance of perhaps one hundred yards to one side, but this was only one night and not several as stated by Van Patten.

Garrett declares that there is positively nothing in the statement of this woman Taylor who rode with the Mexican except that the Mexican and Mrs. Taylor are criminally intimate and the Mexican was afraid of the Edmonds Act. The man who replied to Mrs. Taylor's letter to the Mexican has been found by Garrett and Perry and his name is Johnson, and Perry had run down the men whom she saw and there is nothing in that. He does not think that Ellis the barber at Las Cruces knows a thing about this killing.

Fall may know, but I don't think he was present at the killing. He thinks there were more than three and certainly not more than five. Joe Morgan may have been in it and Oliver Lee, Bill McNew, and James R. Gilliland are no doubt the men who held the Col. up near Chalk Hill and the blood found on the road near Chalk Hill is where the Col. was held up and killed, and those bodies will be found some where within five miles of where he was killed. I had mentioned the names of Lee, McNew, Gilliland and Jack Tucker before Mr. Garrett gave me the names of the people he suspected.

He told me that Jack Tucker was not in it nor was Tom Tucker, but they belonged to the same outfit. Garrett said it would be utterly impossible for any stranger to approach Oliver Lee or this outfit without getting killed, as they were very suspicious and it would simply mean the death of any man who went in here to operate. The outfit was cold blooded and it would be nothing for them to kill anyone whom they suspected.

I questioned Mr. Garrett further to see if there was not some place to put a good man and he said there was only one place and that was to put a good man onto a woman named Richardson at Tularosa or near there. This woman was intimate with one of the gang and she no doubt knew a great deal about the gang. I understood Mr. Garrett to say that she was Bill McNew's woman; Garrett said he did not think it was a good plan for me to go out and interview these people on the Tularosa road as I would get nothing for they had all been talked to and scared to death of this gang of thieves and murderers.

He declared that a trip of this kind would be very dangerous for me to make as Lee and his crowd would not hesitate to kill a man who openly went into that country to investigate this case. From further conversation with Mr. Garrett I saw very plainly that he did not want me to go out and cause a stir by an open investigation. He told me that what he wanted me to do was to try and pull everybody off from the idea that Oliver Lee, Gilliland, and McNew are the men and to stop them from talking so much.

He further stated that if he could be made sheriff in place of the present incumbent he would have things where he could start right in on this gang. He assured me that he and Perry would make a move soon now. There is a contest case now in court at Silver City between the present Sheriff of Dona Ana County (Las Cruces) and the man (a Mexican) who ran against him.

Major Llewellyn's trip to Silver City is to hasten, if possible, this decision from Judge Bantz, and if decided against the present Sheriff, then Pat Garrett would become Sheriff, and would have a chance to disarm this man Oliver Lee and his gang who are, as before stated, Deputy Sheriffs, under the present sheriff, who is also a Mexican. He is said to be an honest man but controlled and handled by this gang. We talked matters over until 12:20 a.m., and after a lunch and cigars retired for the night to meet again in the morning. Garrett thought it would be best for me to wait over for the next train as this would break any connection between us at Las Cruces, where he was to pass through to go to Santa Fe.

I wrote to the Governor before retiring so as to get it off on the same train, also wrote a note for Mr. Garrett to hand to the Governor on his arrival; this note was simply to draw his attention to my letter in his mail so that he would read it before Mr. Garrett left town and be able to question him more fully providing he saw fit to do so.

I find that the various articles that will figure as evidence in this case such as the coins found, also the napkin and piece of boy's shirt waist, and other articles have not been kept together, but are scattered allover; some articles in the hands of one and some in others. I would suggest that all the articles pertaining to the case be properly marked for identification by parties who found them and then turned over to one reliable person and locked safely away. It was near 2:30 a.m. when I got to bed.

Yours truly,
"S"

Monday, March 9, 1896

To-day in El Paso:-

I was up at 7 a.m. and got out my report so as to get it away on the morning train; also mailed my letter to Gov. Thornton in relation to my talk with Pat Garrett. At 9:30 a.m., I went to the depot to see Mr. Garrett again as he was to leave on the 10 a.m. train for Santa Fe. I met him a few minutes before train time and had some further talk with him in regard to the information I had received from various parties in reference to what different people I had seen, etc. I first took up the statement in regard to Col. Fountain's trip from Lincoln to where he was last seen by Barela the mail driver on the Tularosa road near Chalk Hill, as reported in one of my previous reports, and Mr. Garrett said I had it correct. I next took up the statement of S. [Saturnino] Barela the stage driver and Mr. Garrett said that there was no doubt about this man's statement being correct and he was satisfied he told all he knew.

Mr. Garrett I found knew where Fajardo the young Mexican who rode with Barela from Chalk Hill was and he says they had seen all these people. I then asked him about a statement to the effect that one F. W. Pellman of Luna's Wells had seen the men who are supposed to be mixed up in this affair and that he (Pellman) used a telescope which he had to identify them; this Mr. Garrett said was untrue from beginning to end; he had seen Mr. Pellman and there was nothing to the statement.

I next brought up the statement of A. B. Fall in regard to his trip to and from Sunol on the day before and the day of the disappearance of Col. Fountain, Mr. Garrett said that he did not think that Fall was present at the killing of Col. Fountain, but he thought it would be well to find out who first told the story about Fall arriving in Las Cruces as early as 6 p.m. I had suggested running this point down. He said there was no reason to disbelieve Mr. Cox's statement about meeting Fall on the road 16 miles from Las Cruces at a few minutes after 8:30 p.m. on Saturday Feb. 1st, the day on which Col. Fountain was last seen.

Mr. Garrett informs me that the distance from Chalk Hill to Sunol on a direct line is 6 or 7 miles, and the view is very clear from either place. I then asked him what he thought of the Negro barber Ellis knowing anything about this matter; also told him what I knew about Ellis from the conversation with Major Llewellyn, Van Patten, and others, but Mr. Garrett feels satisfied that this gang that did this work would not trust a Negro, they use him to pick up information in town, but they would not let him in on a case of this kind.

Mr. Garrett said he would be back about Thursday and would see me, so as the train was pulling out I jumped off and went up town where I met an old friend of mine named A. Van Cleve, and he informed me that A. W. Hawkins recently of Eddy, N. M. was formerly a law partner of A. B. Fall at Las Cruces and in talking about the Fountain case with Mr. Hawkins a few days after it occurred, Hawkins said that Fall would perhaps know something about that matter and said that Fall was a dangerous man; Hawkins had only spoken of Oliver Lee in the same way for he knew them well. I put in the balance of the day with Van Cleve and some of his friends in hopes of picking up some more information, but learned nothing further, so discontinued at 11:30 p.m.

Yours truly,
"S"

Denver, Colorado, March 10, 1896
Hon. W. T. Thornton
Gov. New Mexico, Santa Fe, N.M

Dear Sir:-

Replying to yours of the 6th, would say that it is a mistake on the part of my clerk not to have enclosed the guarantee, and I herewith enclose the same to you.

I forwarded to you last night reports of Ass't Supt. Fraser and would say that things are certainly in a very bad shape around Las Cruces, but it is too early in the investigation to make any suggestions.

Yours truly,
"S"
Jas. McParland

TERRITORY OF NEW MEXICO
OFFICE OF THE EXECUTIVE
Santa Fe, N. Mex., March 10

Mr. J. C. Fraser
Las Cruces, N.M.

Dear Sir:-

I am in receipt of your favor from El Paso, and also the note sought by Mr. Garrett. I differ with Mr. G. as to the course he is pursuing, and so advised him. I think that you should go upon the ground, examine and talk to every witness, and thoroughly inform yourself of all the different clues, so that you can make up your mind from an inspection of the premises and from known facts as to who the guilty parties are and the best mode of procedure.

I am inclined to think that I shall leave for Washington tomorrow, and if so, I shall leave word with Major Palen of the First National Bank of this city, to honor your draft upon me to the extent of Three Hundred Dollars, and I think when that amount is used up, or sooner, if you can get through your work, quit until I return, when I can put the other man on, if thought desirable. I asked Pat Garrett to stop off at Socorro tomorrow (11th) and examine into the clue of which I spoke to you some days ago, so that he will not arrive in Las Cruces until one day after you get this.

Yours very truly,
W. T. Thornton

Tuesday, March 10, 1896
To-day in El Paso and Las Cruces:-

To-day I left El Paso at 10 a.m. arriving at Las Cruces at 11:46 a.m. When I opened my mail that was awaiting me I found a letter from Gov. Thornton also a statement made by a man whose name is not to be mentioned [Jack Maxwell]; please find copy of same enclosed.

This statement, if correct, may be of considerable assistance in this case. As Mr. Garrett is now in consultation with the Gov., I will see what he has to say about this man Ed. Brown and others mentioned. Gov. Thornton also notifies me that the analysis shows blood in the horse hair clipped from one or Col. Fountain's horses. After dinner I called on Major Llewellyn at his house and was informed by him that the contest over the Sheriff's office (which, I mentioned in previous report) had been decided and the decision was against the present Sheriff.

The present Sheriff is one Guadalupe Ascarate and the new Sheriff will be Numa Reymond and he will no doubt take office at once and that will be one point gained in the case to start with. Major Llewellyn showed me a letter from Jas. P. Meadows, one of the men who is out searching for the men; this letter from Meadows is to the Major and is dated La Luz, Mar. 6, 1896. In this letter Meadows declares that Jack Tucker was not in with this affair, that is he was not present with the men who captured Col. Fountain and the boy, and he says he has found out where he was all that day (Feb. 1st). This man Jim Meadows is one of the men working with Garrett. He seems to be quite sure of success and expresses himself in that way in this letter.

Major Llewellyn then handed me a letter from a Mrs. S. E. Barber [widow of Alexander A. McSween], written at White Oaks, N.M. and dated Mar. 6, 1896. In this letter Mrs. Barber states that a man named Jack Maxwell claims to have stopped at Lee's ranch on the night that Col. Fountain was abducted and this man Maxwell seems to have plenty of money which he claims was left him by a relative who died, but Mrs. Barber does not believe this story and is working on Maxwell to find out what she can and she seems to think that he knows something and feels confident that she can get what he knows. She claims that he said he was going to Old Mexico, but did not know where to go as he knew no one down there.

Maxwell is stopping with one Bud Smith on his (Smith's) ranch and Mrs. Barber says she has also heard that Bud Smith claims to have been at Lee's ranch on the same night that Jack Maxwell was, but she does not seem to know whether this story is true or not. She says that Bud Smith and Oliver Lee are very intimate and she is satisfied that they have worked together and robbed her of a great many head of cattle when Bud Smith worked for her as her foreman. Lee at that time had a brand which covered Mrs. Barber's.

She states in her letter that it is her opinion that Jack Maxwell is one of the guilty men and that Bud Smith is accessory to the crime. She also states that she told Sheriff Perry about this and is sorry she did but thinks he may not have gotten anything from Maxwell if he talked with him. Mrs. Barber is a ranch and cattle owner and a pretty bright woman. She is said to have handled her virtue in a rather reckless manner in former days, but of late she had joined the church, and is now one of the leading members.

She expects to go to Colorado in a short time. I requested Major Llewellyn to find out if she was going to Denver so that our people could take her statement in full; he said he would write her and find out, so she may call at the office of the Agency for this purpose. She is worth considerable money and travels considerable.

I called on S. B. Newcomb who returned to Las Cruces from Santa Fe on the day I left for El Paso. I had a long talk with Mr. Newcomb and advised that all talking by the people on our side of this case should stop as there was too much of it. I had also spoken to Major Llewellyn about this and they both agreed with me. Mr. Newcomb informed me that the new sheriff had wired to Gov. Thornton asking if he had any suggestions to make to him; this was very good, for the Gov. and Mr. Garrett are both together and can come to some conclusion as to what is best to be done. I then received from Mr. Newcomb a copy of the statement of Mrs. E. D. Taylor in which she claims to have ridden with the Mexican mail driver from Mr. William Wait's ranch to a point where they change drivers between Luna's Wells and La Luz; here she was taken up by mail driver Alvino Guerra who drives to La Luz.

At about 2 a.m. on Feb. 2, 1896 she claims to have seen a camp fire to the left which seemed to be 10 or 15 miles away and towards the Mal Pais.

[The Carrizozo Malpais is a large and, geologically speaking, recent lava flow west of Carrizozo. The Spanish words "mal pais" translates literally as "bad lands." The term is often used in New Mexico to refer to lava flows. Striking images of the Tularosa Basin taken from space show the black Malpais formation in the northern end of the Tularosa Basin almost flowing into the white sand dunes to the south.]

"I mentioned this bright fire to the driver. I arrived at La Luz," continued Mrs. Taylor in this statement, "about 4 a.m. Sunday morning with Alvino Guerra on the stage above mentioned for Tularosa. At a point about 3 or 4 miles from La Luz I saw three horsemen coming from the direction of the White Sands towards the road on which we were traveling; these horsemen crossed the road in front of us about 100 yards and then they rode along the road on our right passing us about 40 steps from and coming into the stage road about three hundred yards behind us; as these three horsemen passed us I recognized Oliver Lee and William McNew and the other man I think was Frank Chatfield."

"Alvino Guerra asked me it I knew these men and I told him who they were and he said these men had been to Lincoln to Court. It was broad daylight when we met these horsemen. We reached Tularosa about 10 a.m. Feb. 2, 1896, and I remained until Wednesday Feb. 5, 1896, at Tularosa, and as I was about to leave I heard for the first time about the Col. Fountain affair. I then thought of the three horsemen whom we had met as the probable murderers and on my arrival at Lincoln I spoke of it to several persons. I have known Oliver Lee, Wm. McNew, and Frank Chatfield for the past five or six years and I have attended dances where one or all three of them have been in attendance and cannot be mistaken as to their identity."

The above is not Mrs. Taylor's statement in full but it covers the same and this statement is sworn to before the Clerk of the Probate Court at Lincoln, N.M. on the 8th day of Feb. 1896. In speaking to Pat Garrett about this woman's statement, he said that she was wrong and also stated to me that this Mexican Alvino Guerra drove her over to Tularosa in a private rig and was intimate with her. I promised to see Mr. Newcomb again tomorrow.

I discontinued about 10 P.M. and retired for the night.
Yours truly,
"S"

March 11, 1896.
To-day in Las Cruces:-

I saw Major Llewellyn after breakfast and learned that he was going as far as Albuquerque on the morning train, but would try and be back tomorrow. Also saw Jas. Baird, but did not get a chance to speak to him until after dinner when I questioned him about who first told the story of Judge A. B. Fall arriving here from Sunol at 6 p.m. on Saturday, Feb. 1st; Mr. Baird said that his son was the first one who told him, but the hour was 8 p.m. instead or 6 p.m.

"My son," continued Mr. Baird, "was standing in front of Bull's store next to A. B. Fall's office and old man Fall came along and said, 'Hello, Albert when did you get in?' and Albert (A. B. Fall) replied, 8 o'clock last night."

This conversation between father and son took place on Sunday morning Feb. 2nd.

Mr. Garrett arrived on the 10:05 a.m. train from Santa Fe, but I did not get to speak to him until afternoon, when I went to his room with him. He told me of his talk with the Governor and that he agreed with him about my not making the trip, but later he told me that the Gov. said we could do as we saw fit and thought best, and then Mr. Garrett added that the trip would do no good except to enable me to give them my opinion after going over the ground. I then took up the various points with Mr. Garrett beginning with the statement of Mrs. Taylor who claims to have seen three horsemen on Sunday morning a little after 6 A.M. just out of La Luz and recognized two of them as Oliver Lee and Bill McNew and she thought the third one was a man named Chatfield, but was not sure.

Mr. Garrett said that this was out of the question as they had the statement of a man who stopped Saturday and Sunday at Lee's ranch and who saw Oliver Lee, Bill McNew, and Jas. Gilliland ride into Lee's ranch on Sunday morning about 9 a.m. Feb. 2nd, and they were all fagged out and so were the horses. I asked if the man he referred to as stopping at Lee's ranch was not Jack Maxwell and he said it was; he also said there was another man there at the same time, this man was one John Bleven [Albert Blevin] and he was an officer from Texas who had come over to summon some of them at the ranch to appear in a civil case in Texas. Maxwell was hunting stock in that country. Garrett and Perry both interviewed him. I then showed Mr. Garrett the letter which I received from Major Llewellyn and which was from Mrs. S. E. Barber.

Mr. Garrett, after reading this letter over, said that he knew Mrs. Barber very well and that she had received her information second hand. He had never heard of Bud Smith being at Lee's ranch and did not believe it. I next took up the statement of Slick Miller, and Garrett informed me he had seen and questioned this man while at Santa Fe and was satisfied that he was telling the truth and now thought that Ed. Brown may have been in this job, and if so, the trail leading through the Pass in the Mountains and would account for him as that would be right on his way home and also in the proper direction to dispose of the bodies in the manner planned in 1894, which was to be in the San Andreas Mts.

Brown is said to have left Socorro a few days before the disappearance of Col. Fountain and who was seen in the Cottonwood Groves near Rincon a day or so after the affair happened. Mr. Garrett had talked this matter over with the Governor while at Santa Fe and he (Garrett) had a man on the ground now to get the full particulars about Brown and his movements. This man was a Mexican who was well posted and acquainted there.

I again took up the statement of Mrs. Taylor with Mr. Garrett and found that the distance from La Luz or the place near La Luz where she claims to have seen the men is at least 50 miles from Lee's ranch and they could not ride it and get there at 9 a.m. In her statement she says it was 6 a.m. when she left La Luz and that it was broad day light when she saw these three men.

Mr. Garrett said that the Gov. thought I had best remain here and look after the case and advise them on various points that might come up. I then introduced the statement contained in Gov. Thornton's letter of March 6th in regard to a conversation overheard by a friend of the Governor's at Ruidoso Post Office in Lincoln County about a man who stopped over Sunday and Monday after the disappearance of Col. Fountain at Lee's ranch where he saw Oliver Lee, Bill McNew, and Chatfield, all of whom acted nervous and suspicious and who were heavily armed and who slept out of the house. I had Mr. Garrett make a note about this so as to investigate the same when he went out this time.

During the evening I met Mr. Garrett and Mr. Baird at Garrett's room and here I learned that Judge Warren of Albuquerque was in town, having been engaged to fight the case for Sheriff Guadalupe Ascarate against Numa Reymond and that Judge Bantz of Silver City had already been wired that they had applied or would apply for a new trial and if this failed they would appeal their case to the higher court and ask for an order restraining Numa Reymond from acting. Now this is done and the case is tied up in the higher Court and Ascarate allowed to continue on as sheriff, the progress on the case is bound to be very slow. There seems to be an awful change in Fall and his gang since this decision of the Court and they seem very much put out about it, and no doubt are when they employ Judge Warren to come here and assist them. Warren is said to be one of the best attorneys in the Territory. He has been around Fall's office all the day. A petition is now being signed by some of the best citizens for the removal of Mr. Young the Dist. Attorney.

It was decided that Mr. Garrett should write Gov. Thornton about the new moves to be made by Fall and his gang for an appeal, etc., and I was also to endorse this letter. On an appeal this case would go to Judge Smith at Santa Fe and the idea was to have Gov. Thornton see Judge Smith and lay the matter before him, providing the Gov. thought such a step necessary.

I again brought up the question of the time A. B. Fall arrived in Las Cruces on Saturday evening and Mr. Garrett said he remembered Major Llewellyn stating that he had received it from responsible parties in El Paso that Fall had stated to them after this affair that he had arrived home from Sonol about 6 p.m. I will see the Major about this on his return.

I was around through the stores and saloons as is my custom each day, but did not pick up anything new. I retired at 11:30 p.m.

Yours respectfully,
"S"

Thursday, March 12, 1896

To-day in Las Cruces,

This morning I got out my report and then called on Mr. Garrett at his room and had another talk with him; he is a man who says very little, so anything I learn from him is through questions. I took up the matter of the second man named Bleven [Blevin] being at Lee's ranch on Saturday and Sunday (Feb. 1st and 2nd). Garrett said no one knew his first name, but he was from Toyah, Texas, and works for Perry Altman.

Now this information about Bleven being there comes from Jack Maxwell and should be run down. Garrett says Oliver Lee told him when he questioned him that he was home on his ranch on Saturday, Feb. 1st, which, if the statements of Maxwell and Dan Fitchet [Fitchett] are true, the latter, I understand, waited three or four days at Lee's ranch with a bunch of cattle which he was to deliver, but could not do so as Oliver was not at home. This statement was made by Fitchet to Major Llewellyn when the first searching party went out to look for Col. Fountain and his son.

Jack Maxwell claims he was at Lee's ranch Saturday and Sunday and that Lee, McNew, and Gilliland arrived there on Sunday morning with their horses much worn out, he did not ask them anything about where they had been for he was afraid to do so and at the time had no doubt about their having been up to some mischief. These three men had breakfast after their arrival that morning.

I will try to see this man Jack Maxwell myself and get his statement. I inquired of Garrett where Oliver Lee was now and he said he had heard that he had left his ranch and was staying away; if this be true then he may be laying up with this woman of his who keeps a lodging house in El Paso and whose name and location I will try to get through Major Llewellyn on his return home; he did not come to-day.

Judge Warren who is employed by the present Sheriff Ascarate to fight the decision of Judge Bantz left for Silver City early this morning to file his motion for a new trial. Mr. Garrett went to see Judge McFie, Mr. Christie [Christy], and others and talked this matter over and it was decided that Gov. Thornton had best wait on Judge Smith, the State Supreme Judge at Santa Fe, to whom the case would go on an appeal. Word had been received by Numa Raymond [Reymond] through some source that Gov. Thornton was going to Washington, so it was decided to try to stop him if possible as his presence here was considered necessary at this critical moment.

Mr. Garrett sent this telegram and also sent a letter briefly stating the present situation and at his request and the request of others I enclosed a few lines endorsing what Mr. Garrett had said. Judge Newcomb told me later in the day that Garrett had received a reply to his telegram and the Gov. informed him that he would wait for the mail, but could not come to Las Cruces.

Mr. Perry of Roswell did not arrive here to-day, but will no doubt be in tomorrow. I can see very plainly that Garrett does not want to go out again until the question of Sheriff is settled and he becomes an officer of the County himself. There has been one or two letters come in from La Luz from Jim Meadows for Major Llewellyn, but I will not get at the contents of these until the Major returns.

I received a letter from Gov. Thornton in this morning's mail in which the Gov. states that he wants me to go over the ground and interview the people and to place myself in a position to give an opinion and to discontinue when I am through. I told Garrett that I had decided to go over the ground and see the people and country; he acted very nicely about it and said I should go out with them, which I decided to do on account of their knowledge of the country and of the people that I want to see. I could have gone out with Jas. A. Baird early this morning had I received this letter in time.

I made my usual round of the stores and saloons to see if I could pick up anything in the way of information, but there was nothing new, so at midnight I retired.

Yours respectfully,
"S"

Friday, March 13, 1896
To-day in Las Cruces,

I went to Mr. Garrett's room and we talked the case over until 10 a.m., but nothing new was developed and it was more to get the lay of the land than anything else. We went to the depot and saw Major Llewellyn when he arrived on the morning train; he had some ladies with him and said he would see us later in the day.

After dinner, Judge A. B. Fall came and spoke to Mr. Garrett and sat with him for quite a while; I happened to come along from my room and Mr. Garrett introduced me to him; he said he was pleased to meet me and we had a few pleasant words about the weather, when I withdrew to allow Mr. Garrett to continue his conversation. Mr. Garrett told me afterwards that Fall had told him that he for one wanted him (Garrett) here as a Deputy Sheriff and no matter whether Numa Raymond became Sheriff or Ascarate remained in office he should have a commission just the same and he should have any amount of assistance that he might need providing he had any papers to serve.

I saw Oliver Lee on the street here to-day, he is not a bad looking man, being a Deputy Sheriff he wore his belt and pistol; he was around Fall's office and Ellis's barber shop.

Major Llewellyn came to the Hotel after 2 p.m. and we three went to Mr. Garrett's room; here the Major turned over to me some letters he had received; one was from Jas. A. Brock, the Live Stock Commission Merchant, Room 2, Opera House Block, El Paso, Texas, and enclosed a letter from one H. C. Smith of Mt. Blanco, Crosby County, Texas, in which Smith states that a man named John Thompson, supposed to be a U.S. Marshal from New Mexico, had arrested a man at Emma in Crosby County, who was supposed to be one of the murderers of Col. Fountain. This arrest was made on March 5th and the Sheriff of Crosby County assisted in the arrest.

This is the first anyone here has heard of this arrest, so the chances are that he was arrested for some other crime or we should have heard it ere this time.

The other letter was from Jim Meadows who remained behind when Garrett, Perry, and Van Patten came in. In this letter, which is dated at La Luz March 10, 1896, he states that one Antonio Rey at [Luna's] Well made a statement to some one that he had seen and talked for a long while with a man at the Well about 20 days previous to Feb. 1st, and that he saw the same man with two other men out east of the Wells on Feb. 1st. He (Antonio Ray) also said that there was a boy there named Nicolas, but he would not tell his other name and Nicolas was said to know something, but he was missing and no one knew where he was. Meadows goes on to state in this letter that there is another man named Chatfield who had a finger in the pie and that it was Chatfield and Bill Carr who followed Col. Fountain from Lincoln and there were three men who came in behind Col. Fountain to La Luz from Tularosa; one of the three came through town, this was Bill Carr and the others passed below the town. Bill Carr went southwest from town on Friday and returned from same direction on Saturday.

"I think I can find out who the other two were in a day or so," continues Meadows, "but one I think was Chatfield as he has acted very strange." Meadows also says in this letter that it is rumored over there that some Mexicans followed a trail from where the buggy was left to the Little Whitewater Mts., thence into the White Sands from the east side and found blood on the trail. He (Meadows) closes by saying that he is going to Tularosa to run this story down, for there has been so much told that he does not know what to believe.

It seems from this letter that Major Llewellyn had proposed to send one Florencia Luna to see this man Antonio Rey and get from him the truth about this story, but I don't think this has been done. The Major had not heard from Mr. Skidmore who was to carry my list of questions out to Mrs. Lew Cowan at Sunol, but he was expected in to-night or in the morning. As Major Llewellyn was very busy selecting delegates for the coming County convention, I was unable to have much conversation with him during the afternoon and he goes to El Paso tomorrow in response to a telegram.

Mr. Garrett left for El Paso at 3:30 p.m. and will perhaps remain there until Monday as the people here want him to wait until they can place him in office before he goes out again, and I know that he would prefer this to be done before he went out again, so that he can act as he sees fit to do so. This will keep me here until he goes out, for I fail to find anyone who wants to go out with me on this trip alone as driver and guide. Besides, I can do this trip much better by going with Garrett and Perry, for we will have everything necessary to camp out and can take our time so as to see everybody.

Mr. Garrett thinks the trip from here to Tularosa done properly will take about six days. I of course may find it necessary to go to Lincoln and perhaps to Roswell then to Toyah, Texas, to see Mr. Bleven. I learned from Mr. Garrett that this man who was to look up the Ed. Brown matter could do nothing as the man he was to work on for information was away, but he was to go back again.

I saw nothing of Major Llewellyn again until 9 p.m. as he was busy having heard that a secret meeting was to be held by Oliver Lee and others at a certain place in town. I only met him for a few minutes and he thought it advisable for me to go down to El Paso with him in the morning, as I could do nothing more here just at present, and while in El Paso we could consult and he would find out who the woman was and just where she is located that Oliver Lee lays up with while in El Paso; also, look up the matter of who Judge Fall told at El Paso that he arrived in Las Cruces on Saturday Feb. 1st, at 6 p.m. Both of these points should be looked up as they may be important points, so if nothing new comes up I may go in the morning.

I making my usual rounds of stores and saloons to-night I ran across Deputy Sheriff Casey who was doing some loud talking to an attorney named Pickett from Silver City. He was praising the present Sheriff and claimed that more convictions for murder had been made in this county than in any other. I heard him mention Mr. Christy's name as he was speaking about someone wanting him to swear out warrants for two of the suspected men, but he would not do it, but told them to place the warrants in his hands for Oliver Lee or any one else and he would bring them in dead or alive and that was the kind of a man he was. An old gentleman with a long white beard whom they call Judge and who is, I believe, receiver of the Land Office was present also. At 11:30 p.m. I retired for the night.

I enclose copy of letter from Alvino Guerra to Mrs. Eva Taylor; same is said by Garrett to have been written for him by a man named Johnson.

Yours respectfully,
"S"

TERRITITORY OF NEW MEXICO
OFFICE OF THE EXECUTIVE
Las Cruces, N. Mex., March 13, 1896

Mr. John C. Fraser,
Las Cruces, N. M.

Dear Mr. Fraser:

I have your favors of the 12th inst. And shall do what I can to see that no hitch is made in the effort to have Pat Garrett put deputy sheriff. I feel, however, that what I do, should be done

I hope Mr. Garrett has told you all about the affidavit that I need from a party [Jack Maxwell] who stayed all night at a house near the scene [of the] murder on the same night that Fountain was killed, and who saw three men, some of the parties suspected, come home the next morning. He said that he had some hesitancy in telling you because he had promised the party that he would tell no one about it. I told Garrett that you have this information in order to arrive at a correct solution of the matter.

I fully agree with you that unless a change is made in the sheriff's position in Dona Ana County, that we had just as well get what information we can and then quit the matter for the present.

I leave for Washington City to-night, to be gone probably two or three weeks.

Very truly,
W. T. Thornton

TERRITORY OF NEW MEXICO
OFFICE OF THE EXECUTIVE
Santa Fe, N. Mex., March 13, 1896

Mr. John C. Fraser
Las Cruces, N.M.

Dear Sir:-

Either yourself or Garrett should go to San Marcial and have Librado C. de Baca, or Elfego Baca meet you there and investigate that clue. It appears that the men who have the testimony are J. A. Gallegos and two sons, and that the man who the evidence affects is Ed. Brown. I would attend to this matter without further delay.

Yours very truly,
W. T. Thornton,

TERRITORY OF NEW MEXICO
OFFICE OF THE EXECUTIVE
Santa Fe, N. Mex., March 13, 1896

James McParland, Esq.
Denver, Colo.

Dear Sir:-

I sent you a guarantee yesterday, but failed to write you.

I have deposited with the First National Bank the money to pay Mr. Fraser's expenses, and have directed Mr. Fraser to draw on Mr. R. J. Palen for money to cover his expenses there, such sum not to exceed Three Hundred Dollars, and when he shall have exhausted that amount, to layoff until my return from Washington City where I go to-night, to be absent for about three weeks on official business.

I hope that by the time Mr. Fraser has used up this amount of money to which I have limited him, he will have obtained all of the information necessary to put the secret man on, and when I return it is my intention to put him on at once and keep him at work for some time, providing Mr. Fraser thinks anything can be accomplished.

Yours very truly,
W. T. Thornton

Saturday, March 14, 1896

To-day in Las Cruces &. El Paso-

This morning I called to see Judge A. B. Fall at his office, but he was not in, I called two or three times, as I was anxious to have a talk with him, but he had not arrived at his office up to 9:45 a.m., so I paid my hotel bill and boarded the train for El Paso along with Major Llewellyn and Judge S. B. Newcomb; we had a general talk over matters on the way up in the Pullman, as we had taken seats in that car to be able to discuss matters pertaining to this case; nothing new was developed in this conversation.

We arrived at El Paso at 11:45 a.m. and went to the hotel; here I was introduced to Ben Williams whom this same gang headed by A. B. Fall tried to assassinate in Las Cruces a short time ago; they succeeded in shooting his left arm pretty badly.

Williams is one of the Territorial Cattle Inspectors with headquarters at Las Cruces, but ever since this shooting he has made El Paso his headquarters. Williams is thoroughly satisfied that it was the Oliver Lee gang who did this work and told me that he knew them well, as he had been among them for two years and had to quit them because he would not join them in their murderous work.

Williams is working hard to get a case of murder against this man Lee and others in the State of Texas and says he will be ready in a few weeks to arrest Oliver Lee, who comes to El Paso very often to see this woman who runs the furnished rooming house.

I saw Oliver Lee on the street here to-day, he having come up from Las Cruces yesterday I saw him several times during the day, but not to speak to him; he wore his belt and pistols around the street here just the same as at Las Cruces. During the afternoon I located the furnished rooming house of the woman whom Oliver Lee visits and found it to be kept by a Mrs. Stevens, a widow, 312 and 314 San Antonio Street. I called to see her twice to see her about furnished rooms, but the girl in charge said she was not in.

I did not see anything of Mr. Garrett until near evening; we had a talk in my room and he told me that he had a friend here who knew a Mexican who was now working at the Smelter here who saw the three horsemen who are supposed to have killed Col. Fountain and knew who they were; this Mexican had left the country through fear and was going to Old Mexico soon; this friend of Mr. Garrett's was a friend of the Mexican's so he, Garrett, offered to pay them each $200.00 if the information was correct and the bodies could be found on his information. This man was to see the Mexican and get the information and give the same to Mr. Garrett. I did not get any names as Mr. Garrett did not seem to care to give them. I, however, urged upon him the importance in following up a statement of this kind and he said he would follow it.

He (Garrett) received a telegram from Sheriff Perry and he said he could not get to Las Cruces until the 19th. I asked Major Llewellyn to run down the man while here who first stated that A. B. Fall told him he arrived in Las Cruces at 6 o'clock on the evening of the day on which Col. Fountain was last seen. The Major tried to find the man, but he was out of town and he said he would look it up the first time he came down again. It was about midnight when we returned to the hotel. Oliver Lee was around on the streets and resorts up to that time. I will leave here to-morrow morning with Major Llewellyn for Las Cruces, unless I see a better chance to do something.

Yours respectfully,
"S"

Sunday, March 15, 1896

To-day in El Paso and Las Cruces,-

This morning it was decided that we all return to Las Cruces to be present when Judge Bantz came to answer the motion for a new trial in the contest case, so at 10 a.m. we left for Las Cruces, arriving there at 11:45 a.m. I found my pass in care of the Agent on my return. Oliver Lee came down also on this train and is now in town.

I met Judge Fall at the Post Office and received a warm invitation to call which I promised to do when I had time. I received two letters from Gov. Thornton, both dated March 13th, and in one of those he asks me if Mr. Garrett had told me about an affidavit he had from a man [Maxwell] who stayed all night at a house near the scene of the murder and who saw men return the following morning, etc.

I wish to state that Mr. Garrett has never said one word to me about having received an affidavit from anyone, and any information I get from him is mostly obtained by questioning, so it can be readily seen that I am working at a great disadvantage. This being Sunday, I could do nothing with Mr. Fall as he was not at his office.

The other letter from Gov. Thornton advised me to take up the Ed. Brown end of the case at San Marcial and I will leave here tomorrow and take this matter up while this contest case is being decided. Mr. Garrett showed me a letter from the Governor on this same subject and at first said he did not see what I could obtain down there; but later said I had better take it up and advised me to go to Socorro and get hold of Librado de Baca or Elfego Baca. Attached to this report please find copy letter from Banner to Garrett.

At 11:30 p.m. I discontinued for the day and retired. I also attach list of articles said to be taken from Col. Fountain's buckboard.

Yours respectfully,
"S"

[Letter to Garrett from Banner]

Tularosa, N.M., March 12, 1896
Friend Garrett,—

Since I saw you I have heard a great deal to convince me that Antonio knows a good big lot of importance, or he is a terrible fool. It might be well to see Florencia Luna at Las Cruces and have him give Antonio a good talk. His women folks also made an acknowledgment to Gomez that they recognized the man on gray horse (one of the three), said also that this man came to Luna Well some time before the murder and remained all day, got on top of the house many times, looking over the road. There is also a trail leading into the white sands several miles this side (North) of where we camped at edge of sands the night before you went to La Luz and this trail, it appears from all I can learn, is very familiar to Antonio, but he said nothing to us about it. I will expect to hear from you tonight, if not, suppose I will remain in the neighborhood until I do hear from you. Meadows was here yesterday and may be here tomorrow.

E. E. B. [E. E. Banner]

[List of items taken from Colonel Fountain's buggy when found by the searchers.]

The following is a list of articles removed from the buckboard of Col. Fountain as near as known:-

- 1 40-82 Winchester rifle, rear sight taken off and replaced by piece of white metal in slot of same. Front sight small ivory bead, adjustable Lyman sight back of hammer, nose of stock cut out to permit Lyman sight to fold hack into stock; one side of stock worn crossways about three inches from butt end, caused by rubbing against foot rail.
- 1 Celluoid handled dagger and sheath (drawing of same is new in possession of P. F. Garrett)
- 1 Canteen 9 inches in diameter (mate of which can be seen at Col. Fountain's house)
- 1 Bridle with blinds (mate can be seen at Fountain's)
- 1 One inch rope 40 feet long (old)
- 1 Lap robe, one side black the other red with dogs heads printed in black and two whips crossed behind the dogs' heads.
- 1 Indian Blanket about 5x7 feet, 4 inch red and white stripes running alternately across.
- 1 Indian blanket 3x5 feet, red, white, blue, green, and yellow in saw teeth design.
- 1 Quilt.
- 2 Neck yoke straps.

This list was made up by a Mr. Clausen, a son-in-law of Col. Fountain and is suppose to be correct.

Monday, March 16, 1896

To-day in Socorro,-

I saw Major Llewellyn and Mr. Garrett and received from them letters of introduction to Librado C. De Baca and Dr. Crookshanks [Cruickshank], the former at Socorro and the latter at San Marcial. Major Llewellyn asked me if I had seen the letters from Dr. Crookshanks in regard to this Ed. Brown matter. This was the first I had heard of any letters on this subject so I asked the Major who had them and was informed that they had been turned over to Mr. Garrett. I then went to Garrett and asked about them and learned that he had paid no attention to them. These letters from the Doctor contained the same information as I had already received and that was to the effect that Ed. Brown and two other men had left Brown's ranch which is out from San Marcial (not Socorro as before stated) in the latter part of January and returned a few days after the disappearance of Col. Fountain; their horses were very much worn out.

This information came from one Jose Angel Gallegos who lives at a place called Valverde close to San Marcial. Gov. Thornton had instructed Mr. Garrett to take this matter up on his way up from Santa Fe this last trip and he had wired one Librado C. De Baca to meet Mr. Garrett on the train at Socorro and assist him in this matter as De Baca was acquainted with Jose Angel Gallegos and it was thought he could approach him and get this information from him. He (De Baca) went to Gallegos' place, but found no one at home, so went back to Socorro and said he would go up again in a few days. This information he sent to Mr. Garrett by letter as Mr. Garrett had not stopped off at San Marcial as Gov. Thornton had instructed.

After receiving what information I could from Mr. Garrett I left for Socorro at 11:46 a.m. and arrived at Socorro at 5:15 p.m. I went to the Courthouse to find Elfego Baca who is the County Clerk and one of the men whom Gov. Thornton instructed me in his letter to see. I found that he was not at his office, so went to his house and learned that he and Librado C. De Baca were out in the country on some political business. I left word where I could be found and at 7 p.m. Librado C. De Baca came to the Hotel and I took him to my room and gave him the letter from Mr. Garrett.

He informed me that Elfego Baca had gone to San Marcial yesterday and saw Jose Angel Gallegos with whom he was well acquainted and he learned from him that a Mexican who works for Ed. Brown and who owns a ranch close to Brown's had told him all he knew about it, but that this Mexican could not give the day and date of their leaving and also of their returning and what they said before and after their return.

One of them, Gallegos states, says he was over at Lincoln at Court, but this is not true for no one saw him there. Again they said they were going to get some cattle and drive them in, but they brought no cattle; one of the other two besides Ed. Brown was a man named Green Scott, and this Mexican knew the names of all three and also the horses they rode and can give the brands of the horses.

Gallegos told Mr. Baca that he was positive that these men killed Col. Fountain, but this was simply his own opinion. Mr. Baca at once started a son of Gallegos out to notify this Mexican to come to San Marcial and when he got there to notify him by wire and he would meet him. Mr. Baca claims that he overheard this man Green Scott say he was glad that s—of a b---- Col. Fountain was dead. Librado De Baca further stated that he had found out since his visit to Gallegos' house when he could not find him that he (Gallegos) and his family were all at home, but did not want to see him, as they are afraid to be mixed up in this affair.

It will be three or four days before this Mexican will arrive at San Marcial. He then told me that Mr. Baca had a man who was recently convicted of some crime and sentenced for 25 years, but Mr. Baca and his law partner had succeeded in getting a new trial for him and he was now out on bond. This man was one of Ed. Brown's gang and Brown would tell him anything, so Mr. Baca was going to send him to work on Brown and if this man succeeded then perhaps the Governor will do something for him.

This was all the information De Baca had, so he went out and soon came back with Elfego Baca to whom I was introduced and we went over this same ground with Elfego and almost word for word Mr. Baca told the same story of what he had done and what he was going to do; and then he informed me rather bluntly that he did not think he should be called upon to do this for nothing and it was only a question of money with him.

I explained the condition of affairs and mentioned the reward; he said he knew all about that, but Pat Garrett had been hired and others, and he himself had a good record as sheriff of this county. He then went on to tell of the different desperate men whom he had captured, and I saw at once that he seemed to think he should have been called upon to act. He told me that I could tell Pat Garrett just how he felt about it. He went on to say that it he was in a position to go to this Mexican and say, *"Here is a certain sum of money,"* and place the sum in his hand, *"now tell me what you know, I would get the whole thing."*

Mr. Baca said there was no doubt about these being the men, still I found from our conversation that this was simply his own idea from what little he knew through Gallegos. I went over town and treated them to cigars and drinks and before parting it was agreed to allow Elfego Baca and Librado De Baca to go ahead on this matter and get what they could from the Mexican and through the man who was going out to work on Ed. Brown. I made a few suggestions as to the manner in which this Mexican would be questioned and then we parted, as my time is limited, I could not afford to wait for the Mexican's arrival at San Marcial; so at 11 p.m. I discontinued and retired for the night.

Yours respectfully,
"S"

Tuesday, March 17, 1896

To-day in Socorro and Las Cruces:-

This a.m. I was called at 4:30 a.m. and at 5:15 a.m. left for Las Cruces where I arrived at 10:05 a.m.

I neglected to state in my report for yesterday that I met and was introduced to Judge Bantz at Rincon on my way up and had a chance to explain some of the conditions existing at Las Cruces. He seemed much interested and asked me a number of questions. He expressed himself very strongly as being opposed to the manner in which people were being murdered. I had but a few moments before my train pulled out to talk, but from the manner in which Judge Bantz expressed himself, I should judge that he would decide in favor of Numa Raymond.

On my arrival at Las Cruces, Major Llewellyn met me at the depot and he informed me that he had another letter from Mrs. Barber which he would give me sometime during the day. Att'y Ferguson of Albuquerque came in on the same train with me to take Judge Warren's place in the present contest which will come up for argument tomorrow (Wednesday). He is said to be a very clever man and an enemy to Col. Fountain who at one time slapped his face in Court during some case.

I saw Mr. Garrett but he had nothing new. It was decided that we should leave Thursday after dinner, no matter what way the decision went; if Sheriff Perry did not arrive then, he could follow on horseback the following day when he arrived. There was a terrible dust storm here all day and few people were about.

I met Major Llewellyn during the evening and we went around town together, but found everything very quiet; so after the stores closed we called on Mr. John Riley, now of Denver, but formerly a large cattleman of this county, who moved away on account of this lawless gang. During our conversation I was informed that when Col. Fountain went to Lincoln on the last trip he had several of this gang indicted, among these were Oliver Lee, Bill McNew, Jas. Gilliland, Jack Tucker, and Bill Carr; Ed. Brown I was told had been indicted and sent to jail several times by Col. Fountain.

The letter from Mrs. Barber which was written at White Oaks, March 14, 1896, stated that Jack Maxwell had come back to Three Rivers to Smith's ranch and told that Sheriff Perry had been trying to get something out of him, but he did not have to talk. She says that he stopped but a short time at Smith's then left for Old Mexico. She also says that this man J. T. Smith is a great friend of Oliver Lee's and that Mrs. Smith has told it among her neighbors that Mr. Smith was at Lee's on the night or Feb. 1st.

It was 11 p.m. when I discontinued for the day and retired.

Yours respectfully,
"S"

TERRITORY OF NEW MEXICO
OFFICE OF THE EXECUTIVE
Santa Fe, N. Mex., March 17, 1896

Mr. James McParland:-
Denver, Colo.

Dear Sir:-

As the Governor is out of the Territory (in Washington City) and will not return for three weeks, I desire to ask you to keep all your reports in the Fountain matter until you are notified of his return to Santa Fe. I have written the Governor to-day with reference to this request. The Governor's official mail is turned over to the Secretary of the Territory (now acting Governor) and I am afraid through some error or accident one of your reports or letters might get in his possession, which I know the Governor would not have happen under any circumstances, as he wants this matter kept as quiet as possible.

I will notify you the day Governor Thornton returns from Washington, and in the mean time you will kindly suspend your reports. I think this precaution better than to risk the mails until the Governor's return.

Yours respectfully,
Miss N. P. Crane
Private Secretary

Wednesday, March 18

To-day in Las Cruces:-

This morning I met Major Llewellyn and went to his house with him to get the names of friends of his with whom I could go to on my trip to Tularosa. He gave me letters to W. W. Cox who is located at San Augustine Springs and who is the man who met A. B. Fall on his way in from Sunol on Saturday night, the same day of Col. Fountain's disappearance.

Also a letter to G. W. Maxwell of Tularosa, a brother Mason; another letter to Mr. Skidmore at the Bennett & Stevenson mine. This man is the father of Mrs. Lew Cowan, the woman who fixed the time of A. B. Fall's leaving Sunol as 3:40 to 4:20 p.m. on the day of Col. Fountain's disappearance. Also a letter to Don Benseslado Domingue who the Major says is a good man in case I want to reach any of the Mexicans.

I was with the Major until noon and he was to meet me over town after dinner. I saw Mr. Garrett who had been at Court all day waiting to hear Judge Bantz's decision in the Sheriff's contest case. This case was put off until 2 p.m. He (Garrett) returned to the Courthouse after dinner and about 2:50 p.m. Major Llewellyn called on me and informed me that W. W. Cox was in town. I asked him to bring him to my room, which he did and then left us alone. Mr. Cox made the following statement to-wit:

"My name is W. W. Cox, I have been in this country about eight years, came here from San Antonio, Texas; I own what is known as the San Augustine Springs ranch which is 25 miles from Las Cruces. I have known Col. Fountain for a number of years, but never knew him very well, and I did not like him very well because I thought he slighted the smaller cattle men who helped pay him to prosecute cattle thieves by paying less attention to their cases and more to the cases of the large cattle men; still I was never well acquainted with him, but I am for law and order and don't approve of anything of this kind."

"On Saturday, Feb. 1st, I was here in town and left late in the afternoon, it was perhaps an hour and a half before sundown, I had sent my brother on ahead with the freight team as we were taking out quite a load of truck among which was hardware, cots and a bath tub; I caught up with my brother about half an hour before sundown and found he had hurt his foot by having his toes pinched by the wagon wheel, having got down to fix the bath tub in position as it was rubbing on the wheel; he was not hurt very bad; it was about eight miles from here that I met him and it was still

daylight; he would make about three miles an hour with the freight outfit as it is up-grade."

"I made better time as I rode horseback. After I caught up to him I rode along for about seven miles with him and was three or four miles this side of McCowan's when Judge Fall passed me, this would make it about 15 miles out of Las Cruces. I think this was about 8 to 8:30 p.m. but I am only guessing from the distance we rode and the time we made, I did not look at my watch."

"I did not know Judge Fall was driving the team of mules until he hailed me and pulled up, he was past me then I rode up to him as I had some business with him. I had been summoned as a witness to Silver City in some civil case and wanted Judge Fall to present my Doctor's certificate showing I was unable to come on account of rheumatism. Fall told me that he was not going to Lincoln as he had a case to attend to Monday at El Paso, Texas, but would have his brother attend to it for me, which he did. This was about all the conversation we had and he went on towards Las Cruces, and I continued on with the outfit for a short distance when I thought of something I wanted to do at Mrs. McCowan's so rode on ahead."

"I had met Fall's brother-in-law, Joe Morgan, who is a Deputy Sheriff, just after I got out of the town of Las Cruces and stopped and talked with him and he had asked me to stop at Mrs. McCowan's and have her sign some vouchers for meals which he had at her place and to send these vouchers in by our hack, which comes in from the ranch each day, so that he could get them next morning. I met Morgan just out beyond the graveyard on his way in from Tularosa. He did not look as though he had ridden hard and I saw nothing unusual about his manner."

"I did not look at my watch at any time on the road and can only guess at the time; the road to Las Cruces coming this way is all down hill and hard. No, I did not call to Judge Fall to stop, I was not afraid of being run into, he was driving at a very fair gait, but not at break neck speed; he said nothing about when he left Sunol and I did not ask him."

"I went out to help look for Col. Fountain and his son, but gave it up as there were at least 40 men on the trail and when I got there and tried to do some trailing I found I could do nothing. I worked toward the Pass in the San Andreas Mountains, but did not find anything; still I did not cover the ground very well. I also traced five horse tracks to Bear Canyon and then learned that Albert Fountain and four Mexicans had gone in there for water."

"I knew nothing of this affair until Monday afternoon as I am off the Tularosa road a few miles. My brother's name is Perry G. Cox. My place is 25 miles from Las Cruces. I arrived home about 10:30 p.m. as near as I can tell, but I did not look at my watch or at a clock. I know the folks were all in bed when I got home. I galloped home from Mrs. McCowan's place and left my brother to come in alone with the load. I don't know what time he got home, but it must have been midnight or after as he had a heavy load on."

"I have a gentleman named Devlin and his family out at my place stopping; Mr. Devlin and his family are very nice people; he is an attorney and came from Philadelphia, Pa., is here for his health. When Judge Fall passed me he must have recognized my voice for he called out, "Hello Bill" and when I called to him and stopped him and asked him to hand my Doctor's certificate into the court at Silver City."

"I saw nothing unusual about Fall on this occasion and he acted as usual. When I met Joe Morgan, Fall's brother-in-law, on the outskirts of town he was riding along with a neighbor of mine named Tabor, and I saw nothing unusual about his actions or manner of speech and his horse was in good shape. This is all I know about the matter, and I hope it will help you, for I want to see this matter toned down and if it is not I feel for the sake of my family I should do as John Riley did and that is move out of the country."

"I can't give you any idea as to who did this work, and as there are a thousand rumors it is hard to tell anything about it. I am willing to do anything I can on the side of law and order, still I do not want to get mixed up in this matter any more than I can help on account of my family, still I would keep nothing back to shield anyone. I came from a country where men kill each other, but not children."

This was the substance of Mr. Cox's statement and he impressed me as telling the truth. He is the man whose father and uncle were killed by Harding [John Wesley Hardin] one of the bad men of Texas; he himself has killed one or more men and I am told that he lay in jail for about 9 years in Texas awaiting trial, still he is a good citizen here.

After supper I walked up the street with Mr. Garrett and he heard me say that I would like to have a talk with Judge Fall and Oliver Lee before I went out on the road. I also told him that I would like to get Lee to one of our rooms and question him as to his whereabouts. Mr. Garrett said he would see Lee in the morning and arrange this meeting.

I was introduced to a man named Bascome [Bascom] who was one of the party of searchers for Col. Fountain's body and while I was talking to him Garrett excused himself and walked down the street towards Judge A. B. Fall's office and I could see that he was talking to someone in front of Bull's store. Pretty soon he returned and told me that Judge Fall would see me in his office and that he at the request of Garrett had sent for Oliver Lee to come to the office also. I told Mr. Garrett that this was a mistake as I did not want to talk to these men together, but separately, but it was too late to find fault.

At Fall's office there was quite a crowd in the rear room; I could not recognize any of them except Atty. Ferguson and Judge Fall as I could not get a good look into the room. They were no doubt discussing the [Sheriff's] contest case.

Judge Fall brought a lamp into the front office and said we could talk there and be alone. I lost no time in explaining my errand, as I was anxious to get through with him before Oliver Lee came, but in this I did not succeed. Falls' talk to me was not in the form of a statement, but a general talk as I had come to him to get what information I could, the same as I would go to any citizen.

After explaining my position in the matter and impressing on him the fact of this being an impartial investigation in which politics or reward cut no figure. Judge Fall expressed, himself as being well pleased to have some one come in here who would make an investigation of this kind; he then turned loose by first saying that he would state his position in this case; he did not like Col. Fountain any more than he did a snake; he had had dealings with [Fountain] and the man was not straight and he would mould witnesses and testimony to suit his case:

> "He is a man who has killed several men and I will cite you one case to show you what kind of a man he was. He was conveying a prisoner for horse stealing over a line of railroad down here some years ago and at that time his son Albert was a Col. in the Militia down here; the prisoner was said to have tried to escape and was shot dead by Col. Fountain as he got off the train.
>
> Fountain said he was 90 steps from the car when he shot and killed him, but the truth of this statement was that Col. Fountain, when they came in sight of the camp fires of the militia, told the prisoner that the fires belonged to the militia and that it was their

intention to take him from the train and hang him and he (Fountain) advised him to drop off the train when it slowed up and get away and that he was his friend and would assist him to do this; and he did get the conductor of the train to slow up and the prisoner who still wore handcuffs dropped off the front platform and Col. Fountain stood on the steps of the rear platform and shot him dead as he came up to him on the road where he had dropped off; the body was powder burned so he could not have shot him at 90 steps away as he stated. Now this is only one of many cases in which this man has done dirty work."

Oliver Lee came in at this stage of our conversation and I was introduced, the Judge explained my errand to him and then resumed his conversation. He further stated that Col. Fountain came to him at one time and offered him one thousand dollars to assist him in one of his cases, but he refused on account of the manufactured evidence, the judge did not mention what the case was or who the interested parties were.

He said that Jack Fountain had made some ugly talk about him and told on the street that the murder of his father was put up in his office and that he was at the head of a gang of murderers and thieves. *"Now I want to say to you,"* continued Judge Fall, *"that I believe Judge Fountain is dead; at first I thought he might have left and would turn up in Cuba as he was a Spanish scholar, and as he was inclined to be sensational, this would just suit him."*

I here asked the judge if he thought Fountain would take this child with him, providing he had done anything like that. He replied that he may have had reasons for taking the boy as he was very much attached to the little fellow and there was a rumor, but before going any further, the Judge stopped and said that it was only a rumor and if advanced by him would be regarded as some plan to revert attention or a trick of his to lead the officers off the right track.

I asked him to go ahead and he did so by saying that it was rumored that Mrs. Fountain had caught the Col. in a compromising position with his own daughter just before he went away; he could not tell what truth there was in this, as it might be the same as hundreds of other rumors, but said, *"I got it from a reliable citizen, who got it from some one else."*

Why one of these men who has helped drag this thing into politics claims that the tracks of my buckboard were traced from Sonol to the Chalk Hill where Col. Fountain was killed; and this man was none other than Major Llewellyn and I am only waiting a chance to tell him what I think about this kind of work.

I assured Judge Fall that I had never heard anything of the kind; he said that he believed that, for they knew if I was told anything of the kind I would investigate and explode their story. The judge was pretty hot when he was telling this; he said he had not cut across from Sunol to any of those roads since last April one year ago this coming April, when he drove his wife, mother and another lady friend over to a lake about five to seven miles from Sunol in the direction of Chalk Hill.

The Judge then said there were plenty of chances for people to kill Fountain and get into Old Mexico and there were any number of cattle thieves and desperadoes who knew this road, and Col. Fountain had prosecuted a great many people and had used manufactured evidence to convict, still he had convicted very few men; now some of these men may have run across him by chance and killed him:

> "A man could hide behind a soap weed and catch him where he was caught. Now they say that Fountain was a great prosecutor, but I want to tell you that he has convicted only Slick Miller, Davis, and one or two others and that was done on confessions made by some of the gang with whom they have been working; and I want to say further that as a prosecutor and a lawyer no one had anything to fear as he had no standing before any jury and could not make a conviction in Dona Ana County."

> "How if there are any questions you think of I want you to ask them; if the papers and people had not attacked me as they did I should have been ready and willing to help run this down. Why Judge McFie of this very place went to my old law partner A. W. Hawkins in El Paso and asked him to get me to assist in running this thing down and Mr. Hawkins went for McFie and told him flat footed that he (Hawkins) had heard him (McFie) curse and damn me for my connection with the gang of thieves as he termed Mr. Lee, Mr. McNew, Jack Tucker, Jas. Gilliland, Carr and others, all of whom have been dragged into this thing".

At this stage of the conversation Fall laughed and looking at Lee said:

> "Poor Jack Tucker, he says he can prove where he was, as he was chopping wood for his wife 70 miles from there. Well Mr. Hawkins told Judge McFie to come to me himself and ask me like a man to do so and so and he would find I would do it, and so I would, but the condition of affairs before you came here was

something terrible and no one could tell what might happen any minute. The Republican paper here came out and declared that the Democrats killed Fountain; I tell you sir it was something awful. Yes, things have quieted down since you came and I am glad you outsiders such as Mr. Garrett, Mr. Perry, and yourself have taken hold of this case, for there was no telling what some of these fellows might not try to do."

Lee chimed in on this part of the conversation to agree with the Judge. Both these men occupied positions where they could watch each other and Lee kept his eyes on the Judge during the entire conversation. The Judge then asked me if I heard that there had been warrants sworn out for Oliver Lee; I admitted having heard something about them; "Well, Major Llewellyn is the man who wrote the names in these warrants."

I asked Judge Fall if he would tell me when he first heard of the disappearance of Col. Fountain and he said he thought it was on the following Monday when he was on his way to El Paso. I then asked him if he would explain where he was on Saturday the day of the disappearance of Col. Fountain, at this question both Judge Fall and Oliver Lee burst out laughing and Lee winked at Judge Fall. I told Lee that he need not laugh as I would soon reach him; this caused another laugh as I had made this remark in a joking sort of way.

Judge Fall then stated that on that day he was at his gold property at Sunol. I asked him if he went out on Friday, and he said:

"No sir, I did not, I was there several days but I can't say just when I did go out as I was making so many trips back and forth from the mine; about that time, however, I do remember that on Friday morning, Mr. Young (Dist. Atty.) who was interested in some claims over that way arrived at my place and wanted me to go in with him; I asked him to wait and if Mr. O'Neill (a miner) came in so that if I could fix up my business with him, I could go in. O'Neill did not come and Mr. Young remained all night, and as O'Neill did not come in the morning Mr. Young left and came to town alone and a short time after him came my brother-in-law, Joe Morgan, who had been out to look at some mining property and was on his way home and arrived in Las Cruces at 3 p.m.; this he can prove by a number of people here."

"In the afternoon O'Neill came in and we fixed up our business, which was a mining deal for C. B. Eddy of El Paso and at something near 4 p.m. I hitched up my team of ponies and started for town but had gotten

> only a few yards from the house when one of them balked and I could do nothing with them, so unhitched and went back and roped my team of mules and at 4 p.m. left for town."
>
> "I know the time because I looked at my watch as I started. I arrived at Las Cruces at 8 p.m. No, I did not look at my watch on my arrival but I know the time because I went home and ate my supper and we have a clock. No I met no one on the road that I remember unless it was a Mexican. I did not stop to speak to any one." (This question being repeated afterwards brought forth the same reply).

As I had finished with Judge Fall I turned my attention to Oliver Lee and started to ask him what he knew about the matter when Judge Fall interrupted me and said he would like to explain Mr. Lee's position in this case, and then went on to say that Mr. Lee had been accused of being connected with the disappearance of Col. Fountain; the warrants issued for Mr. Lee were proof enough of that in themselves and he as Mr. Lee's attorney and friend had advised him not to talk to anyone as to where he was on that day or any other day, but when the time came he (Judge Fall) had the papers and witnesses to prove where Oliver Lee was and added pointing his right hand toward Lee, "I have letters that you know nothing about."

Lee took his advice and said nothing of his whereabouts. Fall said he had told me what he would not tell another damn man in the town and that was where he spent his time on Saturday. I then had some talk with Oliver Lee, but learned nothing. I noticed that Lee always watched Judge Fall and the Judge kept looking at him all the time; at one time he started to tell something, but Fall shook his head and Lee, who was looking straight at him stopped short and began talking about something else.

Fall did not think that Gov. Thornton had acted right in this matter and was himself to blame for swinging this affair into politics. I invited them to the corner saloon to have something and they went; Lee does not smoke or drink. Lee and Judge Fall told me that Judge Bantz would decide in favor of Numa Raymond and Lee said he would be defeated in the upper court on the appeal.

Before we left Fall's office he told me that two more men were said to have been connected with this killing and they were men named Hill and Yost and if I wanted any information in regard to them I could come to him before I left and he would tell me where they were and show me that they could not have been there. I assured him that I had never heard these names mentioned, and I had not until I spoke to Mr.

Garrett afterwards and learned from him that he had just received information that Yost and Hill were in some way connected with this case.

Fall left Lee and I and returned to his office where Ferguson and others were waiting for him.

I discontinued at 1:05 a.m.

Yours respectfully,
"S"

Thursday, March 19, 1896

To-day in Las Cruces:-

This morning I saw Mr. Garrett and from him learned that the new sheriff Numa Raymond was not inclined to turn the office over to him, but instead had made several promises to Oscar Lohman and others for positions on his staff to which Garrett would not agree. I spent most of the day and evening trying to get this matter straightened out so that I would meet with no further delay, but when I discontinued matters were even worse than in the morning.

The decision was rendered in favor of Numa Raymond by Judge Bantz in the forenoon and his bond was approved and he was instructed to take charge of the office at 9 a.m. Friday.

When Garrett explained the conditions as understood by him, Viz: that he (Garrett) was to have the office turned, over to him, Mr. Raymond said he did not understand these conditions, but he (Raymond) was willing to make him a Deputy Sheriff and assist him all he could on this Fountain matter; Garrett of course would not listen to this and left then.

I had a talk with Major Llewellyn in regard to this matter and he said he and Mr. Riley would see Raymond and Lohman and try to get this matter fixed up so that Garrett would take charge. Garrett says he can make a showing in this office providing he has full charge and sees where he can make a saving for the county. In a conversation with Garrett to-day I learned that Sheriff Chas. C. Perry had gone away for the purpose of getting warrants to arrest James R. Gilliland on a charge of cow stealing and it was their intention to have Les Dow a deputy sheriff of Chaves Co. come in and make the arrest and run him over to Roswell and place him in jail and keep him there until he squeals and that is what is delaying him now.

This man Gilliland is said to be weak and is thought to be a good man to work on.

Mr. Christy informed Garrett and I that one Santa Rosa Rico had informed him that his brother-in-law Pedro Serna, who was over at White Oaks with Dist. Atty. Young, had told him (Rico) that Mr. Young and he had stopped at Fall's place at Sunol on their way back on Friday afternoon or evening, but that there was no one at home, but about 10 o'clock that night (Friday Jan. 31st) a rap came on the door and Young jumped up and grabbing his gun told Pedro to open the door when he told him to; Young stood back from the door and called to ask who was there, and Fall replied that it was him, so the door was opened and Fall and Joe Morgan, his brother-in-law came in. They talked with Young and Pedro says he heard them cursing some one and heard Col. Fountain's name mentioned. Santa Rosa Rico says that the boys knows more he is sure, but this is all he will tell and he can get nothing more out of him.

John Riley told Mr. Garrett and afterwards told me in Garrett's room, that one Chas. Jones had told his brother-in-law Russell Walters that Hiram Yost and Frank Hill were at Sunol Gold Camp on Thursday, Jan. 30th. Hiram Yost is a first cousin to Tom and Jack Tucker and Frank Hill is a nephew to Frank Graham who was mixed up in the Pleasant Valley Arizona war against the Tewkesbury boys.

Yost and Hill I think work for the Detroit Cattle Co. near Engle, N.M. Mr. Riley said he thought Chas. Bruton would be a good man to give some information on this case and Bruton was under a great many obligations to him. It will be remembered that Bruton is one of the men mentioned by Slick Miller in his statement at the Santa Fe prison, who was one of the parties to the plot in 1894 to kill Fountain. Mr. Riley (who knows nothing of this statement and must not know of it) promised to make it his business to see Bruton and get him to assist in the case.

After supper Mr. Garrett and I walked over to Major Llewellyn's house and talked matters over pertaining to the Sheriff's office, and after this talk the Major went over town to see what he could do to straighten matters out, and I saw no more of him.

At 11:15 p.m. I discontinued and retired for the night.
Yours truly,
"S"

Friday, March 20, 1896

Today in Las Cruces,-

This morning I met Mr. Garrett in front of the hotel and he informed me that matters had taken a turn and it looked now as though he would be placed in full charge of the office of Sheriff; I also met Major Llewellyn and he told me he thought everything would be all right.

I saw Judge Fall in front of the hotel talking with a Government Land officer named Olive. I asked him to walk down the street with me, which he readily consented to do; we stopped opposite Max Shutz's store and I asked him if he did not think it was a mistake not to allow Oliver Lee to make a statement explaining where he was at the time of the disappearance of Col. Fountain; Judge Fall replied very promptly that he did not think it was a mistake and that he had carefully considered the matter before advising him to say nothing to any one.

I had asked first on starting this talk if Oliver Lee had ever made a statement to any one here as to his whereabouts at that time, and Judge Fall stated that he did not. I asked him if in the face of all the talk about this case he did not think it was poor judgment for him not to make a statement and again he said no. He then went on to tell me how this affair was all politics and that certain people only wanted a chance to kill Oliver Lee, how Major Llewellyn and other Republicans had placed armed men in the street on election day three years ago and how a man had been brought in from Nebraska to kill him (Fall) and through all this Oliver Lee was the only man whom he could call on and trust, and Lee had never committed a crime since he had been in this country.

I broke in to say that Lee was not accused of any connection in this case and for this reason I thought he should make a statement. I further stated that I had noticed how bad it looked for him not to make a statement when I came to write up my report.

In reply to this he said that Oliver Lee certainly was accused of a connection with this case; otherwise, those warrants would not have been sworn out for him, McNew, and Jack Tucker. Judge Fall then drew my attention to the fact that as soon as Oliver Lee became aware of the warrant for him he came into town and demanded a hearing before the Justice of the Peace who said he knew nothing of any such warrant; he then went to the Dist. Attorney Mr. Young who was also ignorant of any warrants for McNew and Tucker as they were out there in the country, but by orders of Judge Newcomb the warrants were called in and destroyed.

What they wanted was a chance to kill Oliver Lee and he knew it. At this stage of our conversation a man came up whom I took to be Joe Morgan and told the Judge that some one wanted to talk with him over the telephone. This same man came through Judge Fall's office on the night I was talking with Oliver Lee and the Judge.

I forgot to mention that while on my way to Major Llewellyn's house last night we met Oliver Lee and Judge Fall's brother coming in on horseback. I had not seen Lee around all day, nor had I seen Judge Fall, still they may have been. This ended the conversation between Judge A. B. Fall and myself. I returned to the hotel and wrote my report for yesterday and up to 11 a.m. to-day, I did this because I may not be able to write a report for several days to come owing to the fact that I fully expect to get away after dinner for my trip to Tularosa.

Yours respectfully,
"S"

Friday, March 20, 1896

To-day in Las Cruces,-

After enclosing my report at 11 a.m. today I neglected to state that in my conversation with Judge Fall this morning, he corrected his statement made to me at his office by stating that he had forgotten to say that he had met Mr. Cox and his brother while he was on his way from Sunol to Las Cruces and that he had had a conversation with Mr. Cox in reference to a business matter.

During this conversation I again asked the Judge if he was sure as to the time of his departure and arrival on that day and he again repeated that he had left Sunol at 4 p.m. and arrived in Las Cruces about 8 p.m.

I had a talk with Mr. Garrett who informed me that affairs at the Sheriff's office had not been straightened out and he did not know when he would be able to leave. He said that he was anxious to get away to-day as he had promised me he would, but things were moving very slowly.

So after dinner I called on Major Llewellyn and had a talk with him; he promised to go over town and push matters as rapidly as possible. I returned and had another talk with Garrett and in this conversation ascertained from him that if things were straightened out and he was given charge of the Sheriff's department, he would not be able to leave for two or three days. This was something I had not expected, so I again called on Major Llewellyn and in a short space of time made arrangements with him for his team of mules and his buggy, also for his son Morgan to accompany me on this trip.

Sheriff Perry of Roswell had not arrived on the noon train, and so at 4:10 p.m. I had finished all arrangements and left Las Cruces for the Bennett & Stevenson mine in the Organ Mts. I arrived there at 7:30 p.m. and after putting our team in the coral and getting something to eat I had

Mr. Skidmore go to the cabin occupied by Mr. and Mrs. L. W. Cowan.

I first took the statement of Mr. L. W. Cowan, who at the time of Fountain's disappearance was working for Judge Fall at the Sunol mine, but within the last few days these people have moved over to the Bennett & Stevenson Mine and are now working at that mine.

Mr. Cowan's statement ran as follows:-

"I think Judge Fall came out on Friday to Sunol; he came the same day that my brother Charlie came, who drove out with him. I think he arrived after dark. On Saturday I sold Judge Fall five claims in the San Andreas Mts. about 30 miles from Sunol. The claims were originally located by Chas. O'Neill and Charlie Cowan. The time had expired and I with Jas. W. Cowan, who is my brother, re-located [the mines]; Chas. O'Neill at this time was lying ill at the Sunol camp, but it was on account of this illness that his title to the claims had expired. In making this sale, however, we gave him 1/3."

"These claims were bought by Judge Fall for C. B. Eddy of El Paso, formerly of Eddy, N. M. Mr. Fall paid us $50.00 down; the agreement was to pay $100 more on the 15th of March and $200 on the 15th of April, neither of these two latter amounts have been paid."

"Chas. O'Neill was laid up sick in bed previous to February the 1st, and he was just able to be around when this deal was made. I afterwards talked with Judge Fall about the time of his leaving Sunol on Saturday and I recollect he said 20 minutes to or 20 minutes after 4 p.m. In this conversation with Judge Fall, he told me about some trouble he had with Jack Fountain in regard to some remarks he had made connecting him (Fall) with the disappearance of his father. Fall stated at that time that he was sorry for Mrs. Fountain and the children, but he did not care about the Col. at the time."

"I am quite sure that Hiram Yost was at Sunol several days previous to the Fountain affair, and I think he was there on Saturday Feb. 1st, but am not positive as I was working all the time in the mine."

"There was someone come in in the night while Yost was there, but I don't know who it was. I heard that Frank Hill was there in camp, but did not see him. I think Chas. Jones was at Sunol on Friday, Jan. 30th. He was working in the place of my brother Charlie, who had met with an accident in the mine and had to go to

Las Cruces for treatment. Jones was paid off by me on Feb. the 5th, he was away for a few days during this time to Parker's Well, but I don't know what days or dates. Jones was here to the mine to-day, but left this evening; I think you will find him at Parker's Well."

This concluded the statement of L. W. Cowan, but was not at all clear as to days and dates. I then interviewed Mrs. L. W. Cowan and from her received the following statement:

"Judge Fall arrived at the camp Friday Jan. 31st, he arrived just about dark, or about 6 p.m. Chas. Cowan, my brother-in-law was with him, having driven out from Las Cruces. Judge Fall's house was the next house to ours in the Sunol camp. He stopped at the camp Friday and Saturday."

"On Saturday morning I saw Dist. Atty. Young go from Fall's house in Sunol camp to the shaft house. I did not see much of Judge Fall while he was around the camp, but to my knowledge he did not leave the camp, at least he was not away any distance. He left for Las Cruces Saturday, Feb. 1st, about 4 p.m. as near as I can judge."

"I saw him when he started with his team of ponies and was watching him as he drove away; he had gotten but a short distance from the house, just a few yards when the horses balked on him, he turned and brought them back to the coral, unhitched and hitched up a team of mules, then left and I saw no more of him; he went in the direction of Las Cruces. He did not call at my house at any time during his stay at the camp. I know that Mr. Yost stopped over one night at the camp, and that must have been Friday night, I do not know what hour he arrived at Sunol, but he was coming from the White Oaks country."

"We can drive with a team of horses from Sunol to Las Cruces in five hours with a wagon and have done it quite often, and Judge Fall could drive it with his team in four hours, easy. I had no callers that I remember or during the time that Judge Fall was in camp; I did not have any conversation with him while he was there on this visit. I did not see him have in his possession at that time or any other time a pair of field glasses and I do not know whether he has any at his house, I never saw any."

"I have had no conversation with him since the time or the disappearance of Col. Fountain. I have never heard that he stated to any one what hour it was that he arrived in Las Cruces on Saturday evening.

The Judge ate his meals at his own house. H. P. Niles cooked for him; Niles also helped him rope the mules that he used to drive in to Las Cruces on Saturday night."

Further questioning of Ms. Cowan failed to develop anything additional.

My reason for questioning the Cowan's in reference to Hiram Yost and Frank Hill was on account of a statement one Chas Jones had made to his brother-in-law Russell Walters. It seems that Jones had stated to Walters that Hiram Yost and Frank Hill were seen at the Sunol camp on Thursday, January 30th. Yost is Tom Tucker's first cousin and Frank Hill is a nephew of Frank Graham's. Frank Graham is one of the Pleasant Valley Arizona warriors and is mixed up in the feud with the Tewkesbury boys.

This information came from John Riley the cattleman who received it from Russell Walters. Both Yost and Hill work for the Detroit Cattle Company and their railroad station is Engle on the Santa Fe [rail]road, which is north of Rincon. Both of these men are considered hard cases and are men that might be mixed up in an affair or this kind. I will endeavor to find this man Jones and get at the truth of his statement.

I next called at the camp of Chas. Cowan in the same camp and received from him the following statement:

"I came out with Judge Fall from Las Cruces on the day before the sale of the claims and the Judge went back to Las Cruces the next day, which I am quite sure was Saturday; Dr. Cowan, my uncle at Las Cruces can no doubt give you the date on which I left Las Cruces. I saw no one around, as I was not out of the house. I had not entirely recovered from the accident I had met with. I heard that Dist. Atty. Young was there after I had arrived. I did not see Hill, Yost, or Tom Tucker there. I went into Las Cruces again on Monday following. I rode out only once with Judge Fall."

This was all the information that I could obtain from Chas. Cowan; so at 11:30 p.m. I retired tor the night.

Yours truly,
"S"

Saturday, March 21, 1896.

At 5 p.m. I left the Bennett & Stevenson Mine for Organ, which is 18 miles from Las Cruces. We took breakfast at Mrs. McCowan's. I found that Mrs. McCowan at that time was in Las Cruces where she owns a home. Mr. McCowan and his little son were the only people at the house. I questioned him in reference to the vouchers for J. Morgan which were brought to McCowan's by W. W. Cox on Saturday evening. Mr. McCowan informed me that he had been working in the Mines and did not know what day or date or at what time Mr. Cox arrived with these vouchers, but remembered that there were two as his wife asked him why there were two vouchers to be signed for one meal and he had told her that he supposed one was a duplicate and that it was perhaps necessary to have a duplicate copy.

He did not know on what day his wife would be home, but thought that I would catch her on my return trip. He could throw no light on this matter and knew nothing about Young or Judge Fall passing the place, as he was usually at work in the mines and very often at night, consequently was sleeping in the day time.

After having breakfast here we continued on to Parker's Well, which is 25 miles from Las Cruces; here I saw Mr. Tabor and he informed me that Chas. Jones had not arrived at his place; he knew nothing about the story told by Chas. Jones in reference to Yost and Hill.

After watering the horses here we continued on and at Chalk Hill, 40 miles from Las Cruces, we met Jas. Baird and his party returning from Tularosa. I had a talk with Mr. Baird, but he had learned nothing new; we then continued on arriving at Luna's Well, which is about 60 miles from Las Cruces about 2 p.m. Here I saw Antonio Rey the Mexican who has charge of the station and well; Rey made the following statement:

> "I know nothing about the case. I saw Col. Fountain on the road about 3 to 3:30 p.m. on Saturday and asked him if he saw any wagons on the road, as the boy Santos Alvarado wanted to go to town (Las Cruces) and wanted to ride in with someone. I did not see any horsemen in this vicinity that day, but Santos saw two men about a quarter of a mile from the ranch off of the road East of the main road; he could not tell who they were, but one rode a gray horse and one a bay horse and both wore white hats."

Saturnino Barela told me that Col. Fountain had spoken to him about the men following him, relating the same story in part that Barela has heretofore given and which has been stated in a previous report. Barela said that one of the men was riding a gray, another a bay, and the other a dark horse, but he did not say whether he knew these men or not. This was all the conversation that Barela and I had in reference to these three horsemen.

> "A good while before this Fountain affair Oliver Lee and another man whom I do not know stopped at my place with a prisoner. I did not see Joe Morgan pass on Friday, but was told by my wife that he passed while I was eating my dinner, this would be about noon."

Antonio Rey I found was not very communicative and his "can't sabas" were quite frequent during the questioning, which was carried on through my interpreter Morgan Llewellyn; I found that he understood English pretty well, but he declined to talk in English. Santos Alvarado was seen, but claimed that he knew nothing whatever and was disinclined to talk. Mrs. Antonio Rey was seen but she declined to say anything in reference to the matter.

We then continued on to Gooley [Pellman] Well which is now in charge of F. W. Pellman. Before leaving Luna's Well, however, I had left a note for E. E. Banner and John Meadows who were to return there in the evening; in this note I informed them that I would stop over night at Pellman's and they could find me there; I had word from Mr. Garrett to send Mr. Banner in to Las Cruces, for the change in the Sheriff's office was made and Garrett took charge. Mr. Banner was to be jailor and bookkeeper. I had dinner prepared for us at Pellman's after putting our team into the coral, and shortly after dinner I managed to get F. W. Pellman in my room and from him received the following statement:

> "I saw Col. Fountain on Feb. 1st. He arrived at my place about 12 o'clock noon and stayed until about 2 p.m. [He] fed and watered his horses; he had three horses; he carried a lunch and he and his son ate their lunch near my coral. We had a good deal of talk during this visit about politics, but he never said a word [about] anyone following him, nor did he speak of indictments, cattle thieves, or court matters, and to the best of my recollection no names were mentioned during our conversation."

> "We have been very good friends and I have known the Col. for about 15 years. About 9 a.m. on Saturday Feb. 1st, Mr. Geo. Coe and two men passed my place; the two men seemed to be sickly people or invalids, one of them lay on a cot in the wagon. Mr. Coe lives on the Ruidoso; he is a rancher; the two men with him looked like eastern men."

> "In the afternoon about 3 or 4 p.m., C. R. Scott and H. K. Parker of Tularosa came to my place and left some oats for C. B. Eddy's outfit who were surveying what is known as the El Paso and North Eastern Railway.

They did not stay long, but drove on toward El Paso where they were going for a load of freight."

"I think all of these parties camped somewhere beyond the Chalk Hill, but I do not know where. I asked Mr. Coe afterwards if he saw Col. Fountain, he told me that he had not, but he thought he remembered a light rig passing on the road while he was off shooting some distance from the road, but he did not pay much attention to who went along. His team at that time was being driven by one of the two invalids that were with him. He had known Col. Fountain for 20 years and called him an old friend of his."

"I am positive that no one else passed the house during that time, unless they went along back of the ridge, which lies a quarter of a mile east of my place here, or in the rear of the house. This ridge runs parallel to the main road and any number of men could ride back of it from the vicinity of the White Sands and not be seen, and at the same time could watch any one on the main road."

"On the opposite of the ridge the country is as level as it is at the Salt Well. This would make the ridge from 12 to 15 feet high and the road for horses would be very good and would be a more direct route to Chalk Hill than by the main road."

"I am positive that I saw no horsemen that day and no other parties outside of the ones I have mentioned. I have a pair of field glasses here that belong to an Indian and have heard the statement made that I had seen the horsemen by using the glass and had recognized them; this is untrue. During that time I was at work, most of the time outside, and I am sure would have seen any one who would have passed along the road."

"I do not know Oliver Lee, Bill McNew, or Bill Carr, but I do know Jack Tucker who has often stopped at my place, but he had not stopped with me for some time before this affair. I cannot remember about Mr. Morgan having passed for sometime before and don't recollect of his passing on Friday."

Mrs. Pellman and her daughter made about the same statement and could throw no further light on this matter.

About 4 p.m., E. E. Banner and John P. Meadows called on me at Pellman's having received my note at Luna's Well and we talked matters over for about 2 hours and compared notes. I received the names of several people to call on at Tularosa and La Luz.

Meadows told me that I would not find Jack Maxwell as he was [being kept] "shadowed." Bill McNew and J. Gililland were hiding out in the Sacramento Mts. and Joe Morgan was over at Tularosa drunk. I learned from Meadows that Coe and his two invalids had camped way beyond Chalk Hill, and the rig that Coe saw while he was hunting was probably the spring wagon occupied by the Mexican and the two women mentioned in Barela's statement. Coe at the time they passed was shooting some distance off the road. He was quite a distance ahead of Col. Fountain and claims that he heard no shooting nor did he see anything of the horsemen mentioned so often.

Mr. Banner informed me that they had ascertained positively where Jack Tucker was on that day and that he was not in this affair as an actual participant; still he may have taken a part in it by watching the Col. while he was going through from Lincoln and posted some other members of the gang.

After 6:30 p.m., Meadows and Banner left for Luna's Well where they were stopping, and I retired early as I wanted to get an early start in the morning in order to make Tularosa by noon.

Yours respectfully,
"S"

Sunday, March 22, 1896

I left Pellman's at 5 a.m. and arrived at Tularosa at 11:35 a.m. After putting up the team I went to Mrs. H. K. Parker's for dinner; at the dinner table I managed to get into conversation with Mrs. Parker and from her received the following statement:

> "My husband H. K. Parker and C. R. Scott went over the road after Col. Fountain; they left Tularosa on Friday afternoon, both were drunk at the time they left and they carried liquor with them; they camped about 10 miles from Tularosa in the vicinity of the Lost River; they did not leave camp very early the following morning; they had a load of oats for the railroad outfit which they were to leave at Pellman's and from there they went on to El Paso."

> "My husband had not seen Col. Fountain. I am sure that they did not meet any strangers or any men on horseback or he would have told me, for the Fountain affair has been discussed a great deal in this town. As near as I know, he camped beyond the Chalk Hill on Saturday night, still he may have camped this side of Chalk Hill; I don't know where you can find him now unless he is in the Bank saloon, he is most likely

drunk as he has not come home to his dinner, but I received word a little while ago that he was going to Three Rivers."

Late in the afternoon I met H. K. Parker, but he was so drunk that I could get no intelligent statement from him, the man appeared to me to be on the verge of delirium tremens; I was in hopes I could get him home and after a sleep get a statement from him, but I found this was out of the question and had to leave him without obtaining any information, except that he verified in main the statement made by his wife as to the time of leaving Tularosa and as to the part of the country he camped in on Friday night; also as to arriving at Pellman's, that it was late on Saturday afternoon; he did not seem to be clear as to where he camped Saturday night, but I believe this was owing to his muddled state of mind, but he expressed himself as willing to do anything he could and declared he had seen no one along the road.

It will be remembered that Col. Fountain went from Tularosa to La Luz on Friday and stopped there all night with Dave Sutherland in La Luz and then went by the La Luz road to Gooley's Well; this is an entirely different road from the one over which Parker and Scott would travel going from Tularosa to the point of the white sands where the two roads meet, which is from 4 to 6 miles this side of Gooley's Well or Pellman's place.

I next tried to find the man Johnson who was said to have written the letter for Alvino Guerra to Mrs. Eva Taylor. Alvino Guerra, it will be remembered, is the stage driver who goes to Tularosa and with whom Mrs. Taylor rode when she claims she saw the three men on horse back, two of whom she identified as Oliver Lee and Bill McNew.

I learned that there was a John Johnson who lived out near the graveyard; I finally located him only to find that he was not the man I was looking for, he being a new arrival in this vicinity having moved from La Luz to Tularosa; but after considerable search I found the man in Chas. Johnson who is a part owner in a small grocery store; Johnson is a young man and I took him for a Mexican who speaks good English. He did not hesitate to acknowledge that he was the man who wrote the letter for Guerra to Mrs. Eva Taylor, but he could not remember [the man's] name until it was mentioned. The circumstances of his writing this letter were, that Guerra, who often visited the store had come in while he was busy one evening and had requested him to write a note in English; he (Guerra) dictated the letter which was sent to Mrs. Eva Taylor.

I questioned him [Johnson] closely as to whether or not Guerra had made any statement to him in reference to these horsemen mentioned in this letter; he said that they had had no conversation on the matter at that time, he (Johnson) being very busy at the time that Guerra requested him to write this letter. Johnson positively claimed that he does not know nor did he ever see Mrs. Eva Taylor. Alvino Guerra is now driving the stage or mail wagon from Lincoln to White Oaks and does not come into Tularosa; consequently I could not see him.

When Johnson was questioned as to whether or not he had any conversation with Guerra after the disappearance of Col. Fountain, he remembered that Guerra had told him that the man mentioned by Mrs. Taylor as having crossed the road while they were driving into La Luz was Ben Williams the Deputy U.S. Marshal and some other man; this was all the conversation they had ever had on this subject. He was not at Tularosa at the time Col. Fountain disappeared, but was working in Lincoln. When questioned as to whether he knew Joe Morgan or not, he said that he did and that Morgan was in town yesterday, drunk, but he thought that he went to La Luz. I saw nothing of Morgan around town although I looked for him expecting to be able to pick up something. Johnson offered to render any assistance he possibly could. I told him to say nothing about our interview to any one.

I next called on W. P Shields, whose place is about a mile out of town. He was taking a nap when I arrived at his house, but got up and after we had talked for a few minutes and I had explained the reason for my visit, he promised to meet me after he had taken a bath at Mrs. Parker's.

Mr. Shields is considered one of the best citizens in Tularosa, and is a man who is very much interested in this case. He is a warm personal friend and in the employ of Mr. Riley. I next saw Mr. Jeff Saunders but he could give me no information. C. R. Scott was at Three Rivers consequently I could not see him.

Bernadillo Gomez was not in town but was thought to be out on his ranch some distance from the city. I wanted to see Gomez in reference to a conversation that one Marcus Mestos had claimed to have had with Antonio Rey at Luna's Well in which the latter told him that he could find the bodies of Col. Fountain and his son and also told him that he would find the remains, with the exception of one arm rolled up in a wagon sheet; also told him to follow the trail to where the cattle obliterated it then go over about seven miles beyond and he could pick it up again and follow it. This information came to me through Mr. Banner, and if true, this statement is very important and would tend to show that Antonio Rey had not told all he knew in reference to this matter.

While waiting for Mr. Shields in my room about 3 p.m., Judge Wm. D. Bailey, an old citizen of Tularosa, called at my room and told me that he had heard that I was here and thought he would call in to tell me what he knew. He then went on to state that he saw Col. Fountain on Friday Jan. 31 about noon in front of Adam J. Dieter's store [in Tularosa], and after the Col. had driven away toward La Luz he saw Jack Tucker peeping around in the direction where the Col. drove out to reach the road to La Luz, and that he afterwards saw Jack Tucker riding a sorrel horse which seemed much worn up the road which passes Mr. Shields' and Mrs. McDonald's; Mrs. McDonald is the next door neighbor to Mr. Shields.

Tucker, he [Bailey] states, in riding by acted as though he wanted to avoid being seen, that he (Bailey) called "Hello" to him as he passed and Tucker replied. Mr. Bailey states that if Jack Tucker was going home he should have taken the same road that Col. Fountain took to La Luz, but he seemed to be taking the other road or lane which lies beyond Mr. Shields' house and from which point he might be able to see Col. Fountain for some distance, but his opinion was that Tucker, who was driving toward the Sacramento Mts. had gone to notify some of the gang that the Col. was on the road.

Mr. Bailey further stated that he drew the attention of Mr. Adam J. Dieter to Tucker at the time he was watching after Col. Fountain and asked Mr. Dieter if he knew him, and he (Dieter) said, *"Yes, it is Tucker,"* but did not say whether it was Tom or Jack. He again spoke to Mr. Dieter about this matter as soon as he heard of the Fountain disappearance, which was on Wednesday Feb. 5th.

Bailey further stated that he had heard that Frank Chatfield claimed to have driven over from Lincoln about that time with wagon and team, but that this was not true if he ever said so, and if Perry Kearney, who has a ranch somewhat off the road between Tularosa and La Luz could be seen, he could give some information about this man Chatfield and his whereabouts at that time.

Mr. W. P. Shields and Adam J. Dieter called at my room about the same time, and from Mr. Dieter I learned that he had seen Mr. Jack Tucker as stated by Judge Bailey, but could not learn that he had paid any particular attention to his peeping around the corner as described by Judge Bailey. Mr. Dieter stated that he had seen and talked with Col. Fountain Friday noon, which would be Jan. 31. The Col. had fed his horses in the coral and Mr. Dieter asked him to go over to his house and have dinner, but the Col. informed him that he and the boy had eaten lunch in the coral, and asked Mr. Dieter for some oats; Mr. Dieter gave him 40 lbs for which he informs me he would accept no pay.

Mr. Shields informed me that he was talking to Col. Fountain as he sat in his buckboard ready to leave for La Luz and this was at noon on Friday and in front of Dieter's coral; he had shaken hands with the Col. and also with the boy and noticed that the boy was dressed in a gray suit, but could not say anything about a waist as he wore a small jacket.

All three of these men who had conversations with Col. Fountain stated positively that the Col. had not mentioned having been followed by any men on horseback or anyone else, but the Col. did say to Mr. Dieter that he had an Indian escort from the Reservation as there was an Indian that wanted to kill him. Mr. Dieter was told afterwards by the Agent from the reservation that this was not true, and Mr. Dieter also learned since his talk with the Agent that the Col. had met on the road an old Indian friend who had rode into town with him. After Mr. Dieter and Judge Bailey had left the room I had a talk with Mr. Shields and he volunteered to ride out on his horse and bring Barnadillo Gomez into town so that I might get a statement from him.

Gomez did not arrive until about 6 p.m. and as I thought he was not coming and was anxious to get to La Luz, my time being limited I was preparing to start, but had not yet eaten supper; about 6 p.m. he arrived, however, and I had a talk with him and took his statement in part only as he volunteered to give his statement in full to Mr. Shields who would write it down and send the same to me at Las Cruces care of Major Llewellyn.

Gomez states that Marcus Mestos, who was looking for the bodies, told him that he was at Luna's Well for four or five days after the disappearance or Col. Fountain and Antonio Rey told him that he knew nothing and stuck to this for sometime and Mestos threatened him and told him that he might get into trouble, he also pleaded with him for what information he could give, and little by little Antonio Rey began to drop something here and there and that he finally said that they would find the bodies over in the direction of the San Nicolas Pass in the Sand Hills and they would find them in a wagon sheet and one arm would be gone.

Mestos tried to get the name of the man who went to the top of Rey's house about 20 days before Fountain disappeared or about the time that Fountain passed over the road on his way to Lincoln, but Rey would not give it and claimed to be perfectly ignorant; Mestos tried to get this out of him by threatening him with arrest, but Rey said they could do no harm to him and he had a good horse and could get into Mexico.

This story about a man having stopped over one day at Luna's Well about 20 days previous to the disappearance of Col. Fountain and having gone onto the roof a number of times apparently watching for some one on the road and who was afterwards said to have stopped at the house at Luna's Well on the day before the disappearance of Col. Fountain, has been circulated to considerable extent and was given to me by Meadows and Banner after I had left Luna's Well, which was the first I had ever heard of it.

As I did not have the time to take his statement in full in writing, I concluded to allow Mr. Shields to do this for me, and after supper at 6:40 p.m. I started for Perry Kearney's ranch, arriving there about 7:30 p.m., only to find that he had left for El Paso, Texas, and would not be back for several days. I then drove into La Luz, which is about 9 miles on a direct road from Tularosa; on arriving at La Luz I put up the team at Myers' Corral, then went to Mr. Chas Myers' house and introduced myself; I had a talk with Mr. Myers and he informed me that old man Gililland, father of Jas. R. Gililland, left La Luz on Thursday Jan. 30th, and claims to have camped at one of the lakes north of Chalk Hill on Friday night. This is undoubtedly Parker's Lake which is some distance beyond Chalk Hill. He claims further that he went into camp with D. F. Baze and one Emmet Russ, both of these men live about 10 to 12 miles from La Luz and camped with him at Parker's or near Parker's Lake. It would be impossible for me to see D. F. Baze or Emmet Russ without laying over another day and then I might not catch them at home. The horse which was mentioned as having been found in La Luz and held by the Justice of the Peace and afterwards claimed by Oliver Lee is still held by the Justice of the Peace.

Mr. Myers says there is not truth in the statement that Oliver Lee or any of his men claimed this horse, it was an old stray broken down horse and was claimed by a Mexican from Tularosa, but the Justice was not satisfied as to his claim and would not deliver up the horse. It is nothing but an old stray horse and Mr. Myers is sure it can have no connection with this case whatever as a man who would be connected with this case would not use such a horse as was found.

Mr. Myers took me to the house of Mr. D. M. Sutherland where Col. Fountain stopped over night. Mr. Sutherland was in bed but got up to see me. Mr. Myers left us to talk alone. Mr. Sutherland stated that since seeing Mr. John Meadows here he had learned that there was but two men seen by Mrs. Barunda who lives half a mile from La Luz northwest from the town; she describes the men as two red faced bearded men but could give no other description of horses or men. Bill Carr at that time wore a full beard and was seen in town Friday evening and shook hands with two men whom he knew and met on the road; he was then on his way toward Dog Canyon and on Saturday he had lunch at Mr. Myers' store about 1 p.m. The other man disappeared after he left the neighborhood of Mrs. Barunda's house and was not seen in town; both men she declares were armed and carried packs. This was on Thursday that Mrs. Barunda saw these two men.

Now my reason for seeing Mr. Sutherland in reference to this matter was on account of the statement received from John Meadows while at Pellman's. This information had come to Meadows from Mr. Sutherland and he requested me to see Sutherland and find out if there was anything new. This was all the information Mr. Sutherland could give me, so about 10:30 a.m. I retired at the house of Mr. Reynolds, leaving orders to be called at 3 a.m. so that I could leave on my return trip.

Yours respectfully,
"S"

Monday, March 23, 1896.

At 6 a.m. I left La Luz for Pellman's, arriving there at 10:45 a.m. I met John Meadows at Pellman's and told him of my conversation with Mr. Myers and Mr. Sutherland. Mr. Meadows told me that he had seen Phil Kearney on his way to El Paso the day before and he would catch him on his return and question him in reference to the Frank Chatfield matter; also promised to see Emmet Russ and D. F. Baze and find out from them whether or not old man Gilliland camped with them on Saturday night as he claimed near Parker's Lake. I arranged with Meadows to remain at Pellman's until after I had a chance to again interview Antonio Rey and Santos Alvarado at Luna's Well. Then he could drop in there as though he had not seen me and see what effect my interview had on Antonio Rey.

Meadows promised to give me the statements of these different people by sending them through Maj. Llewellyn who would forward them to me at Denver. After resting up and feeding the team and having dinner, I left Pellman's at 1:00 p.m. arriving at Luna's Well where I saw Antonio Rey and Santos Alvarado, and also Mrs. Antonio Rey.

I went at Antonio Rey in a different manner from what I had on my previous visit. I gave him to understand that he would have a chance to tell the truth or take the consequences of doing so in a court of justice. I questioned him closely in reference to his story told to Marcus Mestos without mentioning the name of Mestos or any one else and he denied this story point blank and claims that what he did say was to a party of Mexicans near the Salt Mines, which is between La Luz and Tularosa. He said that he told them to search in the vicinity of San Nicolas Pass. He said that he had told a good many stories to people who had come to his place just to get rid of them, as he was annoyed and bothered a great deal.

When questioned about the man who had gotten on the roof of his house looking around some twenty days before the Col.'s. return from Lincoln, Rey claimed that he knew nothing of this and said that the only man that had been on the roof of his house looking around was Joe Morgan, but that that was a long time before Col. Fountain made his trip from La Luz to Lincoln; still he could give no definite time when it was, although pressed very hard to do so.

He positively states that Joe Morgan had no field glass and that he did not know what he was looking for. Morgan passed their place on Friday about noon going towards Las Cruces. Santos Alvarado verified this statement about Morgan being there before Col. Fountain made his trip to Lincoln. I then had Morgan Llewellyn go into the house and see Mrs. Antonio Rey while I held Antonio Rey and Santos Rey in conversation on the outside. He questioned her closely but only learned that she verified this statement made by Antonio and Santos as to the time Joe Morgan was at their house and looked around from the roof of the same over the country.

It is hard to tell whether these people are telling the truth, but I am inclined to think that Antonio Rey knows nothing more than what he has already told. Being unable to get any further information from any of these people we continued on to Parker's Well, arriving there about 6 p.m. I found Chas. Jones at Parker's well and questioned him regarding Hiram Yost and Frank Hill being at Sunol at the time of the disappearance of Col. Fountain. The following is his statement:

> "I went to work the last Saturday in January, I don't know what date it was, worked seven days at the Sunol mine in the place of Chas. Cowan who was injured at the mine some time before. I saw Hiram Yost there but cannot say what day or date. I was not well acquainted with Yost; think he stopped with Fall while there. He came in the evening and was there next day; I don't know when he left or where he went. I had no talk with him while he was there, except to pass the time of day when I first saw him there. I never saw

Frank Hill there at any time. I have never stated that I saw him."

"I think that Mr. Fall went into Las Cruces on the day before Fountain disappeared but I am not sure as to that. Mr. Cox can tell you about this as he met him on the road when he was going into town. This is all I know about the case."

I questioned Jones very closely but could obtain no further information from him, and I believe he has told all he knows. The statement credited to him is like a good many others, badly exaggerated.

From here I drove on to Cox's ranch arriving there about 7:30 p.m., having driven 65 miles that day. At Cox's ranch I met Mr. W. W. Cox, but found that Perry was at another ranch and that Mr. Cox had not as yet asked him in reference to the time they met Judge Fall going from Sunol to Las Cruces on Saturday evening. Mr. Cox promised he would see his brother Perry as soon as he reached the ranch and settle this point, would then report the same to Major Llewellyn on his next visit to town. Mr. Cox suggested that I see Mrs. McCowan at Organ, that she would be better able to give the correct time than he would. We stayed all night at Cox's ranch.

Yours respectfully,
"S"

Tuesday, March 24 1896.

At 7 a.m. we left Cox's ranch for Las Cruces, stopped at McCowan's at Organ to see Mrs. McCowan and was informed that she was still in Las Cruces or on her way home. About five miles from there I met Mrs. McCowan going out on the stage and had a talk with her. She states that Mr. Cox came to her house on Saturday evening the same day on which Col. Fountain disappeared between the hours of 6 and 7 p.m., but not later than 7. The reason she places the time is that she was preparing the children for bed and she always does this after supper and it could not have been later than 7 p.m., she was inclined to believe that it was earlier, she knew it was dark, but at that time it was quite dark early in the evening. Mr. Cox had two vouchers for her to sign for Mr. Morgan who had dinner at her house on that day. She was not familiar with these vouchers but signed them and they went in [to Las Cruces] next morning by the hack that goes in from the gold camp.

Mr. Morgan had never eaten at her house before that she remembered of. This was all Mrs. McCowan knew about the case, so we pushed on to Las Cruces and arrived there about 1 p.m. After dinner, I saw Mr. Garrett and Mr. Perry in Garrett's room and was told by Garrett that Perry had not succeeded in getting the warrants for Gilliland which he had expected; however, Garrett's manner in reply to my questions led me to believe that Garrett was perhaps holding back information from me; he did not seem to care to talk on the subject and I did not press him.

Garrett and Perry were preparing to leave town to make a search for the bodies. I gave Garrett all the information that I had and was surprised on several occasions while reading my notes to him to have Mr. Perry say that there was nothing in this or that statement as he had or they had investigated these points before. It seemed very strange to me if these points were investigated that Mr. Garrett and Mr. Perry did not give me the result of their investigation, as I was there to assist them in every possible way that I could.

Mr. Garrett asked me while reading my statement in reference to H. K. Parker bringing a load of oats to Pellman's whether or not I had found out what kind of oats these were. I then learned for the first time that the supposed assassins fed their horses oats where the camp fire was found beyond Col. Fountain's buckboard, the oats fed were unthrashed.

Now this seems to have been a very important point and I was surprised that I had never been told of it before as I was in a position to make a thorough investigation in reference to these oats had I known anything about it. It would have been no trouble to me while at Tularosa to have learned positively what kind of oats Parker had conveyed to Pellman's for the Eddy outfit and at Pellman's I could have verified this statement through Mr. Pellman himself; also through his wife and daughter.

I found in my entire trip that no investigation had been made by Garrett or Perry or any of these people, but that they had picked up information here and there and the same had not been given to me. I should like to have had the time to have visited White Oaks and Lincoln if necessary and have seen Alvino Guerra and Mrs. Eva Taylor, but it was out of the question owing to the fact that my time was so limited.

I found in my conversation with Garrett that he thought that Parker and Scott Day had encountered the assassins of Col. Fountain, as they were on the road behind the Col. and that they may have supplied the oats which the assassins fed their horses; this, however, I think hardly probable, as Col. Fountain was at least two hours ahead of Parker and Scott and the men who were keeping track of Col. Fountain were probably ahead of him, according to the statement of Barela. I had very little time to talk to Garrett and Perry as they were very busy preparing to leave town.

I met Judge Fall during the afternoon, but he was very busy and I had no further conversation with him. I called to see Dr. Cowan at his office to ascertain positively from his records if possible what day and date Chas. Cowan left for Sunol gold camp with Judge Fall. Dr. Cowan informed me that he had no memorandum of the date on which his nephew left town, but did know that he went out with Judge Fall, whichever day that was and it was his impression that it was about the last of the week; this was as close as he could come to it.

Before Mr. John Riley left Las Cruces on Friday last I met him at the depot as he was about to take the train, he was with two other gentlemen at that time, one of whom he informed me was Col. Mothersill, manager for the cattle company for whom Hiram Yost and Frank Hill work.

This I understand is the Detroit Cattle Co. I asked Mr. Riley to talk with Mr. Mothersill on the way down on the train and find out what he could about Yost and Hill, which he promised to do. I called on Judge Newcomb during the afternoon and had quite a long talk with him; also with Major Llewellyn who had just returned from Albuquerque. These people seemed very much disappointed and surprised at my withdrawing from the case, and they talked as though they were going to takes steps to have me return and handle this case. I saw nothing of Oliver Lee in town during the day.

Yours respectfully,
"S"

Wednesday, March 25, 1896.

At 11:46 a.m. I left Las Cruces enroute for Denver.

Numa Raymond, the new sheriff, was on the same train with me and I had quite a talk with him. He seemed to be well pleased with Garrett and his men who had charge of the Sheriff's office as he seemed to have every confidence in Garrett and his men.

When we reached San Marcial, I met Librado C. De Baca and Elfego Baca. I learned from them that they had been out to Valverde which is across the river from San Marcial to see Alexandro Garcia, having received a telegram from him at Socorro the day before; this telegram I was shown by De Baca who told me that this man Garcia was very much frightened and they were satisfied he had not told all he knew; the statement that he had made to them on this visit was that Ed. Brown, Green Scott, and the third man whose name he did not know, but whom they called Gene, had left Brown's ranch on Jan. 29th, and returned to Brown's ranch three or four days afterwards, that they afterwards had told that they had only gone as far as Tularosa, that one rode a gray horse, one a sorrel and the other a buck skin. He stated that they had acted in a very suspicious manner after their return, keeping close to the ranch and evidently always on the lookout for some one.

Garcia promised to get the name of this man Gene and give it to them on his next visit to San Marcial, which would be in a few days when he would bring in a bunch of cattle, he is to wire them again and they will meet him at San Marcial, when they expect to got more information from him.

After leaving San Marcial, I learned from Numa Raymond that Elfego Baca had requested him to put up money so that he might carry on this work on the Ed. Brown end of the case. Mr. Raymond consulted with me in regard to this and I advised him not to put up anything at all for I don't think it would be proper or beneficial to the case to give Elfego money to place in the hands of this Mexican to tell something that I don't believe he really knows, as he is liable to tell something we are not able to prove afterwards. I believe that he has told all that he knows. I don't doubt but what Ed. Brown, Green Scott, and this other man were connected with this case in some way; but I don't believe this Mexican knows anything more about it than he has already stated.

This man Elfego Baca, I don't see why he should not continue on without expecting to be paid for his time; besides, he has learned through some source that Garrett is being paid for his time and at the same time is working for the reward and this has made him feel rather sore, as he considers himself as good a man as Garrett and some of the other people who have been working on the case, and so stated to me on my visit to Socorro recently.

I was on the road all day and night and nothing more of importance occurred to report.

Yours respectfully,
"S"

Thursday, March 26, 1896.

While enroute this morning to Denver I met Mr. John H. Riley at La Junta who was on his way from Kansas City to Denver. I had quite a little talk with Mr. Riley on my way in. He informed me that he had had a talk with Col.

Mothersill and had learned from him that he (Mothersill) feared that Hiram Yost and Frank Hill were in the Fountain killing. The Colonel's wife is postmistress at their place and she told her husband that Frank Hill had been receiving letters through the mail from Santa Fe prior to and one after the murder or disappearance of Col. Fountain and that these letters were in envelopes with United States Marshall on the corner and he believed that they were from Tom Tucker, who was a Deputy U.S. Marshal at that time.

Mr. Riley thought that I ought to have seen Col. Mothersill and had a talk with him, but as Mr. Riley's letter had not reached Las Cruces previous to my departure, I was not aware of the result of his conversation with the Col. Consequently, I will have to take this matter up provided I return. In my conversation with Mr. Riley, I found he and other cattlemen had been talking this matter over and were quite determined that I should return to Las Cruces and take up this case.

I told Mr. Riley how I had been handicapped in my investigation owing to the fact that information was held back from me by parties interested in the case, and the only way for me to do if I returned on this matter again would be to take one of my own men with me, who I could send out to investigate points under our own methods, to handle the case from Las Cruces running down such points as might be necessary at Silver City, Engle, Socorro, San Marcial, and El Paso myself while the man could use a horse and pick up what information he could taking full statements, etc. on the road between Las Cruces, Tularosa, La Luz, Lincoln, and White Oaks.

I arrived in Denver at 5:15 P.M. reported at the Agency and discontinued.

Yours respectfully,
"S"

Denver, Colorado, March 29, 1896

Gov. W. T. Thornton
Santa Fe, New Mexico

Dear Sir:

In view of the future investigation into the murder of Col. A. J. Fountain and son, it would very much facilitate matters if we had accurate maps of Dona Ana and adjoining counties, showing trails, roads, water, mountain passes, etc. I think these can be obtained from the military authorities at Washington, D. C.

If you will, kindly make application for two sets. If they cannot be had in the counties, please get the best map in duplicate of the whole state, either Military or Civil, whichever is the most accurate.

Yours respectfully,
"S"

TERRITORY OF NEW MEXICO
Office of the Executive
Santa Fe, N. Mex., April 1, 1896

Mr. James McParland,
Denver, Colorado,

Dear Sir:-

Gov. Thornton has returned from Washington, and you will please send the reports in the Fountain matter to him, which I requested you some weeks to suspend until the Governor's return here.

Yours very respectfully,
Nellie P. Crane
Private Secretary

Chapter 4 | Status and Recommendations

Following are letters between Fraser, Governor Thornton, and McParland regarding the status of the investigation. In his April 14 letter, Fraser admits his investigation was less than definitive (although he does not label it a failure), and gives his reasons why. He also sends Governor Thornton the bill for the investigation: $299.10. This is 90 cents under the $300 dollar limit imposed by Governor Thornton when he hired the Agency. Fraser recommends that a second Operative, William C. Sayers, who can work undercover, be assigned to the case. Governor Thornton agrees and Sayers is authorized to begin his investigation.

TERRITORY OF NEW MEXICO
Office of the Executive
Santa Fe, N. Mex., April 4, 1896

Mr. J. C. Fraser
Room 50, Opera House Block,
Denver, Colo.

Dear Mr. Fraser;-

I have just returned home and find your favor of the 29th of March, and have this day written to the Secretary of War for the maps requested. As soon as they arrive, I will forward to you.

If you have not already sent me a full report of your work in Dona Ana County, I should like to have it together with your bill up to date, and if you have not fully completed the work, I would like to have you do so at your earliest convenience. If you return you might come by Santa Fe and talk the matter over with me. Wire me when you start.

Yours very truly,
W. T. Thornton

Denver, Colo., April 6, 1896

To His Excellency
Hon. W. T. Thornton,
Governor of New Mexico,
Santa Fe, N.M.

Dear Sir:-

I enclose herewith our bill for $299.10. I have already mailed you full reports of my investigation, also written you a synopsis of the same and this letter went with the reports. I also notified you that I expected to leave for Europe, but this trip is now off and I will be here and will be pleased to hear from you as soon as you have read over these reports and until I hear from you again before taking this work up.

In my recent letter I suggested that Operative Boxwell be detailed on this work to continue the same and if you think it necessary after he is on the ground I can also go forward and make a further investigation and direct his work. This however is merely a suggestion and I will leave it to your judgment as to how this work should be taken up.

Yours truly,
"S"

TERRITORY OF NEW MEXICO
OFFICE OF THE EXECUTIVE
Santa Fe, N. Mex., April 7, 1896

James McParland, Esq., Colo.

Sir:-

I am just in receipt of your favor with reports up to date.

I think that you are a little mistaken as to Garrett. I told you Garrett had an affidavit from some one who saw the horsemen ride along the road the day that Fountain was killed. I did this on information received from Llewellyn; the man I referred to was Pellman. I was told that he saw them and recognized them with a field glass. I have since seen Garrett and find out that this story, like many others concerning the murder, proved to be a hoax. I shall be glad to have your man go back and begin work, and shall have the money ready to pay him.

He ought to keep me posted, however, as to the amount of his expenses, so that when the fund runs short, I can cut him off. I shall write this to John Riley, and have matters there carried through in a systematic manner. I am particularly anxious to have the Ed. Brown and Yost clue run down. I still think they know who the murders are. Your man should stop off at San Marcial, cross the river, and see the Mexican, as I understand he talks Spanish well, and might do this better than anyone else.

No reward or anything should be offered to induce them to talk, or give this testimony as it might throw us off the trail. I shall write to Riley today, and ask him to see certain parties down there who I understand know something about the case. I agree with you as to the importance of keeping his name secret. Put your man at work at once and let him follow up the matter systematically. I have written for transportation for him, and he had probably better wait to see if comes, for a few days.

Upon receipt of this letter, telegraph the name of the man you want to send to J. J. Frey, General Mgr. at Topeka, Kansas, as I have forgotten the name. I am going to have the post office here watched with reference to letters, as in this way, I may find out the whereabouts of some of these people who are missing. I notice in the *St. Louis Republic* of either Friday last or Saturday, a telegram from a little town in Illinois with reference to there being a man, a stranger, in the hospital, who had been wounded six or eight weeks ago, and who is believed from his conduct to be an escaped criminal. The paper spoke of his being a mysterious stranger. I would suggest that you get this paper and examine it, and make inquiry as to the identity of this man. I have lost the paper or would send it to you. It is barely possible that two or three of these men who are missing, it might be that one of them was wounded and sent off East to be doctored. It would do no harm to look into the matter. I suppose you know that Pellman is the father-in-law of Ed. Brown.

As to Garrett and Perry not giving Mr. F. [Fraser] a great deal of information, I do not think it is because they do not want his assistance or help, but because they do not realize the importance of these things.

I tried to get Pat [Garrett] to look into the matter of the oats, because of the peculiarity of their being green, and not in a condition to feed to horses and because they might have been traced to whom they were purchased from, but he did not seem to think it amounted to anything.

I have written to Mr. Frey for the pass, telling him that you would telegraph the name of the man you wanted it for. If it does not come in a few days, he can come without it, and when it arrives you can forward it to him. Please attend to this as soon as this letter reaches you.

Yours respectfully,
W. T. Thornton

Denver, Colorado, April 8, 1896
Gov. W. T. Thornton,
Santa Fe, New Mexico

Dear Sir: -.

In writing you I forgot to mention the fact that I had seen an article in the *Denver Republican* of Sunday, April the 5th. I enclose you the newspaper clipping, and would like to know whether or not this body has been identified; although considerable distance from where Col. Fountain disappeared, still, it would not be impossible for a body to be conveyed to where it was found. True, there may be nothing in this that would connect it with the Fountain case, still, at the same time I am anxious to know what Deputy Sheriff Newcomer learned from the papers found on the body, also as to whether or not it has been as yet identified.

I will be more than pleased to receive the maps which you have sent for. I have not heard whether Mr. Garrett and Mr. Perry have accomplished anything in the way of finding the remains or not.

If I return on this matter I will certainly stop and see you at Santa Fe, and if Mr. Boxwell and I both go forward on this work we will want to see Slick Miller and also Tom Tucker. I want to get a full statement from Tucker as to the time he claims to have been at Sunol and as to what he was doing there. He of course may refuse to talk the same as Oliver Lee, but it will not hurt to try and get this statement.

Yours truly,
John C. Fraser,
Asst. Supt.

Denver, Colorado, April 11, 1896
Gov. W. T. Thornton,
Santa Fe, New Mexico

Dear Sir:-

I am in receipt of yours of April the 7th addressed to Mr. McParland. On receipt of your letter I immediately called upon Mr. Hall, Agent of the Santa Fe, and gave him the name of our Opt. who is to go forward on this work: Mr. W. B. Sayers, who has been mentioned in my previous letters as W. S. Boxwell; as he is somewhat known, I thought it best to use his right name. I am expecting the transportation here by tomorrow or Monday at the very latest.

From your letter I should judge that you have not had time to read over my reports.

In regard to the affidavit of which you speak, I know nothing about it; the first intimation I had of any affidavit was the letter I received from you at Las Cruces.

In regard to Mr. Pellman who is the father-in-law of Ed. Brown, I have his statement in my reports [page 98], as I stopped at his place on purpose to be able to talk to him. He positively denies having seen any one.

You may be correct in regard to Mr. Perry and Mr. Garrett; I have every confidence in both of these men and believe they are good officers, but you will admit that they are very careless about giving any information that they may possess. Had they been as frank with me as I was with them, they would have saved me a great deal of trouble and I would have been able to have made a more thorough investigation between Las Cruces and Tularosa than I did.

Mr. Sayers has handled all of my reports and I have gone over the matter very carefully with him. He is an intelligent and very competent operative and understands exactly how this matter should be taken up. You are mistaken when you say that the Opt. speaks Spanish, you have evidently misunderstood me, I was talking to you about another Opt. who is at the present time is absent, who speaks Spanish, and I have no doubt you have the two men mixed.

Mr. Sayers will stop at Santa Fe and have a conference with you before proceeding on this work. I think it advisable for him to stop at Engle and investigate the actions of Yost and Hill. If you think it advisable, he might see Tom Tucker while in Santa Fe, but if you think otherwise, he will be governed by your instructions in this matter entirely.

I reported fully the conversation I had with Elfego Baca, also with Librado C De Baca, as they were on their way from San Marcial to Socorro after having seen the Mexican Garcia.

Mr. Sayers will have with him copies of my reports so that he can refer to them from time to time when necessary. I will send him forward just as soon as this transportation arrives, but if it does not arrive by Monday I will send him on without transportation.

I tried to secure copies of the *St. Louis Republic* of Friday and Saturday April 3d and 4th, respectively, but after a thorough search in this city was unable to obtain anything but a copy of Friday's paper and a search in this failed to reveal the article which you mentioned in reference to the stranger being in the hospital in Illinois. I have written to the *St. Louis Republic* to send me Saturday's and Sunday's issue of their paper.

Yours truly,
"S"

Denver, Colorado, April 13, 1896

The Hon. W. T. Thornton,
Gov. of New Mexico,
Santa Fe, New Mexico

Dear Sir:-

This will introduce to you Mr. W. B. Sayers, whom I have detailed to take up the matter of the murder of Col. Fountain. Mr. Sayers is the operative whom I intended to send down to you when I first took up this operation, although I gave you the name of Boxwell at that time. He has read over all of Mr. Fraser's reports and is perfectly familiar with the case, so far as we know, and you can confer freely with him. If in the future you should require the services of Mr. Fraser on this matter, I expect that he will be available in a short time.

Yours truly,
James McParland,
Supt.

Denver, Colorado, April 14, 1896

Gov. W. T. Thornton,
Santa Fe, New Mexico

Dear Sir:-

Enclosed please find my reports up to and including Thursday March 26th.

You will see from my reports that it has been utterly impossible for me to complete this investigation in anything like a satisfactory manner, owing to the limited time. You will also note that it was impossible for me to get out on the road to Tularosa and La Luz sooner, owing to the wrangle between Numa Raymond [Reymond] and Oscar Lohman, as the latter insisted on having charge of the Sheriff's office, which Mr. Garrett would not listen to.

Owing to this misunderstanding, I was compelled to leave Las Cruces with the son of Major Llewellyn as my interpreter to make this trip alone; I had but four days and a half to make the entire trip in, and but six days and a half to make the trip and reach Denver, so as to keep within the limit of the amount specified in your last letter.

I feel that this investigation should be continued, and I would suggest that if this matter is taken up again that we be allowed to send one of our men who is a thorough plainsman and an A 1 investigator, to continue this work. Investigations should be made at Engle, Silver City, also investigations that will undoubtedly come up at such points as El Paso, Socorro, San Marcial, and other points over as far as Lincoln and White Oaks, using a saddle horse for this purpose.

I think this should be done, as I find that all previous investigations so far have amounted to nothing, and have been done in a slip shod manner, that a man in the vicinity of Tularosa, La Luz, White Oaks, or Lincoln would soon be able to get at what data we want; in the meantime, let Mr.

Garrett and Perry continue their search for the bodies of Col. Fountain and his son.

I feel satisfied that a good man could pick up a good deal of information around in the country that I have spoken of. You will understand of course that it is impossible for any man to go in there and work secretly on Oliver Lee or any of this gang, but what we do want to get is the statements of these people in full to be used in every case provided arrests are made in the near future. I feel satisfied that this entire matter will come home to Oliver Lee, and that Bill McNew, Jack Tucker, Bill Carr, and others are implicated in this matter.

I am thoroughly satisfied that Judge Fall was not at Chalk Hill, but I am not satisfied that he was not a party to the conspiracy. There is certainly a master hand in this whole affair, and the great legal point would be the proper disposition or disposal of these bodies so that they could be found. There was nothing to prevent Judge Fall from being able to see what was going on, provided he used a pair of field glasses, while at Sunol, for with the naked eye from Chalk Hill you can see Sunol, and if Judge Fall was a party to this conspiracy, there is nothing to have prevented him from knowing whether or not the plan had been carried out by the other people at Chalk Hill.

I consider the statement of Slick Miller very important in this case. In your last letter to me at Las Cruces you desire to know if I had seen the affidavit which Mr. Garrett had in his possession from some one whose name you did not mention [Maxwell]; I wish to state that Mr. Garrett has positively denied to me taking any affidavits or receiving any. I did not let him know that I had received this information from you, but managed to ask him if any affidavits had been taken and he stated positively that none had been taken so far.

You can see how I have been handicapped in this matter and any information I have gotten from Garrett I have been compelled to draw out of him by asking questions direct after having received intimations of what he possessed. I believe he is thoroughly honest in his intentions, but may be a little careless and not consider certain points of much importance. I find that he regards Mr. Perry as quite a Detective and takes his word and advice for the truth or falsity of statements and rumors which come to them.

I found that Mr. Perry treated my investigation at Tularosa and La Luz in a very light manner and it was he who told me while I was reading my notes to Garrett that they had looked these matters up themselves. Now if our man continues on this work, it will not do to incur the enmity of Garrett, Perry, or any of their men. I have been very careful not to let them know that I am aware of their having held information back from me and at the present time we are the very best of friends. I simply write this for your own knowledge, so that you will know exactly how things are going.

I would like to know who this affidavit was from which you mentioned. I, of course, imagine that it is from Jack Maxwell. If we continue this work we should find this man Maxwell and interview him. I also want to get statements from Oliver Lee and others, if it is at all possible, by having them away from their legal advisor Mr. Fall.

If this plan meets with your approval, I wish to state that W. S. Boxwell [Operative William C. Sayers] will be the man whom I desire to detail, and I think it would be well to have transportation furnished to him the same as you had to me.

Mr. John H. Riley does not want to be known in this case to any one, as he has large interests close by where these people live and he has been threatened on several occasions. He is very anxious that this matter be run out and he is willing to give financial support to run the matter down. I expect that he will write you if he has not already done so. In my conversation with Mr. Riley he stated that the depot agent at Las Cruces had informed him that Judge Fall rode up on Sunday morning to his (Fall's) house, which is almost opposite the depot on horseback at a very early hour.

This was the day after the disappearance of Col. Fountain. I did not have time to investigate this point, but Mr. Boxwell will do so if he takes up this work. I wish to state that I made an examination of Chalk Hill and vicinity, but at this late date it was impossible for me to find anything, owing to the lapse of time, still I found things exactly as they had been represented to me before arriving on the ground.

Hoping to hear from you soon, as I am holding Mr. Boxwell in readiness to take this matter up. I would be pleased to take this work up myself in person were it not for the fact that I expect to leave for England to-night on an important matter.

Yours truly,
"S"

Chapter 5 | Sayers Investigates

Operative Sayers begins his investigation with a fixed idea: Ed Brown knows who killed the Fountains, and, further, he probably was one of the conspirators. Sayers is confident that if Brown can be forced to talk, the case will be solved. And he knows just how to crack Brown – confront him with "Slick" Miller.

Gov. W. T. Thornton,
Santa Fe, New Mexico

Monday, April 13, 1896

To-day in Denver:-

As per instructions received from Supt. McParland, I left Denver at 7 p.m. for Santa Fe, New Mexico via A. T. & S. F. R. R. and traveled to La Junta where I was compelled to lay over as my transportation was not good on the limited train which leaves La Junta at 12:50 a.m.

Yours truly,
"S"

Tuesday, April 14, 1896

I left La Junta this morning at 9:30 a.m. enroute for Santa Fe and arrived at the latter place after midnight having traveled continuously all day.

Yours respectfully,
"S"

Wednesday, April 15, 1896

I arrived at Santa Fe at 2:10 a.m. and immediately went to the Clair Hotel and registered; leaving a call for 7 a.m., I retired. At 7:45 a.m., I called at Gov. W. T. Thornton's office but found no one there; so I walked around town and called at the office several times till I found Miss Crane, Gov. Thornton's stenographer in the office, and from her learned that it was the Governor's intention to leave town this morning to be gone several days; but she did not know that he had gone.

I immediately went to Gov. Thornton's house and learned there that he had left town. I returned to the office and some time later Miss Crane telegraphed to the Gov. for me stating that I was here and asking if I should remain until he returned. About 4 p.m. Miss Crane received an answer saying that I should wait.

During the afternoon, Col. Bergamer [E. H. Bergmann], Supt. of the penitentiary, called at the Governor's office and Miss Crane introduced me. I also met Mr. Hall, U.S. Marshal, and had a long talk with him. Miss Crane pointed out to me Tom Tucker and I loafed around town in the hope of falling in with Tucker, as if by accident; but railed as I noticed him go to a livery stable and overheard his conversation from which I learned that he was going out of town to be gone two days.

About 5 p.m., Col. Bergamer in from the Penitentiary and Miss Crane told him that I wanted to see a party there and the Col. said that was all right and for me to come out in the morning to the Pen and see him about 9 a.m.

Miss Crane tells me that there is a letter missing from the Governor's table which was written by Ass't Supt. J. C. Fraser to the Governor some time ago; so I write to Supt. Jas. McParland asking that a copy of the same be sent to Gov. Thornton so he could see what if any information an outside party could gain from it, supposing it to have been stolen by someone having access to the Governor's private office. It may have been an important letter.

Yours respectfully,
"S"

Thursday, April 16, 1896

To-day in Santa Fe.-

This morning I got a rig at the livery stable and drove out to the Penitentiary, where I met Col. Bergamer in his office.

He enquired how long I expected to remain in Santa Fe, and learning that I should be here all day to-morrow he said he thought it best that he should have a talk with his man first and then have me meet him and question him; I did not like this as I would rather see the man myself and have an opportunity to visit him a second time if necessary, but I found the old Col. a most peculiar man and soon saw it was useless to crowd him in any way; he has his own system of handling his convicts and to urge him to do it differently would not do.

The Col. showed me through the Pen and pointed out [Slick] Miller, but told me to say nothing. He called my attention to Miller's face and said that from conversation he had had with the man he was convinced that his story could be depended upon and that he would tell all he knew.

Since the Col. took Miller's first statement, he has spoken to him several times on this subject and yesterday asked him if he knew this man Herrera [Luis Herrera] that Pat Garrett arrested and who was suspected of being the murderer of Fountain. Miller does not remember him and does not think there is anything in it.

He told Col. Bergamer that he believed he could locate the bodies of Col. Fountain and his son and the Col. thinks that we may be able to get some information of value from this man and said that he would talk to him this evening and have it arranged for me to meet him tomorrow. I saw that the Col. was determined on this point, so I did not try to force the matter, believing that Col. Bergamer was acting as he considered best and that he was anxious and willing to assist in every way possible to bring to justice Col. Fountain's murderers.

At 12 a.m., I returned to town and called on Miss Crane; she had heard nothing from Gov. Thornton and said she did not expect to until he came in. During the afternoon I called on Mr. Hall at his office and he informed me that he was going to leave town tomorrow morning and would not return before Monday, so he said that I could come to his office tomorrow that he would give me a commission as Deputy U.S. Marshal which might be of use to me in the future.

Mr. Hall expressed himself as being thoroughly well satisfied that the parties who killed Col. Fountain are resting easy and that is a matter of utter impossibility to do anything with the case and that if Pat Garrett and Mr. Perry could not find the evidence it was utter folly for any one else trying.

I noticed that Tom Tucker returned to town this evening but had no opportunity to speak to him as he was busy at the Courthouse with the Sheriff Mr. Cunningham. I noticed Tucker watched me closely at the hotel and looked over the register carefully but there are a number of strangers at the hotel just now so he could not pick out one man more than another.

Yours respectfully,
"S"

Friday, April 17th, 1896

To-day in Santa Fe,

This morning I received a message from Gov. Thornton telling me to come to his office, which I did at once and remained there until 10:30 a.m. talking over the case and receiving instructions on different points from Gov. Thornton.

At 10:30 a.m., I went to the penitentiary to see Slick Miller, arriving there at 11:15 a.m.

I found Col. Bergamer in his office and he was very busy so that he could not call Miller in at that time, and told me to come again at 1 p.m. I then returned to town and after dinner went back to the pen and about 1:30 p.m. I met Miller in Col. Bergamer's office.

The Col. had explained to Miller what was wanted and I found him ready and willing to talk. He said he had been thinking over the matter constantly since he made his first statement [see page 36], but did not think he could give me any additional information, but one point he had overlooked.

At the time the stock association was formed and prior to the proposition made to him as set forth in his former statement, he was riding with Ed. Brown from San Marcial to Brown's ranch when the conversation turned on the action of the stockmen and Brown said that he could get Maxammeano Greago [Maximiano Griego] to kill W. C. McDonald for $100 and that he had a notion to do so.

Miller does not know that he did make this proposition to Greago, but he says that Greago was a tool in the hands of Ed. Brown and that Brown frequently used him to do his dirty work, and subsequently when the Rustlers determined to kill Col. Fountain, that Brown said he would hire a man to do his part, and Miller believes he had in view this man Greago.

Miller says that Brown is a shrewd cold blooded man and that he always looked for material among the Mexicans to do his dirty work; he was willing to pay for it and thought nothing of hiring a man to kill some one, but if it were possible he would avoid getting into it himself. Miller said he knew Greago was more closely connected with Brown than anyone else, and that he was in a position to tell a good deal about him, so that as Greago was now convicted of murder and could not place himself in any worse position, I might possibly got him to talk.

Miller also told me that a man named Tom Davenport living at San Marcial, also Charlie Allen at the same place, were both connected with Brown in his cattle stealing, also a man named Green Scott, but he did not think that any of these men would say a word about Brown, particularly the latter, who was about the only American that Brown was very confidential with.

I then questioned Miller as to what he knew about the other men who were in the original plot to murder Col. Fountain and asked him to tell me anything he could remember about their friends and associates, or about any crimes he knew of which they had committed. Miller said he did not know of anything which would be sufficient to indict any of these men on, and what he did know was what he learned from hearing the men talk among themselves.

Wm. McNew was completely under the control of Oliver Lee and anything that Lee told him to do he would do, believing that Lee could get him out of any trouble, but if McNew could be gotten away from Oliver Lee he would be easily broken down, as he was a very weak man in many ways, but in Miller's opinion nothing could be done with him so long as Lee was with him to advise.

There is a man named McDonald who lives in Tularosa who used to be a great friend of McNew's and some time ago they had a fight; McDonald would tell all he knew about McNew provided he thought it would not get out; also two men named Williams who live near La Luz might give some information about McNew.

Miller states that McNew always wore boots and to the best of his recollection he used to run one of them over very badly at the heel, but he would not have remembered the circumstance had I not questioned him about his clothing, etc. McNew had married a niece of Oliver Lee's; he was with Oliver Lee when Lee killed the Frenchman in Broad Canyon and tells what he knows about this as follows:

The Frenchman had some cattle and a ranch at Dog Canyon and he was a cranky old man and when Lee had cattle rounded up the Frenchman would go out and look through them and see if there were any stolen cattle in the bunch; he also threatened to have Lee indicted for stealing stock, and Lee was afraid that he would and could furnish the proof, and Miller heard Lee and McNew talking about it several times and Lee said he would kill him.

Then the Frenchman sold his cattle to a man named Riley and still lived on his ranch doing a little farming; he had some dogs and when any of Lee's cattle came around would run them off with the dogs. Lee again threatened to kill him, and one day Lee, McNew, and a man named Dan Davis went to the Frenchman's ranch on horseback; the Frenchman met them at the door with his gun and began cursing Lee and Lee shot him; he fired at him three times, only one bullet taking effect. There was nothing done about it, as the Frenchman had no relatives and no friends to take the matter up, so Oliver Lee jumped his ranch and the matter ended.

Miller learned this from Dan Davis who was present at the killing and who told Miller about it some time in June, 1894. Miller was sent to the Pen on the first of November, 1894, he says he thinks Davis is some place in that country yet, but does not know. Lee once told Miller positively that he intended to kill the Frenchman.

Miller states that he knows Lee and Tom Tucker killed [Walter] Good, and there was a man named Cherokee Bill who was with them. Lee was afraid that Bill, who had no interest in the country, would give it away, that he took him on a trip to Old Mexico to get some cattle and when he got him to a convenient place on the other side of the line he killed Cherokee Bill and returned to his ranch. Miller heard him boasting about it afterwards, but does not know of any way to prove it, as he only has Lee's own statement, but he is quite satisfied that these things are true.

Miller said he did not think that Gilliland would give up any information; he is a young fellow that wants to be bad and he has a good deal of nerve.

Miller is still of the opinion that the body of Col. Fountain was disposed of in the San Andreas Mts. as he says that country is full of caves and deep ravines where no one ever goes and the work could be done in such a way as to leave no trace. The rest of Miller's statement is the same in every particular as that made to Col. Bergamer some time ago.

As he could think of nothing else to tell me, I concluded our conversation and returned to town. Miller said that should he from time to time think of anything else in connection with this matter, he would report it to Col. Bergamer and the Col. who was present during my interview told me if at any time I found any question come up that Miller might be able to answer, to let him know and he would ask Miller about it.

On my return to town I called on Mr. Hall, U.S. Marshal, and he gave me a commission as Deputy U.S. Marshal for Dona Ana County. I then went to Gov. Thornton's office and reported to him verbally my conversation with Miller. The Governor said he knew some of it was true, as he knew that Tucker and Lee had killed Good, but the information about the Frenchman was important as Lee could be indicted for that if the proof could be had, and he instructed me to look up Dan Davis, also Cherokee Bill, and find out all that I could about the killing of the Frenchman when I got to that part of the country.

Gov. Thornton told me he had it from somewhere, which he could not exactly place, that there was some man stopped at Lee's ranch on Friday and Saturday, the 1st and 2nd of February, to see Lee about some cattle he had for sale and that Lee was not at home. This man may be the party referred to as having the conversation with the postmaster at Ruidoso and who is supposed to come from Penasco. I will take this up with Maxwell when I see him and locate this man if possible.

I spoke to Gov. Thornton about the missing letter and he tells me there is no doubt that it was taken from his desk by some one interested in protecting these people.

I noticed that Tucker is very much interested in watching me when I went to the Courthouse to make oath before Judge Langhly; he made it convenient to follow me and wait around to see what I was there for.

I received a letter of introduction from Gov. Thornton to Hon. J. M. Doherty at Socorro and the Gov. also wrote to Mr. Freeman, Elfego Baca's partner, and it was arranged that I should see Maxammeano Greago at Socorro and try to get some information out of him as to Brown or any of the parties connected with this affair; so at 10:10 p.m. I left Santa Fe for Socorro, N.M.

Yours respectfully,
"S"

Saturday, April 18, 1896

To-day in Socorro,-

I arrived at Socorro this morning at 5:15 a.m. and going at once to the hotel went to bed for a few hours.

At 10 a.m., I called on Mr. Doherty and presented my letter of introduction; he was engaged at the time, but as soon as his visitors had gone away he took up the subject of the Fountain murder with me. At first Mr. Doherty wanted to get all the information I had and my authority for the same and give me none in return, but I did not see my way to telling him anything.

He said that he was aware from other sources that Greago could give some valuable information if he wanted to, but that it was impossible for him to know anything about the Fountain murders as he was in jail at the time; and so far as Ed. Brown was concerned his testimony was not necessary as Mr. Doherty had sufficient now to convict Brown of cow stealing and send him to the Pen. Brown's case would come up at the next term of court in May, and the evidence was all ready.

I learned that Greago is at liberty and is living at San Pedro with his family; he is not on bonds. Mr. Doherty tells me that Mr. H. O. Bursum, Sheriff of Socorro County, has been working up this case and that he knows the parties who left Brown's ranch on the 28th or 29th of Jan.; also that since the killing of Fountain, Brown is supposed to have said that he could find the bodies.

Now Mr. Bursum is working on this part of the case and has the party who claims to have heard Brown say this, and it is quite possible that by now the Sheriff has seen this man and got the statement in proper shape; however, Mr. Doherty said he would go no further as he did not know what

Mr. Bursum, the Sheriff, would say about it and that he could not tell me anything more about it unless the Sheriff gave him permission or told it himself. Mr. Doherty is quite positive that Brown did not kill Fountain, but he is equally certain that Brown knows all about the affair. Mr. Doherty suggested that we go to the Sheriff and see what he had to say; accordingly we went to the Courthouse, but found the Sheriff had left town this morning and would not return until some time to-night.

We then called on Elfego Baca and found him in his office. Mr. Baca said that it has always been his opinion that the only way to get at the facts in that killing was to have Maxammeano Greago go to Brown's and get in with the gang he always associated with and through him something definite would be gotten hold of; so when Greago was let out of jail he (Baca) instructed Greago to go to Brown's ranch and try to get some information, but so far the man had done nothing as he was very poor and had to try to do something for himself at his ranch. Mr. Baca had not heard anything new in the matter lately and he did not think Greago would do much for some time as he had no way to meet these men unless they came to where he was.

As to the information Mr. Baca had received about Ed. Brown and his companions leaving the Brown ranch on the 28th or 29th of January, it came in this way: Mr. Baca heard some mention of this from a man named Chaves and learned that Chaves had gotten it from J. A. Gallegos, so he went to Gallegos and found that the story originated with a man named Alexandro Garcia, who is employed on a ranch adjoining Ed. Brown's, which is owned by Mrs. Luz Baca who lives in Socorro.

Baca sent for Garcia and this is the story he tells:

That on the 28th or 29th of January 1896, Ed. Brown, Green Scott and another man that he calls Meana, but does not know his American name, came to the ranch where he was working and told him that they were going to Old Mexico for some cattle and that if anyone came to Brown's ranch enquiring for him, to tell them that he (Brown) had gone for some cattle and would be back in a short time.

The men were all heavily armed each carried Winchesters, one was riding a dun or buckskin horse, one a brown, and the third horse he describes as more blue than white. The three men returned to the ranch in four or five days, but did not bring any cattle, and for several days he saw them around the ranch and noticed that they were armed at all times.

This is about all that Garcia knows and he is the only one that Baca found who knew anything about Brown leaving his ranch. The Gallegos, who live at Valverde, had gotten what they knew from Garcia and there was no one else who had noticed them going away. Mr. Baca said he did not think he could get any thing more out of Garcia except to make him fix the date as to their going; it was either the 28th or 29th of January, but that if Garcia was paid some money and gotten away from the county he might be willing to talk.

Mr. Baca said that he had told Mr. Fraser that it would take money to make Garcia do anything; but when I questioned him closely as to what he expected to get out of Garcia, he admitted that it was not at all likely that Garcia could know anything more than he had already told. Mr. Doherty, who was with me, said afterwards that he believed this story was as straight as it could be gotten and that Mr. Baca was more willing to act in this matter than he had been, from the fact that he had recently gotten himself into a little trouble here which might annoy him a good deal, and he thought that Mr. Baca would do all that he could now to assist in this matter.

I found it would be impossible to get Maxammeano Greago up here today and that the quickest way to reach him was to have Mr. Baca send for him and have him come up to-morrow morning when we could see what could be done with him, and meanwhile I should see the Sheriff and find out if possible what he knew.

Mr. Baca said he would accompany me to Valverde if I wished, but did not see any use in asking Gallegos any questions, because they would tell nothing, only what they had heard Garcia say, and he considered that the best plan to work with Garcia would be to send Greago out there and get him try to get some additional information out of Garcia, because it would not do for Mr. Baca to go out with me to see Garcia as someone about Brown's would notice us and Garcia is so badly scared now that he would not say a word if he thought there was a danger of Brown's learning of it.

Spending the evening in talking with Mr. Doherty, he said that he could do a good deal with Ed. Brown, as he had him in a tight place and Brown was aware that his chances of going to the pen were good, so that Mr. Doherty thinks that if he is not in this murder as a principal, that to save himself he will give up all he knows, and even if he was in it, he believes that Brown will give up if he can by so doing help his own interests.

Mr. Doherty thinks that the point the Sheriff is working on is a sort of a feeler from Brown with this end in view, and yet it is in such a shape that Brown could easily say he never said such a thing and the party who repeated it could say that he only gave it as his opinion that Brown could do so and so.

In reference to Green Scott, he is employed at the C. N. Ranch and left there to go, as he said, to Lincoln to attend court and when he returned after the murder of Col. Fountain, he told at the ranch that he had been to Lincoln. The C. N. Ranch is about 100 miles from Socorro and Mr. Doherty said that he was well acquainted with some of the men there and would find out exactly what Green Scott said about his going away at that time; also when he left, what horse he rode, and date of his return, and where he said he had been. Mr. Doherty thought he could get this information in the near future and do it in a way that would arouse no suspicion. It was known that Scott was not at Lincoln as Mr. Doherty and Mr. Baca were both there and did not see him. Mr. Baca said that he spoke to Scott once about the killing and Scott said he was glad of it and wished to God they had gotten the rest of the family.

Mr. Doherty has some affidavits in connection with the cattle stealing and gave me the following list of men who are implicated in the different deals: Bob Springs, Sandy Hightower, Wain Wilson, Fred, Joe, and Chase Spence, Tom Carter, Oscar Hill, Jas. Campfield (called Jimmy the Tough) and also Sherfield, John Latham, Walter Roberts, Chas. Henley, Punch Collins, and Geo. Carter.

Punch Carter was the main witness against Green Scott and he has mysteriously disappeared, he is supposed to have been killed by Scott, his body was not found. On account of his death, the cases against Green Scott had to be dismissed. Geo. Carter is a very important witness against Ed. Brown, but Brown made him leave the country and he cannot be located; he is supposed to be in Texas. There is also a man named Antonio Valdez, at present supposed to be in Trinidad, Colo., who was with Greago at the killing of Prieto at St. Pedro nine years ago and who is wanted as a witness against Ed. Brown, as he was as closely associated with Ed. Brown as Greago, but Mr. Doherty does not know his exact location.

[Apparently referring to the killing of Owen Gleason by William C. Reese at the St. Pedro mine as a result of a labor dispute.]

I failed to see Sheriff Bursum to-night but Mr. Doherty arranged to have me meet him at his office to-morrow at 10 a.m. As nothing further could be done, I discontinued at 7 p.m. and finished writing my reports.

Yours respectfully,
"S"

Sunday, April 19, 1896

To-day in Socorro,-

   This morning I met Elfego Baca and he told me that Maxammeano Greago would be here this evening. He had found a man yesterday who was going directly to where Greago was and had sent a letter by him. At 10 a.m., I called on Mr. Doherty; he told me had seen the Sheriff and that Mr. Bursum was quite willing to tell me all he knew, and assist me in every way in his power; but at present Mr. Bursum did not have his evidence in good shape and it did not amount to much. Mr. Doherty told me that Mr. Bursum had a great deal of influence over Greago and that he could do more with him than Baca.

   Mr. Doherty learned from Geo. Smith last night that he (Smith) had seen Green Scott at Magdalena on or about the 8th of Feb., 1896. He was with a man named Buck Graham. Smith will find out for Mr. Doherty how long Green Scott was at Graham's place and where he came from to there. Geo. Smith is at present living near Socorro and is connected with the C. N. Ranch which is owned by H. M. Porter of Denver, Colo.

   After leaving Mr. Doherty, I looked around for the Sheriff and at dinner time I met him at the Windsor Hotel. After dinner we went to his room and talked over the Greago murder case and what the chances were for getting any information from him. I found Mr. Bursum a very intelligent man and he seems to know the people here thoroughly. He had heard the story told by Gallegos and his sons at San Marcial and knew that they had gotten it from Garcia, but did not think it was quite straight, because he could not get any one to corroborate the statement that Green Scott was with Brown when Brown left his ranch and Scott certainly did not return to the ranch with Brown, that he knew positively.

   Ed. Brown came into San Marcial a few days after Col. Fountain was killed and his horse was in bad shape; there was a man with him whose name Mr. Bursum had not yet gotten, but the horse he was riding was completely done out and was said to have lain down as soon as he was put in a stable, but still Scott may have been one of the party.

   The way Bursum gets his information is this; he has a deputy at San Marcial named Donaldson Walker, who was at one time a cow thief and a great friend of Brown's; but Bursum has been able to render him a number of favors in times past and got him out of some serious troubles so that Walker is devoted to him and will do anything for him.

   Now a short time after Col. Fountain was killed Ed. Brown came to Walker and talked to him about the Fountain case, and told him that there was no reason why he (Walker) should not earn the reward which was offered for the recovery of the bodies of Fountain and his son, as he (Brown) would give Walker a letter to a man over there who could show him where they were. Brown first said he could tell him where they were and later spoke of giving him a note to this man, but did not mention the man's name.

As soon as Walker saw Bursum [...unreadable] see Walker, and as soon as he did get time to visit him, he found that Walker was not yet able to do anything; they consulted about what was best to do and concluded to get a man named Dick Brown (a distant relative of Ed. Brown), a great friend of Ed's, also a cow thief, to go to Ed. Brown and make a bluff; they instructed Dick Brown to go to Ed and tell him that the officers had gotten some very damaging evidence against him in the Fountain matter and that he had been traced from the other side of the San Andreas Mts. over to Rincon and up to San Marcial and that there were some things known that would tell against him if he were tried, etc., and that as the cases now in court against him for cow stealing were conclusive and the proof was forthcoming that he was in a closed box, so the best thing he could do would be to make some friends for himself and turn over the Fountain matter at once and that was the only way he could save himself.

Bursum says they succeeded in getting Dick Brown thoroughly alarmed for the safety of his friend Ed and it was plain that Dick believed Ed was mixed up in the killing. Bursum mentioned the Rincon route because he was told by a man named McKee who lives at Rincon that Brown's horse, was seen there the day before Brown got to San Marcial, and from the way Dick acted he thinks he hit it just right and that Dick knew Ed came up that way.

Now Bursum has not been to San Marcial since that time, and he told Walker and Dick Brown not to write him, that he would go down there and see them, so he knows nothing of the result of this plan; however, he will go with me to San Marcial to-morrow and find out all that he can and get dates as to when these men were seen in San Marcial, etc. He will also give me a letter of instruction to a man named Best; an old cow thief who will do anything that Bursum wants him to and if Brown came up from Rincon he will be sure to know it as Best is in with the gang and lives on the road where Brown would have to pass.

Mr. Bursum said he had kept very quiet about this, because it was uncertain and he knew it would not do for any one to go to Walker about it, as Walker would shut up and say nothing, but as Ed. Brown had come to Walker of his own accord and told him about the bodies he believed that between Walker and Dick Brown they could finally get a squeal out of Brown.

At 5 p.m., an uncle of Maxammeano Greago came to town saying that Greago could not come up as he had met with an accident and was in bed.

Mr. Bursum said he would see him as soon as he got well and find out if Greago knew anything; so I thought best to pass Greago by at present; as he is not living at San Marcial; and in order to reach him I would have to go out of the way a good deal and it seems more important to go with Sheriff Bursum to San Marcial to-morrow and see what is new there; besides Sheriff Bursum seems to take the proper view of this affair and is quite willing to assist all he can, so that he can do more with Greago and if Greago can furnish any additional in formation against Brown, Mr. Bursum will get it from him in the form of an affidavit.

About 6 p.m., I met Mr. Doherty and walked to his office from the depot with him. He said that Ed. Brown's case would come up for trial in about two weeks, the first Monday in May, and he hoped if nothing turned up between now and that time that he would be able to bring sufficient pressure to bear on him then to get him to squeal; meanwhile, if he learned of any new points he would send them to Gov. Thornton and if we had any information that he could use to assist him with Brown, he would be glad to have it. I learned that Mr. Freeman had returned and called at his office, but did not meet him, and at 8 p.m. I discontinued for the night and retired.

Yours respectfully,
"S"

Monday, April 20, 1896

I left Socorro, NM, this morning at 5:15 a.m. accompanied by Sheriff Bursum and came to San Marcial, arriving at the latter place at 6:30 a.m. After breakfast we called at Don Walker's house and found him at home. Sheriff Bursum introduced me and told Mr. Walker my business in San Marcial; he then went over the case so far as Walker was acquainted with it and asked him what was new in the matter. Mr. Walker said there was nothing; he said he had just recovered from his illness so that he could get out, but was very weak still and Dick Brown was out at Ed. Brown's ranch and was in bed sick with pneumonia; he has sent word in that he is in bad shape, and further than this Walker did not know; he wanted to go out there, but was not strong enough to make the trip.

Ed. Brown had been in town last week, but Walker saw him for only a few minutes and Brown left town before he had a chance to have any talk with him. Walker had not found out anything more about the horses and did not know where they had been seen or who saw them, but supposed it was at Lohman's ranch outside town. As Sheriff Bursum was in a hurry to get back to Socorro on the next freight, we left Walker and I arranged to meet him later on and visit Lohman, and the Sheriff and I came to town where he introduced me to a number of people and told me who might give some information. I also met Dr. Crookshanks [Charles Glanville Cruickshank], based in San Marcial, died Oct 12, 1904] and the Sheriff told him what my business was, and the Dr. said he had some information to give me later.

Sheriff Bursum also gave me a letter to Jack Best at Engle and told me to use Jack in any way I could. Mr. Bursum was sorry he could not remain but there was a burglary in Socorro this morning before we left there and he was compelled to return at once and look into the matter; so at 8:15 a.m. he left San Marcial for Socorro and promised to let me know should he hear of anything more around Socorro.

After the Sheriff left on the train I looked up Mr. Walker and had a talk with him; I saw that I had to convince him that I was not interfering with his claims to the reward and that it would be to his interests to assist me, and as soon as I succeeded in this I found Mr. Walker to be a good ally and willing to do all in his power to help me. We loafed around town for a while in the saloons, looking for a man named Harry Lohman, but did not succeed in finding him and just as we were about to go to Lohman's ranch, Mr. Walker was called away to arrest some parties, so I had to wait until he had attended to that and then we walked out to Henry Lohman's ranch.

We saw Mr. Lohman, his wife, and son and soon learned that there was a mistake somewhere, as no one had stopped at that ranch during the month of Feb. We then came back to town and found Dr. Crookshanks and had a talk with him; before seeing him, however, I had gotten from Walker the story of the note Ed. Brown offered to give him, which is exactly the same as that given in my report for yesterday and related to me by Sheriff Bursum in Socorro, but in addition, when I questioned Walker closely, he said on that occasion he had a long confidential talk with Ed. Brown and when Brown came to talk about the note he did so in this way:

Brown said, *"You remember the man that wanted you to get bonds on that cattle stealing case?"*

Walker said, *"Yes."*

"Well," said Brown, *"I can give you a letter to him and he will fix it so you can find Fountain's body all right, he knows all about it."*

Walker said all right and it was settled that whenever Walker was ready to go, Brown would give him this letter. Now, though Walker said he knew this man that Brown mentioned about the bonds, as a matter of fact he could not place him and could not recall his name, though he knew him and remembered he had only one eye, but he could not recall his name.

I asked him if he would remember the name if he heard it and he said yes, so I asked him if the man had not gone under the soubriquet of "Goodeye" and he said yes; then I mentioned a number of names of men in that country and when I came to the name Wm. Carr, he stopped me and said that was the man; Carr was the name he could not remember and now he knew all about the bonds. Carr wanted him to help and get bonds for a man who was in jail, a friend of Carr's, and Walker had refused as he was not in a position to do so.

Walker was quite positive on this point and he went on to tell me the reason the deal was not carried out was that two days after this conversation with Ed. Brown he was taken sick and he has not been out of his house since that time till about a week ago. During his illness Ed. Brown called on him and they had some further conversations on this matter in one of which Brown said that the men who were ahead of Fountain on the road were not the men who killed him at all, that they only led Fountain into the trap, and that the boy was all right and was not killed.

Walker said that Brown made these statements like a man who had some knowledge of what he was talking about, but at the same time Brown might have been simply giving it as his opinion, for he often spoke in that positive way about things of which he had no personal knowledge. Walker was too sick to remember what else was said at that time, but there was nothing important; since he got out of bed, he has seen Brown only once and then he thinks Brown avoided him, but he may have imagined this.

When I met Dr. Crookshanks, he told me that last Thursday, April 16th, he had had a long talk with Ed. Brown, and Brown had broached the Fountain matter, saying that he had been informed by Mr. Perry that there were some stories afloat about horses having left his ranch before the murder and that they had been traced back to his place and that he was suspected of being mixed up in it.

He said he cared nothing about the suspicion, they could suspect all they pleased, but it did not concern him; however, if any one could find the bodies he believed he could, and if Dr. Crookshanks would take the matter up and fix it so that a large reward was offered for the bodies, he would go over among those people in Dona Ana County and he might induce some of them to give him some pointers as to where the bodies were; might get some of them to go drive a stake or mark the locality so that he could find it and discover the bodies.

He would give a written guarantee that he would not claim the additional reward but use it only as an inducement to get some one to tell him where the bodies were; but of course he would claim his portion of the present reward. He said it was an outrage to kill the child and he thought it would be an easy matter to work the matter up and get the men after the bodies were found.

Ed. Brown asked the Dr. to take this matter up with Gov. Thornton and see what could be done and let him know; and Dr. Crookshanks told me he believed that Brown was sincere and that he could do more toward finding the bodies than anyone else. I also learned from Dr. Crookshanks that he had heard the story about the horses coming into town played-out from a man named Blood and he had understood Blood to say that he had heard it from Wm. Steen, who was the boy who attended to the corral where they were stabled, so I left the Dr. and looked up Mr. F. O. Blood; when I questioned him he had nothing to say, all he knew was a story he had heard from Steen and he did not know anything personally about the matter, had seen neither horses or men and had not seen Brown for months before or since the murder. Mr. Blood talked fairly enough and evidently knew nothing about this except by hearsay.

I then hunted up Wm. Steen and found him at work in the corral of S. J. Hanna where I spoke to him about this business. He said he did not want to have anything to do with it and he would say nothing, as Ed. Brown would kill him, but after talking to him a little while I succeeded in showing him that it was his duty to tell me what he knew, so he finally consented and told his story.

As soon as he was finished I went to my room and wrote it out in the form of an affidavit and then got him to come to a room in the rear of Hanna's store and told him I wanted him to sign it; I read it over to him and then handed it to him so he could see for himself; he said it was the truth and that he willing to swear to it, but only on condition that I would keep his name quiet, and not let Ed. Brown get hold of it; I reassured him on this point and then had him meet me at J. M. Broyles store where he signed the affidavit and I had it properly witnessed by Mr. F. J. Haftey, clerk in the store. I enclose the affidavit with this report.

I then saw Dr. Crookshanks and had him write a letter to Ed. Brown saying he had communicated with the Governor and that the Governor had sent a man down here to see what could be done in this matter and for Ed. Brown to come to town at once and see him. I did this because I found that Brown's ranch is 40 miles from San Marcial and that I would lose so much time in going out there; besides the Doctor could not go along and as the opportunity presented itself to get a statement out of Brown I did not want to miss it, because Brown would not refuse to talk as he had asked Dr. Crookshanks to send word to the Governor and the whole play could be made quite natural and I would be able to get Brown's statement under the most favorable circumstances.

I instructed the Dr. as to what he should say and do to assist me, telling him, to let me do most of the talking. Dr. Crookshanks did not like the proposition at first, but finally consented; the Dr. was afraid to mix up with it and said he did not want to have to change his range, but I showed him how it could be easily managed, and Brown might easily fall into his own trap and his statement, if false, could be used against him later on to tell the truth.

I had a good deal of difficulty in getting a messenger to go to Brown's ranch; and Walker searched the town but could not find one, at last we got a man for $3.00 to go out there and started him off. I expected to get out of San Marcial this evening, but concluded it was best to remain until I had gotten all the information possible at this point. I had some further conversation with Wm. Steen but it developed no more than already contained in the affidavit.

I also saw Mr. S. J. Hanna, but he did not know anything and seemed very unwilling to tell that he saw Brown at all on the 3rd or 4th of February, but he did acknowledge to having seen him in the store at that time. As it was getting late and I could not do much more to-night I discontinued about 8 p.m. and went to my room to write up my reports. I found the people very curious, but I succeeded in keeping under cover fairly well all day, and became acquainted with about half the men in town.

Yours respectfully,
"S"

[Statement of William Steen]

Territory of New Mexico.
County of Socorro.

William Steen of the town of San Marcial, in the county of Socorro, Territory of New Mexico, being first duly sworn deposes and says:

"That on Monday the 3d day of February, 1896, he was attending to the corral and stable of S. J. Hanna in the town of San Marcial, County of Socorro,

Territory of New Mexico, when about 5 o'clock in the evening one Ed Brown and one Emerald James rode into the Coral and unsaddled their horses."

"Affiant says that he noticed the condition of these horses and remarked to Ed Brown that he must have been riding very hard as the horses were completely tired out, and both animals laid down as soon as the saddles were removed. Affiant also asked Ed Brown where he had come from and Ed Brown answered both questions, saying they had come from across the river and acknowledged he had been riding hard."

"Affiant asked Ed Brown if he had heard of Col. Fountain's murder, or that Col. Fountain had been carried away; Brown stated that he had not, and asked for information about it; affiant told him that it was in the newspaper, and Brown asked where the paper was, and subsequently affiant said Brown got a paper in Mr. S. J. Hanna's store and read the account, remarking when he had finished that there was nothing in that and that they had not gotten descriptions of the murderers."

"Affiant says that he noticed when Ed Brown got off his horse that he was wearing boots and that both of his boot heels had been cut or chopped off, he noticed that this had been done quite recently as the nails which fastened the boot heel on were sticking out and the leather was quite fresh looking; showing that the boot had not come in contact with the ground very much since the heel had been taken off."

"Affiant remarked to Ed Brown that his boot heels were chopped off and said to him that a plan like that would have been a good one for the men who killed Fountain to adopt, as the paper stated that the tracks around Col. Fountain's buggy all showed high heels."

"Affiant said that Ed Brown seemed to be somewhat worried at his remark and did not make any answer. Affiant says that Emerald James who accompanied Ed Brown did not take part in the conversation and that he left the corral and went up town without saying anything to affiant."

"Affiant describes the horses ridden by Brown and James as follows: One was small sorrel horse, sway backed with a sweeney blemish on one shoulder and to the best of the affiant's recollection at this time the horse had two white front feet. The other horse was a large brown animal. Affiant does not remember any particular distinguishing points. Affiant says that both animals were too tired to eat and refused food for some time after they came to the corral."

[Sweeney is an atrophy or decrease in the size of a muscle or group of muscles. It is most common to the shoulder muscles extending from the withers downward about two-thirds of the distance to the point of the shoulder. Sweeney is not very common to light horses. It may be associated with lameness from another source in the same limb.]

"Affiant further states that Ed Brown came to the corral the following day and prepared to leave town, but found the horses in such a condition, that they were unable to travel, so he concluded to wait until the following morning; at this time affiant says that Ed Brown asked him if he had heard anything about the Fountain murder, and if they had caught the men; affiant answered him, but had no further conversation."

"This was on Tuesday, the 4th of February, 1896."

"On Wednesday, the 5th day of February, affiant says that Ed Brown and Emerald James came to the Coral and saddled up their horses and affiant asked them if they intended to leave town; Emerald James said yes, to which affiant remarked that the horses were not fit to go, Emerald James said, 'Well they will have to stand it.' Affiant noticed on this occasion that Ed Brown was wearing a new pair of boots; affiant did not see the old pair, but Ed Brown had a package of something which he tied on his saddle which was large enough to have contained the boots."

"Affiant further says that some time later, about the 16th, or 17th, or February, 1896, Ed Brown came into San Marcial and he was wearing a pair of boots which were very much run down at the heels and looked much worn; affiant said to Ed Brown that he must be hard on boots to have used up that new pair so soon; Brown said yes, that he had been doing a good deal of walking lately."

"Affiant says that he did not notice any fire arms either rifle or revolver with either Ed Brown or Emerald James when they came to town, nor did he see any arms with them on their departure. Affiant said that Ed Brown had another horse with him when he left San Marcial on Wednesday the 5th of February, 1896. Affiant does not know where Brown got this horse, but he led it out of town when he left, and further affiant saith not."

William C. Steen

Subscribed and sworn to before me this 20th day of April, 1896.

Tuesday, April 21, 1896

This morning I went across the river to Valverde to see Gallegos but could not find him, so had my trip for nothing. Valverde is four miles from San Marcial and I got a horse from a Mexican to make the trip on. On my return from San Marcial, I got an introduction to Tom Davenport and during the day I made a strong effort to rope him for some information about Brown, but got nothing; I find, however, that he is not in a position to know anything on the Fountain case; he was here all the time and has not been with Brown much lately.

I had a talk with Wm. Wilton who is yardmaster here and one of Sheriff Bursum's deputies. Dr. Crookshanks seemed to think that Wilton knew a whole lot that he had not told, so I went after him and I find all that he knew was the story Blood started, and he had that mixed up in a terrible shape; it seems that he and Blood have been talking the thing over at different times and they have figured it out and theorized on the subject a good deal.

Wilton does not like Walker, and told me that Dick Brown was a great friend of Walker's, etc., and that they were both cow thieves and would tell Ed. Brown anything they could learn. He had a great deal of this to tell me, which does not amount to anything in this case because he had nothing definite except his own ideas. One point he established; that was the day that Ed. Brown and Emerald James came to San Marcial after the murder. Wilton could not remember the day and said he thought it was about ten days after the murder, but he recollects seeing the two men, Brown and James riding into town from the south and places the time at a little after 5 p.m. as he was going home when he saw them, they were apparently very tired and could hardly travel.

His wife was running a boarding house at that time and Brown and James came there to eat; neither man had any money and Mrs. Wilton charged the meals to Brown who agreed to pay for both, and Wilton said that the entry on the book would show the date; I had him get the book and it showed the names of both men and the dates were Feb. 3rd and 4th, which corresponds exactly with Wm. Steen's statement. There is also an entry for Ed. Brown on the 12th of February and Walker says that that was the time that Brown made the proposition for him to go and find the bodies.

I spent a good deal of time in locating where Brown bought his boots and find that he and James both bought new boots at H. Bonham's store, but I did not dare question Bonham too closely as he cannot be trusted and I am doing my best to keep covered till after I have had my talk with Brown for there are a number [of men] here who would post him if they could find out that I was looking up the record and actions of Brown.

I asked Steen about James' boots and he said he did not notice anything wrong with the heels, but remembered that James had a new pair on when he left town. About 3 p.m., the Mexican we sent to Brown's came in and brought a note from Brown saying he would be in to-night or early in the morning, as he was bringing some cattle for Mr. Elly, the butcher, and he might have to stay across the river to-night. I was much disappointed, but concluded to remain and see him, as he was evidently acting all right and anxious to talk; the cattle were not an excuse as Elly expected them any day.

I finished up my reports to date and send them in by Express as I did not like to trust the office here; the people in it seem altogether too curious.

At 7 p.m. Brown had not arrived, but I heard from a cow puncher that he was seen coming into Valverde across the river, so he will be sure to get in early tomorrow.

Yours respectfully,
"S"

Wednesday, April 22, 1896

To-day in San Marcial.-

This morning after breakfast I met Walker and together we went to the river and watched for Brown to come across. The wind was blowing very hard and the river had risen during the night, so that the Mexicans were afraid to cross, they had some boats, however, and were using them.

We waited until some came from Valverde and questioned them about Brown, but got no satisfaction, none of them seemed to know anything about him and we could not learn whether he had gotten in last night with his cattle or not. By 10 a.m. the wind had freshened until it was a regular gale of dust and storming so bad that one could hardly get across the street, but I could not hear anything of Brown, and as I had waited to see him, I made up my mind to work it some way without letting him think I was very anxious, so at 1 p.m. I had Walker get some Mexicans to ferry him across the river and he got a horse and went to Valverde to find Brown.

I posted him what to say and do and then waited the result; meanwhile I had gotten hold of a story about some woman who had made remarks about Col. Fountain while stopping at Mrs. Wilton's boarding house; I saw Wilton and he said he was now trying to locate that woman. It seems that about two weeks after the murder, a man named Chas. Parrett came to San Marcial with a woman who claimed to be his wife and signed herself Mrs. Chas. Parrett; she talked with Mrs. Wilton about the murder and told her that the officers in Dona Ana County were all at sea about the man who did that job and that they had better look some place else for the people.

This woman was a bitter enemy of Col. Fountain's and Mrs Wilton says she talked as though she knew something. Wilton claims she is not married to Parrett, but is at present living with him and they went from here to Deming, N.M., and he expects to hear from them in a few days. The woman talked as though she wanted to throw someone off.

At 4 p.m., Walker returned and said he had found Brown, who had only just arrived at Valverde with some of the cattle, and Emerald James and a butcher from Santa Fe were coming with another bunch, but had not yet gotten in. Brown said that as soon as James came and they could get the cattle across the river he would come into town and see me; that the reason he did not get in last night was he had trouble with the cattle and the storm to-day split them up and James was with the others.

Walker said that Brown acted all right, but he could not get him to talk much. Walker asked him what he meant by going to Dr. Crookshanks and also what he has said to Crookshanks, claiming that I would not talk and the Dr. would not tell him. Brown answered, *"Oh, I was just joshing with Crookshanks and did not mean much, but all the same if they will offer a big reward I'll fix it so you can go and find the bodies all right and we will whack up on the reward."*

At 5 p.m., I saw Brown and James cross the river and after they had corralled the cattle I told Dr. Crookshanks and he came downtown and met Brown and introduced me, we stood on the street for a few minutes and talked; Brown said he believed he could be of some help in this matter but said he did not want to be seen in conference with me on the street and that he would not have these men in town get on to him for anything, but he would meet me after supper and talk the matter over; he then left me and I watched him closely for some time after; he kept on the move and attended to his business around town and did not pay any attention to James.

I was talking with a cow man named Johnson when James came in and spoke to Johnson, so I asked him to take a drink and invite his friend and so got an introduction to James and some other men who were with him at the time. I told Walker to take James off with him some place while I was waiting for Brown, and the last I saw of James he was going with Walker in the direction of the latter's house. At 8 p.m. I had Brown go with me to my room and I kept him there until 11 p.m.

The following is in substance our conversation:

Brown said that he had been joshing with Dr. Crookshanks about looking up this murder, and that in one way he was in earnest; he believed if any man could find the body he could, and gave it as his opinion that once the body was found it would be an easy matter for him to get the rest and he would get the information and turn it over to the officers so that they could do the rest and get all concerned provided he could get half the reward.

In order to do this and assist him he suggested to Dr. Crookshanks that someone post a reward in the papers to say $5,000 for the recovery of the body, and let it be put in at once and the people in Dona Ana County would read it and talk a good deal about it and then he would go over there and get among those fellows and use this argument, that some of them might just as well have that reward as not, and as he had their confidence, he believed that he could get one of them to tell him where it was, on condition that he (Brown) would split the reward with the party giving the information, and then he said, *"as soon as they show me the body, it will come quite natural to talk over how it was carried there, and how the killing was done, so that I can get all the information at one time if I get any at all."*

Brown then goes on to tell how he used to live in Dona Ana County and was intimately acquainted with all the men in the Organ and Sacramento Mts. and that none of them would suspect him for a moment; and he knows that if either of three parties he has in mind did the work or knows of it, that he can get all the details and do it easily. He would not tell me for some time who these three men were, but in the end he said that he figured on Bill McNew, Wm. Carr, and Jack Tucker.

Later on he said there was one party down there that, *"I can go to visit and take my wife along, and if any of the gang are into this job he will know all about it and by going there on a visit I can stay two or three days and get all he knows."*

He would not tell me who this was, but intimated that it was McNew. Another time he said that if Oliver Lee and Wm. McNew did the job alone, that settled it so far as ever finding out anything was concerned, but he was sure there were more in the deal than that.

Then he went on to say that if Oliver Lee, McNew, Tom Tucker, and Carr killed that boy, they were no longer his friends. He said he had two boys of his own and he did not want to think that either of them might be killed for some crime he might do or because some one had it in for him; that the child should be killed for convenience sake and any man who could kill a child was too dangerous to be let remain at liberty.

He went on at some length in this strain and said that while Col. Fountain was very active in prosecuting him and others for cattle stealing, yet he never dreamed of his being murdered on that account; but the fact that Col. Fountain had had him indicted and that he was soon to be tried for cattle stealing would help him to get the necessary information to turn this thing over, as everyone in that county knows of the trouble he is in and he could stand in quite easy and never be suspected.

I told Brown that there had been some stories circulated about him connecting him with this job, he said he knew about it, but did not care as they were all false and he gave me the following statement as nearly as he could remember dates of his whereabouts at that time.

He takes a starting point from a date he remembers and says that on the 20th of January he went to Engle for a load of corn; he took his wife with him and returned from Engle to his ranch on the 24th of January; on the way home he met John Carter who told him that Tom O'Donnell had some steers for him at Mound Spring; Brown told him all right and said he would go after them.

When he was down at Engle, Col. Mothersill asked him when he was going to come and round up some cattle he had bought from Mothersill, and Brown said he would come as soon as he got home with his corn, so about the 25th or 26th of January went with a man named Thergood (who is working for him) down to Col. Mothersill's ranch and began gathering the cattle; he worked several days, does not remember how long, but thinks he got back to his ranch about the 29th.

He brought the cattle to Thergood's corral and put them in there and afterwards turned them loose as he concluded it would not pay him to take them at the figure Col. Mothersill asked; he then went with Emerald James to Mound Spring and got the cattle there, drove them to the Mocking Bird Spring and camped there all night and returned next day to the ranch; he does not remember what he did on his return to the ranch but knows he did not go any place tor several days.

He might have been at Mound Spring on the 1st of Feb., but thinks it was earlier than that and it may have been later about the 3rd or 4th. I asked Brown where he was when he first heard of Col. Fountain's murder, and he said at the ranch; he was at Thergood's place and Harry Crawford came out there and brought the mail and told the news.

I asked him how long this was after his return and after the murder. Brown said about a week because Crawford had the eastern papers and the murder was written up in them. He said the date of his going to Col. Mothersill's ranch could easily be fixed as he arrived there the same day that one of the Directors of the company from Colorado did, and also while he was there a Negro was discharged and the date of his time check would show; as to the time he was at Mound Spring. Tom O'Donnell might know when that was, or Randolph Reynolds, who was there at the time.

At any rate Brown says that he believes he can show where he was every day during that time and he cares nothing about the stories that may have been circulated; he would just as soon they would suspect him if he is to go down there and try and turn this thing up, but he wants to be sure that I do not mention this matter to any one, because if he does not do anything he does not want any of the gang to get onto the fact that he had ever made such a proposition as they would kill him sooner or later.

I questioned him very closely about coming in here at any time with played out horses and he positively states that he did not come here last February or any other February or time that he knows of with tired stock, and any Mexican who says he did is lying. He said so far as his own troubles were concerned that when he was in the hole here, and indicted for cattle stealing, Oliver Lee or any of the gang in Dona Ana and Lincoln Counties did not come to hold him out and that he would have got in bad shape if a few of the Mexicans had not stayed with him; and as far as his trial was concerned which comes up in May, he was not much worried, he had some friends left yet.

He said he believed that the men who killed Fountain had some witnesses staked out who would prove an alibi for them when called upon to do so and that the whole thing was cut and dried, but it will only be a question of time to get a squeal and the first one who gives it up will save himself; and wanted me to say that I should see Gov. Thornton at once and fix it so some bogus reward could be reported in the papers in Dona Ana County and he would go down there about the 10th of May and work among the friends he had there till he got the necessary information and then he would prepare to leave this country at once as he could not stay here after the thing was turned up.

I noticed just talking with Brown that he always used the word body and not bodies when speaking [of] Col. Fountain and his son, and at first he was very nervous but soon got his self possession; he has studied the situation closely and is a very shrewd man in his way, but the whole drift of his conversation seemed to be to make some sort of an arrangement by which he could be made safe himself and then he would be willing to do something for the sake of the [unreadable] said if he did not succeed in doing anything in the [unreadable] he would be willing to tell all he could and give all the pointers he could but he wanted to try for himself first.

A little after [unreadable] p.m. I went out to find Emerald James but he had gone off somewhere [unreadable] waited around until after midnight I did not find him; Walker had, however, got a partial statement out of him and it was very much mixed as to dates, in fact, James claimed to know nothing at all, but said he was with Brown all that time and that he first learned the news of Fountain's death at Thergood's ranch. When James left Walker he went to the Mexican town and Walker did not think he would come back to-night, so I concluded to wait till morning to see him. Brown said he supposed James could tell where they were about those dates without any trouble.

Yours respectfully,
"S"

Thursday, April 23, 1896.

This morning at San Marcial I got up at 6 a.m. and went out to look for Emerald James but did not meet him till about [unreadable] a.m. He had not yet had breakfast, so I waited till he had eaten and then took him aside and asked him about his trip to Good Fortune (which is Mothersill's ranch) and also a statement as to his whereabouts from the 20th of January 1896 to some time in February.

James said he could not remember just what date it was that he went to Col. Mothersill's place but it was some time in January near the end; he went there with Eugene Thergood and Ed. Brown and they were about a week at the ranch. He had no idea as to the date he left there; remembers of bringing some cattle from there and corralled them at Thergood's place, but when it came to dates he could not place anything; all I could get from him were answers to direct questions. I asked him if he gathered any cattle at any other part or the country about that time and he said that he and Ed. Brown made a trip to Mound Springs and the Mal Pais Spring and stopped at Tom O'Donnell's place at Mound Springs; says they remained there about a week and brought some cattle from there to Brown's ranch; he believes he made this trip about the first of February, because he remembers saying afterwards when they heard of Col. Fountain being killed, that if they had known about it at the time they would have had a good joke on Tom O'Donnell who lives in that country and he knows that Tom did not say anything to them about it.

There was also a man at Mound Spring named Randolph Runnels. James states that when they got back to the ranch they laid off for a while and remained around the ranch; also made a trip about that time into the San Marcial with cattle, but does not know what the date was, but Ely the butcher would remember and he would ask Ely when they delivered the cattle.

I questioned him closely about coming into San Marcial with tired horses and he positively denies ever having ridden into town with a played out horse and while some of their horses were gaunt and in poor flesh, yet he never had any played out stock this past winter. He said he had heard some talk about Ed. Brown being connected with this killing of Fountain, but that it was all foolishness as he knew that Brown was not in any way mixed up in it. He had been stopping at Brown's ranch all winter and during the latter part of Jan. and Feb. he was with him every day and knows that Brown was not in that section of the country at the time of the killing. As for himself, he did not know Col. Fountain and had never had any dealings with him, he had always tried to avoid trouble and never been arrested or indicted in his life and he certainly would be a fool to mix up in some outside job that he had no interest in, besides he did not sympathize with the killing of anyone.

It could easily be proven at what time he and Brown were at Col. Mothersill's as they camped at the ranch and there was a man named Brady with them every night they were there, also Eugene Thergood was there. As to the trip over to Mound Spring, James said he might be altogether mistaken as to the time and it might be possible that the time he refers to may have been in January as they have been over there a number of times this winter and came from that country a few days ago.

In talking with James, I noticed that he was uneasy and that he took a long tine to answer any question I asked and usually prefaced his answer by saying, "I am not sure," or "I don't know." I asked him where he was when he first heard the news of Col. Fountain's death and he said Eugene Thergood told him; Thergood saw it in a paper, some Eastern paper, he does not remember what one. He places the date at about the 10th or 12th, maybe later. He had come down to Thergood's ranch and was spending the evening there when he heard it. Brown was also present; he was very much surprised and so was Brown.

I concluded to let him go for a while, so I walked away saying I would see him later and I noticed he went at once and hunted up Ely and had a talk with him; then he came back to me and said, *"Well, I guess I was mistaken about the time we were at Mound Spring because Ely has the date on his books which shows that we delivered the cattle to him on the 1st of Feb."* I told him that was all right and would be a good means for him to remember where he got those cattle and where he was before the first; he said he was not sure what bunch of cattle that was, but at any rate if he and Brown were here on the first of February they could not have been at the Mal Pais and could know nothing about Col. Fountain.

I did not go with him to see the entry of the books at Ely's for I wanted to get all I could and not get Brown or James suspicious of them and I was aware that Ely was in a position where he could not possibly falsify dates. I saw Brown coming along the street so I called to him and when he came over I said, *"I have been talking with Mr. James about where he was on the 1st of Feb. and tells me about the trip you made to Mound Spring and that it was possible you were over there then."*

James at once put in with the remark, *"Yes, I thought so but I was mistaken because Ely has a date on his book that shows that we were here on the first with cattle."* Brown looked very much surprised and said it could not be possible, that Ely must be wrong and that they could not have been here then. He said to James, *"Don't you remember when I came from Engle with the corn that I met John Carter and he told me Tom O'Donnell had some cattle for me and I sent for you that night and the next day we went to Mound Spring, got two head of steers from Tom O'Donnell, and came back to the ranch and brought the steers into town; that was before we went to Mothersill's and when we went back we went to Good Fortune and gathered the steers there."*

While Brown was talking James was watching him closely and assented to everything he said and then went on talking about it being hard to remember dates when a man was on a ranch. Both men now began arguing about the trip to Col. Mothersill's and then James said, *"Well you know we wrote some letters there at Engle and we know who we wrote to and could get those letters back so that the dates will show."*

They also spoke about when they first heard of the killing and Brown said that Crawford brought the news, but James claimed it was Thergood; at any rate they both agreed that it was at Thergood's they heard it and it was ten or twelve days after the killing of Col. Fountain. James then said that Tom O'Donnell would be a good man to ask for information about that murder as he was well acquainted and could give some help. Brown thought this a good idea and said that Tom was a straight fellow.

Both men then separated and left me and I went at once and got Dr. Crookshanks and we watched till Ely left his shop and then went in and examined his brand books and receipts. There is no entry on the first of Feb. of any cattle received from Brown; but on the 12th of Feb. there is an entry of two head of cows bought from Brown and a bill of sale for the same in Brown's handwriting; also an order on Ely from Brown to pay to Luce Chavez for the same. In looking over the brand book I find no entry of any cattle bought from Brown or James in the month of Jan., but on Dec 12 there is an entry for two cows. Ely may have an entry on some cash book or blotter, but I did not want to ask him for it at the present time; I can see it later.

About 12 p.m., Walker came to me and said Ely had been talking to him and, said, *"I don't want to go to Sayers, but you can tell him that if the indictments against Brown in the cattle stealing cases are quashed by the Governor, that Brown will dig up some information on the Fountain matter."* Walker asked him why he would not tell me; Ely said he would not do so and did not intend to mix up in the affair at all, but he knew this much and wanted me to know it.

After this I met Brown on the street and we had some further talk; he said he had a good many friends left and did not expect to get a hard deal at Socorro (meaning when his trial came up next week). He also said in a significant way that he had some friends at Santa Fe.

I then found Harry Crawford and he stated that he remembers going to Thergood's place in February, he cannot recollect the exact date, but has a means of fixing it accurately; he went there to locate a spring close to Thergood's and has the location certificate on record and when he goes home he will bring the certificate down and show me. He only remained one day and thinks it was the 16th, but it may have been earlier. He took out some papers with him and had among them the *St. Louis Republic* and in it was an account of the Fountain murder. Thergood found the article in the paper and read it and all present seemed surprised. There was Jean Thergood, John Carter, Baldy Russell, Ed. Brown, Emerald James, Fred Richards, and himself; at the cabin that evening. Brown said that was the first he had heard of it, so did all the others.

I had a talk with Dr. Crookshanks and he told me that he thought from what he could learn that Brown felt satisfied that he could beat the suits against him at Socorro and that Elfego Baca had done a lot of jury fixing and could fix Brown's jury for $200. The Dr. also explained to me how Brown was tied up with the Gallegos and Ely.

So after thinking the matter over, I concluded that it was of sufficient importance to take some immediate steps to prevent any crooked work at Socorro and that Gov. Thornton ought to know all of this evidence at once; so I had Dr. Crookshanks wire the Governor and ask him if he could come to Socorro so as to be there in the morning; at 3:30 p.m. We received an answer from Gov. Thornton saying he would be there and at 4 p.m. I left San Marcial for Socorro to meet him there in the morning.

After wiring the Governor, I went with Dr. Crookshanks to H. Bonham's store and examined his books but could find no charge against Brown in Feb. for boots or anything else so we were compelled to question Bonham and he stated that he did remember selling Brown a pair of boots at that time, but Brown paid cash tor them, so there was no entry made except in the cash book and that would not show it, but he remembers the transaction quite well, because Brown came in and said he wanted a pair of boots and that the last pair of $4.00 boots he had were no good, the soles came off.

He kicked a good deal about them and said he must get a discount on the new pair; so Bonham to satisfy him said he would throw off some and sold him a pair at $2.50, which were marked $3.50; he then turned to the cash book and pointed to the item but it does not show the date, because he does not do a large cash business and neglects to put down dates, but he locates it from a sale he made the following day which he remembers and that bears the date of the 4th of Feb.

Mr. Bonham did not examine Brown's boots and does not remember that there was anything peculiar about them; they seemed to be much worn and he did not care about it anyway, and gave the discount because Brown generally traded there.

I tried to see Montgomery, another butcher in town, but failed to do so, as I could not find him; so, at 4 p.m., I left San Marcial for Socorro. At San Antonio I met Sheriff Bursum and we traveled to Socorro together. He had while at San Antonio tried to see Maxammaneo Greago, but failed to find him.

Bursum told me that Wm. Steen who gave me the affidavit had told him something about those horses, but he had forgotten all about it, and never thought to mention Steen's name to me. At Socorro I met Elfego Baca and he told me that Greago had been up there to see me and I was not there so he could do nothing. It seems he did not question Greago at all, at least so he says.

Before leaving San Marcial, Dr. Crookshanks told me to tell Gov. Thornton that he had heard a Deputy Sheriff of Eddy Co., N.M., name unknown, make some remarks about Col. Fountain, saying he was glad Fountain was killed, it served him right and that he had no sympathy with him or the boy; that Col. Fountain had prosecuted him for cattle stealing and that he had made up his mind that if ever Fountain had him indicted again and attempted to prosecute him that he would take his gun in the court room and kill him before every one, so he was glad he got killed.

This man went to Socorro with a prisoner some time ago and Bursum gave me his name, which I gave to Gov. Thornton, but do not now remember.

Yours respectfully,
"S"

Friday, April 24, 1896

This morning I got up at 4:30 a.m. and met the train from the north at the depot.

Gov. Thornton was on board and we walked up town together and while waiting for breakfast I told Gov. Thornton what had been done in the case since I left Santa Fe. The Gov. understood what Brown meant by his friends in Santa Fe and was glad I had wired him, as he is now of the opinion that Brown can be made squeal. Mr. Doherty was absent at Silver City, also Judge Freeman and Judge Hamilton, and it was important that Gov. Thornton should see these parties.

After breakfast about 9 a.m., I met Mr. Bursum and Gov. Thornton; Bursum and myself talked the matter over thoroughly during the day and arranged for the future action in the case so far as Brown was concerned; the plan finally agreed on being that Bursum should at once arrest Brown and put him in jail on the cattle stealing case which is to be tried next month. Brown's bond which is worthless has disappeared and he will be arrested on an order from the court and will have to file a good and sufficient bond, which he cannot do, and the Sheriff will not accept any bond unless it is right; this gives plenty of time and Brown can be kept a close prisoner till court opens.

Bursum is to say nothing about the Fountain case at all, but every point is to be worked on the cow stealing cases. I am to finish collecting the evidence along the line to Engle and at San Marcial and see Brown and work him for a confession on the murder; if necessary confront him with Slick Miller and also Greago and by separating him from the rest of the gang and bringing all the pressure possible to bear on him he will in all probability tell all he knows to save himself. Gov. Thornton thinks it advisable that this thing be worked quietly here and that Pat Garrett or any of the people in Dona Ana County should not be informed, as it might complicate matters at this time.

I spent the day in Socorro with Gov. Thornton who left for Santa Fe at 5 p.m. In the morning the Gov. telegraphed the Stock Inspector to go to Santa Fe and examine the car load of cattle that Brown shipped from San Marcial on Thursday to Arnold, the butcher in Santa Fe. When the train came in Mr. Doherty and Judge Hamilton were passengers, also Judge Freeman, and Gov. Thornton had a few minutes conversation with them before the train started.

The Gov. also told me to acquaint Mr. Doherty with the evidence in the case and have him get a warrant for Brown from Judge Hamilton. After supper I attended to this and Judge Hamilton issued a warrant. Judge Hamilton had just returned from Silver City and he said he met A. B. Fall over there and Judge Fall had a map showing the country around Chalk Hill and where the murder occurred and stated that a Pinkerton Detective had been down there and figured out the place where he (Fall) stood and saw Fountain killed, and Judge Hamilton said that Fall seemed to try to get a whole lot of amusement in exhibiting this map to every one and trying to make the side of the prosecution look as ridiculous as possible.

About 10:30 P.M. I discontinued.

Yours respectfully,
"S"

Saturday, April 25, 1896

This morning I left San Marcial at 6:15 a.m. with Sheriff Bursum and went to San Antonio, arriving there at 7:10 a.m. After breakfast the Sheriff got his team and we went across the river to find Maxammeamo Greago at San Pedro, but he was not there; we spent about two hours searching for him and at last found he had gone down the river and would not be back till to-morrow. Bursum then started for Brown's ranch and I walked back to San Antonio and waited for a train for San Marcial; I caught a freight and got into San Marcial about 4:20 p.m.

I hunted up H. Crawford and he gave me the date of his going to Thergood's ranch when Brown claimed that he first heard of the murder, it was the 10th of Feb. I then went to Ely's and asked him to show me his books, he did so, and on his ledger I found an entry of two head of cattle bought from Ed. Brown on the first day of Feb.

The entry was made in pencil and looked quite fresh; the entry before that was on the 11th of Feb. and after the 28th; I asked Ely for his blotter which should correspond with this and he produced it but the entry did not tally, as the same two head of cows were marked on the blotter on the 13th of Feb. He then said he must have neglected to put down the three after the one and that the bill of sale would have to correspond with the blotter and would be right. I asked him for the brand book and receipts, he showed them and the bill of sale was for the same cattle on the 13th; and the brand book tallied.

Ely was confused by the way I questioned him and I finally told him he would have to keep his hands off this business altogether and that he did not stand in a very good light himself. I also told him not to touch that entry, but let it stand as it is. Ely then told me that Brown told him to tell me that if the indictments were thrown out of court, which now stood against him for cattle stealing, he would do his part and find the bodies, and that the Governor could fix it and hold the indictments over him till he did do as he agreed to. I had a good deal of talk with Ely about his books and I do not think he will try any more crooked work on this deal.

I then called on Mr. S. J. Hanna and examined his books but could find no entry in them for the 3rd, 4th, or 5th of Feb. Mr. Hanna remembered that Brown and James came in about that time with played out horses and put up in his corral, but he does not charge Brown for hay when he puts a horse or two in, as he is a good customer in other ways and he lets him have his horse feed free.

I saw Will Steen and he told me that Brown saw the account of Col. Fountain's death in the *Albuquerque Democrat* or *Sentinel*, he does not remember which, as they took both papers; it was the first account of the murder that came out. I then called on Montgomery and examined his books but they show no entry of cattle bought from Brown this year, and Montgomery claims that he has not purchased any cattle from Brown since Feb. 15th, 1894, and his brand book shows this to be so.

It is reported here that Brown said he was going to Tularosa at once, and Dick Brown sent Walker word that he was coming into town tomorrow, so I told Walker what to do to keep track of James in case he wanted to go to Dona Ana County after Ed. Brown was arrested and also told him not to do any business with Dick Brown at all, but let the matter rest till I came back as I would go to Engle in the morning. I had telegraphed to Col. Mothersill from San Antonio to send out for Jack Best who was with Saunders' beef heard close to Engle and had a letter from Bursum to Best.

At 10:30 I discontinued for to-day.

Yours respectfully,
"S"

Sunday, April 26, 1896

I left San Marcial at 6:15 a.m. and came to Engle arriving at the latter place at 7: 35 a.m.

I found that Col. Mothersill was not at home; he had gone to Good Fortune last Thursday, so did not receive my telegram. I also learned that Jack Best was not in this part of the country; Saunders had started nearly a month ago with his beef herd for the Panhandle [of Texas] and Best had gone with him on the drive. I saw Mrs. Mothersill and she told me that the Col. would surely return to-day so I concluded to wait and see him.

Mrs. Mothersill asked me if there was any news at Socorro, as it had been reported down here that there was a good chance of the Fountain mystery being cleared up. She did not tell me where the report came from, but I learned later from E. J. Westervelt, the Agent at the depot, that Dr. Crookshanks had told him that a man had offered to get the bodies provided he was shown favors from the Governor; the Dr. did not mention names, but he might as well, because Westervelt has a good idea who he meant.

I found that Robert Martin, foreman for Mr. Waddingham, was also absent and there were no men at Engle at all who could give me any information; however, I learned from the Agent Westervelt that Ed. Brown had telegraphed to San Marcial for his mail last January and on hunting up the date of the telegram we found that it was on the 20th of January; he had came here with his wife and bought a load of corn from Col. Mothersill.

At 1 p.m., Col. Mothersill came in from his ranch and I called on him at once, but he wanted to clean up and take a bath so I did not get to see him until after he had eaten dinner and was rested; meanwhile the train coming from Las Cruces came in and I met Major Llewellyn who was on his way to Albuquerque. He informed me that there was nothing new at Las Cruces and that Garrett and Perry were still working on Luis Herrera, but had not developed any further information. At 3 p.m. I went to Col. Mothersill's house and remained with him most of the evening and the following is in substance the information he gave me.

Col. Mothersill is accurate as to dates because he keeps a diary and does not trust to memory. On or about the 20th of January, 1896, Ed. Brown came to Engle and bought a load of corn from the Col. and took it to his ranch, and at that time they did have some talk about Brown gathering some cattle for the Col., so on the 26th of Jan. Brown came to Good Fortune, one of Col. Mothersill's ranches, and camped there; a man named Brady was in charge of the ranch, as Cole Railston, the Col.'s foreman was away at the Hot Springs near Las Cruces.

The Col. was at Good Fortune when Brown, James, and Thergood arrived there; this was Saturday, Jan. 25th. Col. Mothersill remained at the ranch on the 26th and left on the 27th for Engle. Brown, James, and Thergood were at the ranch when the Col. left and Brady says they remained there two or three days and went away on Wednesday evening or Thursday morning, at latest, which would be the 30th of Jan.

Brown did not get any steers and did not take any cattle with him when he left Good Fortune. Mr. Holmes, one of the members of the Detroit Cattle Co., arrived at Engle on January the 22nd and was at Good Fortune when Brown was there. After the Col. and Mr. Holmes came back from Good Fortune they went south to visit some of the other ranches and on the first of Feb. at noon they stopped at Summerford's place at Leesburg and ate dinner at Summerford's house.

Hiram Yost was there; he is one of Col. Mothersill's men and so is Summerford, and Yost told the Col. on this occasion that he looked to see some trouble on the other side before long (he meant the east side of the San Andreas Mts). The Col. told him that he hoped not as they had had trouble enough in the county and could get along without it.. Yost said he did not intend to mix up in any way and would attend to his own business.

After dinner Yost drove Col. Mothersill to the depot. He also told the Col. that Frank Hill was at his, John Yost's ranch at Detroit the night before and was going to Engle later on the same day, the first of Feb. Col. Mothersill saw Frank Hill on horseback and leading a loose horse riding toward Engle; he was then about 12 or 14 miles from Engle and close to his own ranch where he stopped that night, and next day came into Engle.

On Monday the 3rd of Feb. Cole Railston came into Engle and reported the death of Col. Fountain, which was the first Col. Mothersill knew of it.

On the 11th of Feb. the Col. and Railston went to Good Fortune camp and met Brady on this occasion; the Col. questioned Brady as to when Brown and his companions left the camp and Brady said the 29th or 30th of Jan. He also told Brady the news of Col. Fountain's death and thinks that this was the first Brady had heard of it.

Col. Mothersill tells me that on the 3rd he was told by some one, he thinks it was Bob Martin, foreman for Waddingham, that he (Martin) was at the home ranch on the 1st or 2nd and that he met Jack Tucker coming out of Dead Man's Canyon in the San Andreas and this is where Frank Hill had a ranch which is now abandoned. The Col. is not sure about this, but knows someone did tell him about meeting Jack Tucker at Dead Man's Canyon about that time in Feb. Holmes went home on the 3rd of Feb.

A short time after the murder a letter came through the Engle post office from the Sheriff's office in Santa Fe for Frank Hill and Hill answered it and addressed the letter to Tom Tucker. This is the first correspondence that Col. Mothersill has noticed between these parties for some time and there has not been any lately.

Col. Mothersill received a letter from Ed. Brown to-day asking him if he remembers the date or about the time that he (Brown) was at Engle. About 5 p.m., Robt. Martin came into Engle and Col. Mothersill sent for him and questioned him about his statement as to meeting Jack Tucker; Martin does not remember ever saying any such thing and claimed that he does not know Jack Tucker, except by reputation; he does not know that he came from the home ranch on the 3rd of Feb., but does remember that he came into Engle that day as he has made a memorandum of it. He suggested that it may have been Carver who told this; Carver is a man who works for Waddingham at the home ranch and was in Engle some time in February.

Col. Mothersill tells me that he heard a story from McClintock at noon about two or three horses being seen at Rincon, but he did not get it very clearly, and Judge McFie also knows something about it. These horses were seen about the 2nd of Feb. and did not come in town. Mr. J. R. DeMier, the night operator at the depot here is a brother-in-law of Judge McFie and he tells me that McFie has talked to him about this story but he is unable to give it to me in detail. The Judge is expected to be at Rincon tomorrow on his way to Hillsboro where Court is in session and I decided to go to Rincon on the early train and meet Mr. McFie, also Mr. A. McClintock.

Col. Mothersill said he would try and find out if anyone in this section had seen these horses going towards San Marcial; he will also find out about this man Carver who works for Waddingham.

There is no one else around Waddingham to be seen, so I discontinued for the day. I neglected to state that I spoke to Col. Mothersill about his foreman Railston and he says that he is quite sure that Railston and Oliver Lee are not now on good terms and never have been, but that Railston and Hill are old friends; also Tom Tucker; however, Col. Mothersill believes that Railston is all right so far as mixing up with this gang is concerned.

Yours respectfully,
"S"

Monday, April 27, 1896

This morning at 7:30 a.m., I left Engle for Rincon and on arriving at the latter place I called at once on Mr. McClintock. I found that it was he who had given the information to Judge McFie and that he had received it from his partner, Mr. H. Bignell; the story is this:

On Monday the 3rd of Feb. a young man about 18 or 19 years of age came to Mr. Bignell's house and wanted to buy some corn. Mr. Bignell was not at home, but his wife sold the corn to this young man and asked him where his horse was; the man said he was on his road to Cook's Peak and his horse had played out, so he was left behind, his companions going on.

Mrs. Bignell told her husband about the man and next day, Tuesday the 4th, a man came to Mr. Bignell's house and asked for some meat, he told the same story and said he was on his way to Cook's Peak, later on Mr. Bignell saw this man and boy riding close to his house and he questioned them asking if that was the boy who had come to his house the previous day for the corn, the man said yes. Mr. Bignell became suspicious and wondered why they did not move on; so he followed them up an arroyo and found their camp, he concluded they were stealing cattle, but as there was a good deal of talk about the Fountain murder at the time he thought it best to let the officers know so he came over to Rincon and told Mr. McClintock who at once wrote to Judge McFie and gave him as good a description as he could of what Mr. Bignell had seen.

Mr. Bignell lives across the river from Rincon and some distance out so I got a Mexican to take a horse and go over with a note from Mr. McClintock to have him come over as I wanted a description of the horses and men; the Mexican came back and said the river was too deep to cross, so after some time we got a boat and had him go in that; meanwhile I found a man named Harry Butler, a brother of Mrs. Bignell, who had met these men about 12 miles from Rincon late in the evening of Tuesday the 4th of Feb; they were riding a sorrel and bay horse and leading a sorrel horse who was packed with bedding, etc.

They were headed for Lake Valley and said they were going to Cook's Peak and were taking the proper direction when Butler came into Rincon; he heard Bignell talking about this and told of having met the men.

I learned that Judge McFie had passed through Rincon on his way to Hillsboro yesterday morning, so concluded that I had better not go to Las Cruces as I did not want to meet Pat Garrett just now and there was nothing for me to do at Las Cruces.

The messenger to Bignell's ranch returned but did not bring Mr. Bignell; he was not at home so as Mr. McClintock assured me there was absolutely nothing Mr. Bignell could tell me further except a description of the horses, I concluded to return to San Marcial or Socorro, because these men seen by Mr. Bignell could not have been Brown's party, and besides Brown is known at Rincon and the men seen were strangers, so at 2:40 p.m. I took the train north.

At Engle, Col. Mothersill joined me and went to Socorro on some business. At San Marcial, I met Dr. Crookshanks and he said there was nothing new. Walker had gone out to Brown's ranch to-day, he is looking for a man who is supposed to be in that country and is to remain a day or so at the ranch; he has good cover and can probably learn something from Dick Brown, who is still sick at the Ed. Brown ranch. The Dr. promised me he would not make any more bad breaks and would not talk to any one; he said he knew he did wrong to say anything at Engle. As there was nothing to do just now at San Marcial, I came on to Socorro as to meet Bursum and Brown there and have a talk with Brown.

I arrived at Socorro at 5:30 p.m. and met Mr. Doherty at the depot. He told me Bursum had not returned yet, so there was nothing to do but wait, so I went to the hotel and did nothing more to-night as there was a terrible sand storm blowing and one could not get out of doors.

Yours respectfully,
"S"

Thursday, April 28, 1896

To-day in Socorro,-

I remained all day in Socorro and waited for Bursum to come in, but was disappointed. There are some important matters here in the Sheriff's office to be attended to which Bursum told me about, so that I feel sure that this delay is altogether unavoidable, and I believe he had to go to Tularosa to get Brown, so I will wait until he does come here, which cannot be later than tomorrow.

Maxammameo Greago is in town and I called on Judge Freeman with Mr. Doherty. Mr. Doherty said that Judge Freeman was all right and for me to go ahead and talk freely to him and tell him what we wanted of Greago and all about this case, but after I had talked some time with Judge Freeman I concluded it would never do to tell him anything, because he seems to have altogether too much confidence in what people tell him and he believes that Elfego Baca, who is his partner, is the proper man to act as interpreter, so I did not tell the Judge much and asked him to have Greago wait here till Bursum returned telling him that it was quite possible that Greago would be more likely to talk if Elfego Baca were not present; Judge Freeman agreed with me in this when I had explained my reasons and said he would try and put off the conversation till Bursum came; but I noticed that Baca was with Greago a good deal about town and seemed determined to be the one to do the interpreting. Baca met me with Greago and said that he and Judge Freeman would go at him in the morning and learn all he knew.

Mr. Martin seems very anxious to find out what is going on and came to me several times to try and get some information; I also saw him with Greago. Martin told me he had some very important information for Bursum and wanted to know if I could wire to him; I told him that I knew nothing whatever of Bursum's movements. Martin is one of Sheriff Cunningham's supporters and is doing his best to get at the inside of what is going on here, but so far has learned nothing. Bursum knows the sort of man he is and will not enlighten him in any way.

I wrote to Albuquerque for copies of the *Democrat* and *Sentinel* of Feb. 3rd and 4th to find the article which Steen, at San Marcial, said he gave Brown to read; Steen said he would recognize the article and I want to show it to him later on.

Yours respectfully,
"S"

[April 29, 30, May 1 Reports are missing. On one of these days, probably May 1, Ed. Brown was arrested.]

Saturday, May 2, 1896.

To-day in Socorro,-

This morning I went to the Courthouse and at 9 a.m. Dick Brown and James came to the Sheriff's office and asked Nado Baca, the under-sheriff, if they could see Ed. Brown; Baca refused them admission. They then waited till Mr. E. V. Chavez [Ed. Brown's lawyer] came in and they went to his office and had a long talk. Mr. Chavez prepared a bond for Ed. Brown and then James and Dick Brown left town to get it filled. Ed. Brown takes the matter cool, but he is under the impression that he can get a new bond.

Mr. Doherty and I talked the situation over at some length and we concluded that it would not do to crowd the thing just now and it would be better to see first whether Ed. Brown would send for me or not, so I contrived to let him see me from his window; he is confined by himself in the second story of the jail; Sheriff Bursum saw him several times and Mr. Doherty spoke to him once, but Brown did not say a word about his case and is evidently waiting for Dick to get a new bond for him.

Mr. Doherty is afraid he cannot hold Brown long enough and that it may be necessary to swear out a warrant for him charging him with Col. Fountain's murder, in which event he will have to be taken to Dona Ana County, and then the Dist. Att'y there may let him get out. I concluded that as the play had not come as we expected it, but might drag along, that I would visit Brown in the morning and open the Fountain matter; from the way he has acted today he looks as if he had turned sulky and he may not say a word.

Tom Davenport came up from San Marcial on the evening train and when I spoke to him at the depot, would not answer me. He is a great friend of Ed. Brown's. Mr. Doherty saw Mr. Chavez this morning and had a talk with him on this matter, the result being that Mr. Chavez will not make any fight to get Brown out of jail, and will assist in any way he can in this affair. Mr. Doherty told him enough to show that the object of keeping him in jail was in the interests of the Fountain case, and Mr. Chavez was satisfied; as he is willing to do anything to assist in that.

Yours respectfully,
"S"

Sunday, May 3, 1896
To-day in Socorro,-

This morning I went to the Courthouse with Sheriff Bursom and at the door met Nado Baca, who told the sheriff that Ed. Brown wanted to see him; Mr. Bursum went up stairs and in a few minutes came down and told me that Brown had sent for him to tell him he wanted to see me. I went up at once and remained talking with Brown about two hours.

When I first went in, he said he wanted me to go to Mr. Doherty and see if I could not get him out, as he had contracted for some cattle which he was to receive on the

6th and he wanted to get over to Tularosa in time to keep his appointment; and besides it would be a good excuse for him while attending to his own business to make some inquiries about the Fountain murder. He said it was all nonsense keeping him in jail, that he had filed a good bond and when Dick Brown got back he would have the names of men who would go on his bond that would make it gilt edged and he wanted to be sure that it would be accepted.

I talked with him about this bond for some time, and then when he led off on the Fountain murder I explained to him that I had called on Gov. Thornton as Brown had requested and placed his proposition before the Governor, but I found that the matter was in an altogether different light. I then went ahead and outlined the evidence which I claimed the Gov. had collected and intimated that the information came from Chas. Spence, but did not mention any names.

Brown let me go all through, and then just laughed at the whole thing and said that any one who ever said that he did at any time speak of killing Col. Fountain or any other member of the Stock Association, was lying and could not prove a word of it. He said that a short time after he was indicted he wrote several letters to Col. Fountain, and had a friend of his who was a warm personal friend of Col. Fountain's go to the Col. and talk to him about the cases against him and that Col. Fountain sent him word by this mutual friend that he need not worry any, but to go ahead and attend to his business, that the cases would not be pushed.

"Now," Brown said, *"is it likely that after a man had sent me such a message as that that I would make an attempt to kill him."*

He did not give me the name of this man, but said he could get him on the stand to swear to this at any time and that this man was at the present time doing all he could to assist in uncovering Fountain's murderers. Brown then took exactly the same line of argument that he used in my interview with him in San Marcial and dwelt on his splendid chances of his being able to find out all about this murder.

He said he positively knew that if Wm. Carr and Tucker or McNew were in this thing that he could find out all about it and he was willing to do so for half the reward, but he would not attempt to do anything unless his name was kept quiet and he was given a chance to get the confidence of these men. He repeated his statement that these men, Carr, McNew, Tucker, Lee, and others in Dona Ana County were all good friends of his, but if they had done this job he wanted to know it and would very willingly turn the thing up, as such men were too dangerous to live with.

Brown makes a strong talk on this head and he then said it makes no difference to him whether he can or cannot prove his whereabouts at the time of the murder, he knows he was not there and that he cannot be convicted for a crime that he did not commit. So far as his being able to make a statement now, he claims he cannot do so and that all he could say would be to give his opinion, which would be of no more value than that of any man who had read the newspaper accounts, and he positively would not tell any lies for the purpose of getting out of his present difficulties as they would be proven to be lies and then he would have no friends left at all; the officers would all be down on him for trying to fool them, if anyone was arrested nothing could be proven and they would all know that he had made the statements and consequently would feel bitter toward him and take some form of revenge.

If he was to make any statement now it would be all guess work and no one could be convicted on that unless he was turned loose and given a chance to work he could and would do nothing.

Brown puts up a strong talk and seems determined to stick to his first proposition, so I left him for a while and promised to go and see Mr. Doherty and find out something about his bond. I met Bursum and Mr. Doherty in the Judges' Chambers and told them the result of my interview, and so far as Ed. Brown's manner goes he did not appear to be half as much worried to-day as he was when I saw him in San Marcial.

Mr. Doherty is of the opinion that it will be utterly impossible to hold Brown, as the bond is only $300 and it is quite likely Dick Brown will return in a day or so with some good names on it and than it will be hard to refuse acceptance. Mr. Doherty is also afraid that Judge Hamilton will accept the bond, and if not Mr. Chavez will get Brown out on a writ of Habeas Corpus. I think that Mr. Doherty is not very anxious to make too hard a fight in this matter, at the same time he professes himself willing and anxious to do anything in the world to further the case, at the same time there has been so much talk around Socorro that Mr. Doherty is not in a very enviable position and he knows it.

Mr. Doherty suggested that we send at once for the Governor and ask him to bring Slick Miller down with him, but I thought that this was too fast; so after dinner I called again on Brown, told him that I had seen Mr. Doherty and I found there was but little chance to get him out to keep his appointment at Tularosa, as I had read some of the evidence in the case against him for cow stealing and Mr. Doherty told me the case would come up among the first so there would be no chance for him to have time to go and receive his cattle; beside this from the evidence in the cow stealing case I could see no chance for him to expect an acquittal.

Brown showed a little uneasiness when I told him this, but he quickly regained his composure and treated the whole thing lightly, said he did not fear the trial at all and that he would not have any difficulty in getting out of it all right; I tried to worry him all I could on this point, and told him that Judge Hamilton would not try the case, it would probably come up before Judge Collier, and spoke about the evidence on the side of the prosecution in such a way as to make it appear as strong as possible.

I succeeded in getting Brown very much interested, but he soon turned on the Fountain matter and began to describe to me how he would proceed to get the desired information from the Rustlers who did the work; he suggested if he could get some one of them to tell him where the bodies were that he would manage to let me know and then go with this party to where the bodies were and have me follow them and have several other officers around and arrest them both, then get the bodies and when Brown was put in jail with the other man or course it would be quite easy to find out the whole affair.

Brown suggested half a dozen such schemes as this and made them look as plausible as possible, but whenever I got him back to his own connection with the deal he would not give it any attention and treated it as a great joke to think that he was in the killing. However, he expressed a desire to see Gov. Thornton and find out what this evidence was the Governor had, for he said there would not be any use in his going out to hunt the thing up if the Governor thought he had any connection with the murder.

I saw Mr. Doherty again and as he seems to think that Brown may slip through our fingers at any moment, I concluded it would be well to wire Gov. Thornton at once and see it he could come down here and bring Miller with him, so that Miller could be used if it was desirable to make the attempt. Mr. Doherty would also do much better if Gov. Thornton could see him and go over this matter with him; accordingly I wired to Santa Fe asking the Governor if he could come down on the morning train and bring Miller.

I can see that Mr. Doherty is anxious to talk to the Governor and there must be some quick action taken, as the court opens tomorrow.

Green Scott arrived in town to-day and will remain during this term of court.

When the train came from the south I met Mr. Blood at the depot, he told me that Dick Brown and James were trying to rustle a bond in San Marcial, but up to the tine of his leaving had not succeeded. He also said that Ely was making a good deal of talk and seemed to be worried about this arrest; Dick Brown and James were very uneasy, Ely told Dr. Crookshanks that they were all good friends together and must stay with one another. Mr. S. J. Hanna came to me and asked what Brown was arrested for. I told him some irregularity in the bond, etc. Hanna said Dick had come to him to go on a new bond, but he had refused, he did not propose to mix up in this matter at all. I did not enlighten him further.

At 6 p.m., I got a wire from Gov. Thornton saying he would either come or send a man with Miller tomorrow night. I knew that would not do, as we do not want Miller unless the Governor can come, but concluded to wait till morning and then wire again.

After supper I again visited Ed. Brown and remained with him a long time. There is no question but that the man is uneasy but he has settled upon a certain line or argument and will not change it. He seems quite confident that he can get bonds, as if it is necessary [Patrick] Coghlan at Tularosa will sign them.

Brown wants to know why he is not allowed to see his friends and that it was by accident that Dick Brown had gotten to see him; I did not know that Dick had reached him but it seems the first night Dick came here he managed to go up stairs and see Ed before the guard noticed him. Ed expects Dick back tomorrow: He asked me if I could not go to the Dist. Atty. and give security for him.

Yours respectfully,
"S"

Monday, May 4, 1896

This morning I met Mr. Hall, U.S. Marshal, and he told me that Gov. Thornton was at Las Vegas and would come down on to-night's train; also that the Gov. wished me to go to Lamy Junction and meet him there to-night and I should also meet Col. Bergamer at Lamy Jct. and the Col. would turn Slick Miller over to me there.

About 9 a.m., I visited Ed. Brown and remained with him most of the forenoon; there is no change in his conversation or bearing. While speaking to-day of the Fountain murder and that he had been connected with it, he said, *"Of course some one may have gone to Gov. Thornton and made a statement implicating me, but it is a lie, the chances are good that it is some one who is in a hard hole, probably in the Pen and who would make any sort of a statement in order to get executive clemency, but if such is the case I have no fear, because no one can be convicted in this Territory on the evidence furnished by some convict or half a dozen of them at that."*

I passed it off as if I did not have the least idea who the party was that had made this statement; but Brown has evidently been thinking over the talk of yesterday and remembered that Miller is in the Santa Fe Pen, so he sprung this on me to see if he was right.

I told Brown that I heard from Gov. Thornton and that if the Governor could find time he would come down to Socorro tomorrow; he said he would be glad to see him and show him that he was all right; also arrange for some definite plan that he should work on when he went to Dona Ana County. He then referred to his case now in court for cow stealing and told me that if I knew his side of that transaction I would not think he had a very hard suit to beat. I tried to get him to talk freely about it but he would not; he takes the ground that he is entirely innocent and can prove he had nothing to do with the cattle at all.

I visited Brown several times during the day and did everything I could to get some admission from him, but had no success.

At 5:15 p.m., I left Socorro for Lamy Jct. and met Dr. Crookshanks [Cruickshank] at the train traveling with him as far as the Junction. He had nothing new to tell.

On arriving at Lamy Jct., I met Col. Bergamer at the depot and he told me he had put Slick Miller on board the south bound train. It seems the railroad company had made a change in its time card and the north and south bound trains which heretofore have met at Lamy Jct. now pass each other at the stock yards two miles south of Lamy; this change was made at midnight last night and I knew nothing about it, neither did Col. Bergamer, but he told Miller that there would be a man on board who knew him and who would watch him, so he did not feel uneasy.

I immediately wired Gov. Thornton on board the train, and caught him at Cerillos, that Miller was on board and that I would follow as soon as possible. Col. Bergamer returned to Santa Fe; he said he felt that Miller was all right but asked me to be sure and bring him back all safe to him.

Tuesday, May 5, 1896

I found I could not get out of Lamy Junction on a freight train, I tried every Conductor that came along, but was refused, I wired to the dispatcher in Las Vegas and tried to get permission, but could not succeed: the company's rules are strict and the conductors positively will not carry any one on freight trains, however, I tried every one and did not give up till I found that I could not make any time by taking a freight.

At 2 p.m. I left Lamy on the accommodation and arrived at Albuquerque at 8 p.m. where I had to lay over for the passenger.

Yours respectfully,
"S"

Wednesday, May 6, 1896

To-day in Socorro,-

I arrived in Socorro this morning at 5:30 a.m. and went to my room at the Windsor.

After breakfast I met Gov. Thornton at Mr. Doherty's office and he told me he had not yet seen Brown or taken any steps in the matter; Miller was at the hotel and ready to be brought face to face with Brown. I then went to the jail and saw Ed. Brown, he had nothing to say which differed in the least from the line or talk he has adopted all the way through.

I told him that Gov. Thornton was here but was not anxious to see him at all unless he (Brown) was ready to talk and tell the truth as there was plenty of evidence to convict him of conspiring to kill Col. Fountain and if he was not willing to tell all he knew the Gov. did not want to waste any time with him.

Brown did not move an inch; he said if that was the way the Governor felt that it was no use of his trying to do anything, as he had nothing to tell and would not swear to a lie to get out. In the end, however, he said he would like to see Gov. Thornton and thought he could convince him that he was mistaken in his opinion and that he (Brown) had nothing to do with Fountain's murder.

I then came down to the Judges' chambers where Gov. Thornton and Mr. Doherty were; Miller was also in an adjoining room where he could be called at a moment's notice. I told the Governor what Brown had said and the Gov. instructed me to bring Brown to him at once and he would take his statement, I did so and the following is the statement made by Brown as to his whereabouts at the time of the murder:

He commenced by saying that he wanted it understood he did not know anything about the killing of Col. Fountain, but he was willing to do what he could to assist in turning up the guilty parties. He went to Engle on the 20th, 21st, or 22nd of Jan., 1896, he does not remember the exact date, but finally said the 21st; he went there to buy a load of oats and the date could be fixed easily as he wired to San Marcial for mail and the dates on those letters he received would show what time it was.

He returned to his ranch on the 23rd, remained there that night; on the 24th went to Tom O'Donnell's place at Mound Spring, received two head of cattle from O'Donnell and returned to his ranch on the 25th; on the 26th or 27th he went to Col. Mothersill's ranch in the San Andreas Mts. and met Col. Mothersill there; Brown remained at the Col's camp till the 1st or 2d of February when he returned to his own ranch.

Brown fixes these dates, but the time Col. Mothersill left the cow camp, which he thinks was on the 29th or 30th and he stayed there four days after; he says the date of that could be fixed as Dallas McComb, one of the Col's men came to the ranch the day that Col. Mothersill left, and he is quite sure he remained there four days after McComb arrived.

The first he heard of Col. Fountain's death was from Harry Crawford at Thergood's ranch on or about the 9th of February, and he came to San Marcial the next day. He states positively that he was at his own ranch from the time he returned from Col. Mothersill's ranch on the 1st or 2nd of Feb. till he went to San Marcial on the 9th of February.

In answer to questions by Gov. Thornton he states that he never was at any time east of the San Andreas Mts. during the latter part of January or in February till after the 9th of Feb. Also that he did not come into San Marcial on the 3rd of February with a tired horse; that he did not eat any meals at Mrs. Wilton's boarding house at that time or any other time; he admitted that he lodged there when he came in with the cattle on the 9th of Feb. He denied having ridden into Hanna's corral in San Marcial with his boot heels cut off on the 3rd or at any other time.

He states that on the 9th of Feb., he and Emerald James came in with cattle for Ely and that he bought a pair of boots that evening and had them charged to Ely on account of the cattle; he claims he wore a pair of shoes to town on that occasion; he rode a small sorrel horse. James rode a small brown pony; they remained two days in town and returned to the ranch; he led a horse out with him.

This is in substance what Brown had to say.

Gov. Thornton then cross questioned him at some length and then called Slick Miller in and had him tell before Brown the story of the conspiracy of two years ago which is the same as what has been given in previous reports. Brown seemed to be surprised when Miller came into the room, and as Miller told his story and called Brown's attention to different points in it he became uneasy and did not contradict Miller in anything; he showed signs of weakening and was evidently worried over Miller's statements.

As soon as Miller left the room, Governor Thornton again questioned and talked with Brown for about half an hour, but did not succeed in making him admit anything; he stuck to his story and denied everything. He said he thought he could go over to Dona Ana County and find out all about it, and that if Bill Carr, McNew, and Jack Tucker were in it he knew he could find out; he also said he believed McNew and Tucker were in the killing and that he never would believe otherwise, unless it were proved to be so.

When I took him back to his room, be regained his confidence and said to me, *"Oh, all that sort of talk does not amount to anything; they can do and say what they please, but can't convict a man for a crime he did not commit."*

After dinner Bursum took Maxammameo Greago to his room and Greago told him that he had seen Brown brand five head of cattle one day which he had stolen off the range; there was another Mexican present named Garcia Greago and Garcia also knows of seven head of cattle that Brown stole from a man named Johnson and took to Lincoln County. Greago further said that he could tell a good deal more about Brown, but would not now, as Brown had never told anything about him.

Bursum said he would get both of these men before the Grand Jury now in session and have Brown indicted on that charge; however, he could not succeed, as Garcia denied it and then both he and Greago got drunk and that put a stop to the chance of using them to-day. Greago went off and hid and neither Bursum nor I could find him during the evening though we looked all over the town.

The Governor decided to remain until tomorrow evening and see if there would be any change in Brown, but at the last visit I made to him he was just the same and does not show any signs of weakening.

Yours respectfully,
"S"

Thursday, May 7, 1696
To-day in Socorro,—

 This morning I called at the jail and saw Brown. I remained there about an hour, but did not succeed in doing anything. I then assisted Bursum in looking up Garcia and Maxammameo Greago, but neither man was to be found, and about 12 p.m. we learned that Greago had left town. It is evident that James has induced him to go away; so it will be impossible to indict Brown on this charge. Mr. Doherty and Gov. Thornton have talked over the situation and the Governor is inclined to the idea that Brown was not present at the murder of Col. Fountain and it is possible he may not have been in the last deal at all; so that it might be a good scheme to let him out and let him see what he could do toward finding the bodies and any other information he may get. Mr. Doherty does not like to turn him loose, but admits that we cannot hold him unless we get a new indictment and keep him on that. The plan with Greago having failed, it puts us where we were before.

 I made several visits to Brown during the day but developed nothing new. About 3 p.m., Mr. Doherty went to Brown, this was on Brown's request. He told me he wanted to see the Dist. Atty. and I sent Mr. Doherty to him. Brown said he would do anything to get out; and when Mr. Doherty went after him hard about Slick Miller's statement, Brown admitted that he might have forgotten the conversations Miller spoke of, but it did not amount to anything and could not be proved against him. Mr. Doherty said he succeeded in making Brown feel very uneasy, and Brown wanted him to remain, and talk the situation over, but Mr. Doherty said he had no time just then [and] would come back this evening, provided Brown was willing to tell the truth, but he would not come there to listen to a lot of lies; Brown asked him to come, [saying] that he would tell him the truth and nothing else and so Mr. Doherty intends to visit him after supper and do his best to get some admission which will be of use.

 At 5:15 p.m., I left Socorro for Santa Fe with Miller to take him back to the Pen, and was enroute the rest of the evening and night, arriving in Santa [Fe] after midnight. I took Miller to the St. Clair hotel and went to bed, as it was too late to go out to the Pen.

Yours respectfully,
"S"

Friday, May 8, 1896.

This morning after breakfast I took Miller to the penitentiary and turned him over to Col. Bergamer; I then returned to town and reported to Gov. Thornton and received instructions from him to return to Socorro and stay there for a few days till something was done with Brown and he would send me further instructions. At 10:10 p.m., I left Santa Fe and was enroute to Socorro the rest of the night.

Yours respectfully,
"S"

Saturday, May 9, 1896.

This morning I arrived in Socorro at 6 a.m. and after breakfast called on Mr. Doherty; he said the result of his conversation with Brown on Thursday night was unsatisfactory; Brown put up a smooth talk, but on the main stuck to his story. Mr. Doherty said that he gave Brown a hard deal and did everything in his power to break him down, but could not get any information.

He pressed Brown on the point of why he was so sure he could make Bill Carr or Tucker tell, and Brown, repeated his statement that he was certain these men were in it, as on one occasion when he and Carr were coming from Lincoln, Carr said that it was no use in talking, something would have to be done, and they would have to kill off some of the men who were fighting them so hard. Brown said he knew Carr was in this last deal and he felt confident he would be able to get the whole story from this man, if he had an opportunity to see him.

Mr. Doherty is of the opinion now that Brown is in earnest and that he will get the necessary information provided he is let go out now on bond; in any case he cannot be held much longer in jail and will have to be allowed bond; so if he must be let out it will be best to stand in with him, and Mr. Doherty was in favor of letting him go at once. Brown had sent for Bursum last night at 11 p.m. and Mr. Doherty did not know the result of that conversation.

I then left Mr. Doherty and hunted up Bursum. He said he had failed completely in doing anything with Maxammameo Greago as that Greago had gone back on his first statement and it was evident that some of the gang had gotten hold of him and scared him so that he is afraid to testify; so for the present it must be dropped. Bursum believes he can force this from Greago yet, but must wait a little while.

Bursum then told me of his conversation with Brown last night. It came about in this way: Emerald James succeeded in getting a bond filled which he presented last evening and

Bursum refused it; then James began to rustle for another bond and got Tom Davenport and several others to help him and they all showed that they were much worried over the refusal of the first bond; Brown knew of this and sent for Bursum, they had a long talk and this is the first time that Brown and Bursum have talked over the Fountain case. Brown told him the same story he has given all the time and used every argument to show that he wanted to get out and try and earn his own salvation by turning up this job; he also agreed to do it now for one-fourth of the reward and a clean bill of health for himself on the cow stealing cases.

Then they got up a plan by which Brown was to go to Carr's ranch and get Carr to steal a bunch of cattle and drive them to Brown's ranch. Brown was to notify Bursum and Bursum would be on hand and arrest Carr with the cattle also put Brown in at the same time; then Carr was to be confronted with the evidence against him on the conspiracy and Brown was to talk the whole thing over with Carr in jail and get him to make a full confession.

I did not like this plan at all and told Bursum I did not see how we could possibly go into such a scheme as it would give Brown all the power he wanted on his side of the fence. We would be sending him out to commit a crime and induce another to do so, which, when it became necessary to try Brown for the cases already standing against him for cow stealing, would be a strong lever in the hands of the defense and might result in the prosecution getting fooled and beaten all the way through.

Bursum had not thought of looking at the matter in this light, but saw at once where it would be a mistake, and also that in any deal we might make with Ed. Brown, it would be better to keep Mr. Doherty out of it, as he would have to prosecute Brown and the defense might make use of it.

I walked to the Courthouse with Bursum and found that James, Davenport, Selman, Brown's wife, and mother were all there and wanted to know why Bursum would not accept the bond. They were evidently determined to force matters so I told Bursum to stand them off, refuse the bond and give me a little time to get around and we would put up a plan that would look all right.

I then went to Ed. Brown's room and talked to him. I told him I was anxious to see him get out and help himself by turning up this murder and that I had all confidence in his ability to do so, but that it was impossible to get the sheriff to let him go. I represented that I had done everything I could to induce the sheriff to accept the bond and I had some hope of his doing so. I then went on and talked openly and plainly with Brown about his position and the utter uselessness of his trying to deny his share of the conspiracy to kill Fountain and McDonald two years ago, and that he would be a fool not to take advantage of the Governor's offer and clear himself as he could do so safely and also make some money.

Brown did not contradict me and seemed to be in earnest. He said all he wanted understood was, that if he did this, the moment he gave the information he wanted all the men who were connected with it arrested and kept in jail, as he did not want to be loose in the County if one of the gang was left out, for he certainly would be murdered. When I left him, it was with the understanding that I should try and get Bursum to accept a bond and let him go at once.

When I next found Bursum he was surrounded by Brown's friends who were trying to make him take the bond; I signaled to him not to do so and he refused them flat and got away. Brown's mother then took it to Mr. Chavez and had him take it before the Court then in session, but we got word to Judge Hamilton and he refused to allow the bond. I then saw Mr. Doherty and he gave it as his opinion that we could not hold this out much longer and had better compromise and let him go; but I thought it well to let Brown remain as long as we could on the anxious seat and have him understand that his bond could not be forced on Bursum or the Court.

At 4 p.m., Mr. Bursum and I went to Brown's room and talked to him and Bursum gave him a strong talk. Brown spoke of his scheme to get Carr to steal some cattle, and I told him that I would have nothing to do with it; I should not give him any such instructions or authority; he could do as he pleased and work any plan he wanted to but would have to do it on his own responsibility. Finally we turned him loose and Bursum accepted the bond, apparently upon my recommendation; this was in order to show Brown that the bond could not be forced.

The agreement as it now stands is that Brown is to come here on the 18th of May to stand trial for cow stealing and if on that day he can offer something material in the Fountain case such as the location of bodies or some evidence which will convict any or all of the parties concerned; then his case will be continued for another term and he will be given a chance to assist in the work of getting the rest of the evidence in the Fountain murder; meanwhile, he is to report to me at San Marcial or the Sheriff's office by wire as soon as he has had a chance to get over to Dona Ana County and back.

Sheriff Bursum goes to Santa Fe to-night with a prisoner to the pen and will report to Governor Thornton in the morning and send me by wire the Governor's instructions or what point he wishes me to go to from here. I watched Brown closely when he got out and I am afraid he is going to try and defeat the whole case, but there was nothing else for it. He managed to miss the train and did not go to San Marcial this evening.

I saw him about 11 p.m. and he began to talk as if he would not get back here by the 18th, he said he had told Mr. Doherty that he would be among those fellows by the 21st and expected then to get the information. I said, "Brown you will come in here by the 18th and have that information or I will bring you in here; you must stick to your agreement or take your medicine." He just gave me the laugh and said, "Oh, it makes no difference about a few days and Mr. Doherty will say nothing it I don't come till the end of the month."

He is going to try and do something to avoid coming in and try to get his case put off without giving up any information, but I shall see Mr. Doherty and explain matters so that he will be prepared to thwart Brown's plans. I loafed around the saloons and watched Brown and James till evening. They had a good many private conversations together, and James came to me in a friendly way and tried to get me to talk about the Fountain case, but I did not enlighten him much. It would be a good plan to have Brown's movements watched when he goes east of the San Andreas Mts., but this can only be done in a general way.

Yours respectfully,
"S"

Sunday, May 10, 1896.
To-day in Socorro, -

I went to the depot this morning and saw Ed Brown leave. He seems to be quite confident that his case will never come for trial and that he will have no difficulty in getting some valuable information about the Fountain murder; but the way the fellow talks makes me think he is going to try and put up some smooth story and try to get his own cases put off for another term without giving any definite information on the Fountain matter. I talked with Mr. Doherty about it and he said he thought that Brown would either turn the bodies up and do as he agreed to or that we should never see him again; but he admits that Brown would surely have gotten out of jail and we could not do any better than let him go and stand in with him.

About 2 p.m. I received a telegram from Sheriff Bursum in Santa Fe to wait his return, so I spent the evening in Socorro talking with Mr. Doherty about this case.

Yours respectfully,
"S"

Monday, May 11, 1896

To-day in Socorro:-

    This morning Sheriff Bursum came home from Santa Fe and told me that Gov. Thornton would write to me in a day or two and send instructions, but meanwhile the Governor wished me to see Arcadio Saiz [Saez] and get a statement from him. Bursum know this man Saiz and on the way from Santa Fe he made inquiries as to his whereabouts and learned that he had left San Jose and gone to a ranch about 30 miles from Socorro. The only way to reach him would be to take a team and drive out there, and then it was not certain that the man would be at home.

    I called on Librado C. de Baca and asked him what Arcadio Saiz had told him; Librado said that he learned from Saiz that the latter had met Barnadillo Gomez and his brother Pablo two days after Col. Fountain's murder riding into Tularosa, both men were heavily armed and seemed anxious to avoid being seen. Saiz claimed that one of the Gomez brothers is considered a hard case and Col. Fountain had succeeded in getting indictments against him.

    I wanted to get Sheriff Bursum to go with me and find this man Saiz, but he could not spare the time, he had to go to Santa Fe with a prisoner to the penitentiary. I found that the trip was so uncertain that I concluded to make a trade with Bursum and have him go and find Saiz tomorrow and I would take his prisoner up to the pen. Bursum had to serve some papers at a ranch close to where Saiz lives and he would take his team and if possible bring the man in.

    I thought this would be the best arrangement, so at 5 p.m. I left Socorro for Santa Fe with a prisoner for the pen.

Yours respectfully,
"S"

Tuesday, May 12, 1896

To-day in Santa Fe,-

    I called on Governor Thornton and he told me he had written to Supt. McParland in Denver to recall me for the time being as he did not consider it advisable for me to go to Las Cruces now, but as soon as Ed. Brown came in for trial he wanted me to return and work at Socorro.

I remained in Santa Fe all day leaving at 10 p.m. for Socorro.

Yours respectfully,
"S"

Wednesday, May 13, 1896.

I arrived in Socorro at 5:30 a.m. and after breakfast saw Bursum; he informed me that he had failed to find Arcadio Saiz but had located where he was and had sent him a message; he expected him to come into Socorro to-day. I waited all day but Saiz did not come, and we heard nothing from him, however, I made arrangements with Bursum to take a statement from Saiz. Mr. Doherty said he would put it in writing.

At 5:15 p.m. I left Socorro for Denver and was on the road all night.

Yours respectfully,
"S"

Thursday, May 14, 1896.

To-day enroute,-

I was enroute all day Socorro to Denver, arriving in Denver at 10:15 p.m. and discontinued.

Yours respectfully,
"S"

[End of Reports]

Chapter 6 | The Trial

As the Reports document, Garrett limited his cooperation with the Pinkerton Operatives to a few laconic conferences. About one of these, Operative Fraser wrote:

"[I] called on Mr. Garrett at his room and had another talk with him; he is a man who says very little, so anything I learn from him is through questions" (page 68).

This partly was because Garrett was by nature taciturn. But it was mostly because Garrett had no interest in Fraser solving the crime. Garrett wanted – and intended – to do it himself.

Garrett's investigation led him to believe that Oliver Lee, James Gililland, and George McNew were the three men who had abducted and killed Colonel Fountain and Henry. He believed that William Carr ("Goodeye") was one of the men who had followed the Fountains from the Lincoln County Courthouse.

Because of the influence of Albert Fall, Garrett knew that he could not get a Dona Ana County grand jury to indict these men, as they were all clients (and friends) of Fall. So he used an alternate route to obtain arrests -- he sought bench warrants. Bench warrants could be obtained by presenting the court with affidavits certifying that, he, as county sheriff, had sufficient evidence against the men named in the affidavits to arrest them.

On April 4, 1898, he filed the following affidavit with the Dona Ana County court:

"Patrick F. Garrett of lawful age being first duly sworn by the undersigned authority, upon his oath deposes and says, that he knows persons and can have them before the court, who identified the tracks of Oliver M. Lee, William McNew and James Gilliland [Gililland] at the first camp where they stopped with Colonel Albert J. Fountain and his little son, Henry Fountain, after the said Lee, McNew and Gililland had captured Colonel Fountain and his little son."

"He can also bring before the court a witness who saw Lee, McNew and Gilliland early on Sunday morning, February 2, 1896, being the very next morning following the supposed murder of Colonel Fountain and his son Henry. This witness will testify that he was at Oliver Lee's ranch at the time that Lee, McNew and Gilland arrived there and that both of the men and horses were in a very tired and worn out condition."

"He will also have witnesses before the court who will show that William Carr shadowed Colonel Fountain all the way from the town of Lincoln to the town of La Luz; that Colonel Fountain and his son Henry remained at La Luz all night Friday night the last day of January A.D. 1896, and Carr passed La Luz in the evening on the same day going in the direction of Oliver Lee's ranch. He will also have other evidence before the court going to substantiate the fact that Oliver M. Lee, William McNew and James Gilliland are the parties who

murdered Colonel Albert J. Fountain and his son, Henry Fountain." – Signed P. F. Garrett [1]

Garrett submitted additional affidavits along with his, the most substantial of which was by Colonel Fountain's son Albert. See Appendix A for a copy of that affidavit.

Garrett timed his bench warrants so that they were issued when he knew that the four men he wanted to arrest were in Las Cruces. Still, the word of the warrants leaked to Oliver Lee and James Gililland, and they fled before Garrett could act. Not so William McNew and William Carr, who were arrested.[2]

Six days after their arrest, McNew and Carr had a preliminary examination to determine if there was sufficient evidence to hold them. The court ruled there was, for McNew, but not for Carr. Carr was released and never again faced legal jeopardy for the Fountain murders. The court ruled that McNew was to be held until trial without bond.[3]

Lee vowed he would never be arrested by Garrett, claiming he would be murdered in cold-blood if Garrett ever got him into custody.[4] The story of the serpentine, 1.074-day, cat-and-mouse game between Lee and Garrett until Lee surrendered is given in *"Killing Pat Garrett, The Wild West's Most Famous Lawman – Murder Or Self-Defense?"* It will not be repeated here.

The Fountain Murder Trial began May 25, 1899, in Hillsboro, New Mexico, the county seat at the time of Sierra County, on a change in venue from Dona Ana County. The defendants were Lee and Gililland. The charge was murder in the first degree of Colonel Fountain and Henry.[5]

Drawing of Hillsboro at the time of the Fountain Murder Trial. Courtesy *El Paso Herald*, June 17, 1899.

The prosecution team consisted of Richmond P. Barnes, district attorney for Grant and Sierra Counties, William B. Childers, U. S. District Attorney for New Mexico, and Thomas B. Catron. The defense team consisted of Albert Fall, Harry M. Daugherty, and Harvey B. Ferguson.[6]

On opening, the prosecution surprised the court and the public by requesting that the count for the murder Colonel Fountain be dropped. The prosecution only wanted to proceed against Lee and Gililland for murdering Henry Fountain. They also announced that they wished to drop the murder charge against McNew, who was ordered released from jail.[7]

The reasoning for the decision to drop the charge for murdering Colonel Fountain apparently was that the prosecution felt the jury would be more sympathetic to the killing of a child, and also, they could prosecute Lee and Gililland for the killing of Colonel Fountain later if the result of this trial went against them.

The day-by-day events of the trial are given in great detail in *"Killing Pat Garrett."* They will not be repeated here.

The prosecution provided convincing evidence that Colonel Fountain had been killed. But they could provide no direct evidence that Henry had been killed, only that he had been abducted.

The primary evidence provided against Lee and Gililland was the testimony of John "Jack" W. Maxwell. Maxwell said he had visited Oliver Lee's ranch on February 1, 1896, the day the Fountains disappeared. He said Lee was not there. He said he spent the night at the ranch. He said Lee, McNew, Gililland, and a hired hand rode up to the ranch the next day, on fresh horses. He said he later saw, in a pasture about a mile from the ranch house, *"used-hard"* horses, suggesting the men had switched horses before appearing at the ranch house.[8]

This testimony was what Garrett had relied on when he had signed the affidavit to obtain bench warrants for Lee, Gililland, and McNew.

Prior to filing that affidavit, Garrett had signed the following contract with Maxwell:

"Tularosa, N. M., March 26, 1896"

"This is to certify that we, the undersigned, agree to pay John Maxwell two thousand dollars ($2000) in case he give us information that will lead to the arrest and conviction of murderers of Col. A. J. Fountain and son, the said $2000 to be due as soon as the conviction is had."

"P. F. Garrett and C. C. Perry" [9]

This contract was introduced by the defense, which also introduced evidence that Maxwell had told other versions of what he had seen that day.

The defendant's defense was an alibi. Oliver Lee's mother and several other witnesses testified that Lee and Gililland were at Lee's ranch the day the Fountains disappeared.[10]

The evidentiary portion of the trial, including the judge's instructions to the jury, ended at 11:20 pm, June 13, 1899. The court recessed until the following morning.[11]

Fall waited until the lawyers, jurors, and spectators had returned to their lodgings, then he went to the judge's quarters and insisted on his client's right that the jury begin its deliberations immediately. Bizarrely, the judge agreed. (It is unclear if there was such a "right.") [12]

The jury was reassembled – and returned from deliberation in just eight minutes with a verdict:

> *"After they were in the court room, it was found that most of the attorneys were absent and the court took an informal recess until they could be sent for."*
>
> *"At exactly one minute before midnight, Foreman Bentley handed the verdict to the clerk and it was read...."*
>
> *"'We find the defendants, Oliver Lee and James Gililland, not guilty.'"*
>
> *"Immediately the people in the court room rose in mass, cheered and clapped and stamped...."* [13]

Based on the trial details available today, the prosecution did not meet the standard of proof beyond a reasonable doubt. The prosecution made a mistake in trying the defendants for Henry's murder rather than Colonel Fountain's, as the blood evidence did not prove Henry was dead. And the jury deemed Maxwell's evidence not credible, because he appeared to have been offered $2,000 to lie.

No one was ever tried for the murder of Colonel Fountain.

Note: For a day-by-day description of the trial, see *"Killing Pat Garrett, The Wild West's Most Famous Lawman - Murder Or Self-Defense?"*

The "Coffin Notice"

The "coffin notice" was not introduced in the trial. Because it was not introduced in the trial, many historians have doubted that it ever existed.

Mrs. Katherine Stoes, in her notes of her investigation of the Fountain case, writes:

> *"In the buckboard was found and secreted a crudely written note. Albert Fountain [the Colonel's son) knew nothing of this until it was handed to him in the court room at the trial. It read 'If you drop this, Fountain, we will be your friends. If you go on with it you will never reach home alive.'"* [14]

That the "coffin notice" was only discovered during the Oliver Lee/James Gililland trial, 1,238 days after the abduction, too late to be introduced into the trial, is confirmed by oral history remembered within the Fountain family.[15]

The "coffin note" proves that Colonel Fountain knew exactly how serious the threat to his life was. He refused utterly to give in to the threat.

That Colonel Fountain hid the "coffin notice" somewhere in the buggy – and hid it extremely well – indicates he wanted to make certain that if he was murdered, his killers would not get away with his killing.

We know now why the buggy was so thoroughly ransacked. The killers were looking for the "coffin notice!"

Would the "coffin notice" have changed the outcome of the trial? Maybe not, but it would have removed any doubt that there was a conspiracy to kill Colonel Fountain and Henry. And evidence of a conspiracy would have added weight to Maxwell's testimony.

Appendix A | Albert J. Fountain Affidavit

"Albert J. Fountain, of lawful age and being duly sworn, on his oath deposes and says: That he is the son of the late Albert J. Fountain, who is known by the title of Colonel Fountain, that his father lived in the town of Las Cruces several years prior to his death; that on the second day of February in the year of our Lord one thousand eight hundred and ninety six, he and his mother were expecting his father to return from Lincoln, that his mother had received a telegram that he would return at ten o'clock that day."

"He did not return and late in the afternoon, one Satuino [Saturnino] Barela, who was carrier of the mail between Las Cruces and Luna's Wells, came to affiant's house and related to him the circumstances which are set forth in the affidavit of Satuino Barela hereto attached."

"Affiant immediately proceeded to Mesilla and started from that place with Antonio Garcia, Catirino Ballegos, Casimiera Chacon and Pedro Chopa. They started from Mesilla about seven-thirty P.M. on the night of the said day for the point where it was reported my father had last been seen. We travelled all night by moonlight (the four of us) and got to Luna's Well by sunrise. The others stayed behind with the expectation that if they found the buggy, to promptly notify us. My purpose in going to Luna's Wells was to find the tracks of the buggy. I asked the man, Antonio Rey, if he had seen my father the day before. He said yes, he passed here about ten o'clock with his little boy, they stopped in front of the house for a minute and then went on. He was travelling very fast."

"The boy at the ranch came out after the Colonel had passed, and told me that he had seen three men at the well. Before the Colonel stopped here that they were going across the country about a half mile from the house. One of them was off from the road going west, another one also out from the road a good distance from the house, also came this way. The boy said he was suspicious and tried to follow them, but they would not let him get close to them, and he could not recognize them. One was mounted on a gray and one on a black."

"Said Rey put me on the track of my father's buckboard and showed me the tracks of the horse, on the right side of the buckboard which my father was leading. Then we followed the tracks, two on each side of the road, until we come to the place where my father met the mail driver, and came to the Chalk Hill. Then I went to the right side of the Chalk Hill where there was a bush, a kind of an evergreen, high enough to cover a man sitting down by this bush opposite to the direction my father was coming. There was a track of a man made by a fine cowboy boot heel, it appeared as if he had been sitting there quite a while, and as if to place his feet first to the Chalk Hill, and hold up my father."

"From there we followed the tracks and found them just like the mail carrier had described them. We followed carefully along about half way from the pont where the buckboard turned out to the Jarillas. The other men met us there and informed me that they had found the buckboard. They had with them a couple of shawls found on it, and also my father's belt full of cartridges. They said there was not trace of my father or brother. We watered our horses and went ot the buckboard, where I made a careful *examination of the situation. I discovered that the neckyoke straps were gone and one bridle and all three horses."*

"I sent my brother to Las Cruces and I and four men followed the tracks of three men around the buckboard. The harness was there. We slept there that night and in the morning we got on the trail and found they were traveling on a line behind the other. They took right straight for the Jarillas, but about four miles from the buckboard they stopped and took lunch and I made a careful examination of the tracks. They tracks of one man were made by a cowboy boot with a pointed toe and high heel, and the tracks of the two others were made with fine cowboy boots with box toes, one was a smaller foot than the others."

"All of my father's beding was gone from the buckboard. Also my brother's overcoat. From there we followed the same trail toward the Jarillas. About one mile from the camp they turned loose my father's white horse. I satisfied myself of this and retook the trail of the rest of the horses. After awhile I found the track of one of the horses leaving the other."

"I sent two men to follow three tracks and I followed the others. It was made by the buggy horse with shoes on. These men who followeed it were Antonio Garcia and Pedro Chopa, they reported that they followed it to the second pass south from the north end of the Jarillas, and noticed two more tracks of horses there. They came back and went close to the Jarilla mountains, following the tracks of three horses. One of them being made by my father's mare. Major Llewellyn and party had been behind us the night before, and I recognized the facts stated in the affidavits made by him and Thomas Branigan as being true." – Signed Albert J. Fountain.

For the Barela affidavit, see page 46.

Notes

1 – Introduction

1. *Rio Grande Republican*, March 31, 1894.

2. *Rio Grande Republican*, July 7, 1894.

3. *Rio Grande Republican*, July 28, 1894.

4. *Carlsbad Current Argus*. March 27, 1895.

5. *SF New Mexican*, November 26, 1894.

6. *Carlsbad Current Argus*, March 27, 1895.

7. This is the same Lincoln County Courthouse that Billy the Kid had escaped from.

8. Cree, Letter from Colonel Albert J. Fountain, Oct. 3, 1895. Mary Daniels Taylor Papers, Archives and Special Collections, NMSU.

9. Lincoln County Court Records, William A. Keleher Papers, MSS 742 BC, Center for Southwest Research, UNM. Brand defacing was charged when it could not be proved that an animal was stolen, but it could be proved that its brand had been changed.

10. A. M. Gibson, The Life and Death of Colonel Albert Jennings Fountain (Univ. of Oklahoma Press, 1965), p 227.

11. C. L. Sonnichsen, Tularosa, Last of the Frontier West (Devin-Adair Co., 1980), p 117.

12. *El Paso Times*, Apr. 16, 1898.

13. *El Paso Herald*, June 2, 1899.

14. Pinkerton Report, March 5, 1896.

15. *El Paso Times*, Apr. 12, 1898; *San Francisco Chronicle*, May 31, 1899; El Paso Herald, June 1, 1899.

16. *El Paso Times*, Apr. 12, 1898.

17. *El Paso Herald*, June 2, 1899; *El Paso Herald*, May 31, 1899.

18. *El Paso Times*, Apr. 12, 1898.

19. *El Paso Herald*, June 1, 1899.

20. *El Paso Herald*, June 1, 1899.

21. *El Paso Herald*, June 1, 1899.

22. *El Paso Herald*, June 1, 1899.

23 Katherine D. Stoes, "Major A. J. Fountain," Katherine D. Stoes Papers, Archives and Special Collections, NMSU.

24. *El Paso Herald*, June 2, 1899.

25. *El Paso Herald*, May 31, 1899.

26. *El Paso Herald*, May 31, 1899.

27. *El Paso Herald*, May 31, 1899.

28 *El Paso Herald*, June 5, 1899.

29. *El Paso Herald*, June 6, 1899.

30. *El Paso Herald*, June 5, 1899.

31. *El Paso Herald*, May 31, 1899.

32. *El Paso Herald*, June 2, 1899.

33. *San Antonio Daily Light*, Feb. 8, 1896; *The Eagle* (Bryan, TX), Feb. 11, 1896; *Brownsville Herald*, Feb. 22, 1896.

34. David G. Thomas, Killing Pat Garrett, The Wild West's Most Famous Lawman – Murder Or Self-Defense? (Doc45 Publications, 2019).

35. John Conklin Fraser, Letter to New Mexico Governor William T. Thornton, Feb. 27, 1896. Pinkerton Reports Regarding Disappearance of Colonel Albert J. Fountain, Arrell Gibson Collection, MSSU Archives and Special Collections.

36. *Las Vegas Daily Optic*, May 16, 1896; Las Vegas Daily Optic, May 29, 1896.

37 Pinkerton Reports, April 15, 1896.

38. Pinkerton's National Detective Agency records, 1853-1999, Library of Congress Manuscript Division, https://lccn.loc.gov/mm75036301.

39. C. L. Sonnichsen, Tularosa, Last of the Frontier West (The Devin-Adair Company, 1972), p 144.

40. A. M. Gibson, Letter to C. L. Sonnichsen, Dec. 7, 1960, Arrell Gibson Collection, MSSU Archives and Special Collections.

41. C. L. Sonnichsen, Letter to A. M. Gibson, Dec. 10, 1960, Arrell Gibson Collection, MSSU Archives and Special Collections.

42. A. M. Gibson, Letter to C. L. Sonnichsen, Oct. 16, 1962, Arrell Gibson Collection, MSSU Archives and Special Collections.

43. Pinkerton Reports, Katherine D. Stoes Papers, Archives and Special Collections, NMSU.

44. Gordon R. Owen, The Two Alberts, (Yucca Tree Press, 1996) p 270; Rio Grande Republic, December 15, 1894.

45. *Rio Grande Republic*, Jan. 12, 1895; Rio Grande Republic, Feb. 2, 1895.

46. *Independent Democrat*, Mar. 25, 1896.

47. *Independent Democrat*, Apr. 1, 1896.

48. *Independent Democrat*, Mar. 25, 1896.

49. *Independent Democrat*, Mar. 25, 1896.

50. *Rio Grande Republican*, Aug. 14, 1896; Independent Democrat, Aug. 12, 1896.

51. Trial Records, Case 94-104, Chavez County Records, NM State Records Center and Archives.

52. *Albuquerque Citizen*, Jun. 22, 1901

53. *Albuquerque Citizen*, Jun. 33, 1901

54. *Albuquerque Citizen*, Jun. 33, 1901

55. *Albuquerque Citizen*, Jun. 33, 1901

6 – The Trial

1. Garrett Affidavit to Court for Warrant, William A. Keleher Papers, MSS 742 BC, Center for Southwest Research, UNM.

2. *El Paso Herald*, Apr. 4, 1898.

3. *Albuquerque Citizen*, Apr. 18, 1898.

4. *El Paso Times*, Aug. 2, 1898.

5. *SF Daily New Mexican*, Mar. 13, 1899; *SF New Mexican*, Mar. 13, 1899.

6. *El Paso Times*, May 26, 1899.

7. *El Paso Herald*, May 27, 1899.

8. *El Paso Herald*, June 2, 1899.

9. *El Paso Herald*, June 3, 1899. Charles C. Perry was sheriff of Roswell, New Mexico.

10. *The Call*, June 9, 1899.

11. *El Paso Herald*, June 16, 1899.

12. *El Paso Herald*, June 16, 1899.

13. *El Paso Herald*, June 16, 1899.

14, Katherine D. Stoes, "Major A. J. Fountain," Katherine D. Stoes Papers, Archives and Special Collections, NMSU.

15. Keith Bird, Interview with David G. Thomas, Feb. 22, 2020.

Index

A

Allen, Charlie 120
Altman, Perry 63
Alvarado, Santos 24, 26, 47, 92-93, 101-102
Arnold, 148
Ascarate, Sheriff Guadalupe 17, 21, 27, 58, 62, 64-65

B

Baca, Elfego 21, 23, 68, 71, 73-74, 105-106, 113, 123-125, 127, 146, 155
Baca, Librado C. de 21, 68, 71, 73-74, 105, 113, 170
Baca, Mrs. Luz 124
Baca, Nado 155
Bailey, Judge William D. 98
Baird, James A. 21, 45, 49-50, 52, 61-62, 65, 92
Baird, Tom 45
Ballegos, Catirino 177
Banner, E. E. 21, 53-54, 71-72, 93-94, 97, 100
Bantz, Judge Gideon D. 17, 21, 23, 25, 27, 39, 55, 62, 64, 71, 75, 77, 84-85
Barber, George B. 21
Barber, Susan Ellen McSween 21, 26, 58, 62, 75-76
Barela, Saturnino 9, 21, 23, 31, 41-42, 46, 48-49, 56, 92, 177-178
Barnes, Richmond P. 175
Barunda, Mrs. 100
Bascom, Frederick H. 21, 44, 80
Baze, D. F. 100-101
Bentley, Foreman 176
Bergmann, Colonel Edward H. 21, 118-120, 122, 160-161, 166
Bernal, Juan 1
Best, Jack 128, 130, 149-150
Bignell, H. 153-154
Bignell, Mrs. H. 153
Billy the Kid, 11, 21, 23, 25
Blazer, Doctor Joseph F. 7, 21, 41
Blevin, Albert 21, 61, 63, 67
Blood, F. O. 132, 136, 160
Bonham, H. 137, 146
Boxwell, 22, 30, 112, 114, 116
Brady, 143, 151
Branigan, Thomas 22, 45-46, 50, 178
Brock, James A. 65
Brown, Dick 22, 34, 36-37, 73-74, 123-124, 128, 131-132, 139-149, 151, 155-156, 158-159, 160, 161-169
Brown, Eduard W. 1, 19, 22-23, 27, 35, 62, 67-68, 71, 73, 76, 105-106, 110-111, 117, 120, 126, 129, 133-135, 150, 152, 156, 160, 169-170
Brown, Henry 1
Brown, Mrs. 167
Broyles, J. M. 132
Bruton, Charles 35-36, 86
Bursum, H. O. 22, 123, 124, 126-130, 146-148, 154-156, 158, 164-171
Butler, Harry 153

C

Campfield, James 126
Carr Bros, 19, 35
Carr, William Bill "Goodeye" 22, 36, 66, 76, 82, 101, 115, 131, 139-140, 157, 164, 166-168, 173-174
Carter, George 126
Carter, John 144-145
Carter, Tom 126
Carver, 152
Casey, Deputy Sheriff 67
Catron, Thomas B. 175
Chacon, Casimiera 177
Chatfield, Frank 22, 34, 60, 62, 66, 98, 101
Chaves, 124
Chavez, E. V. 19, 23, 155-156, 158, 168
Chavez, Luce 145
Cherokee Bill, 51, 121-122
Childers, William B. 175
Chopa, Pedro 177-178
Christy, Albert L. 20, 23, 33, 41-44, 51, 64, 67, 86
Clausen, 72
Coe, George 23, 93, 95
Coghlan, Patrick 160
Collins, Punch 38, 126
Cormack, 38-39
Cowan, Charlie 89, 91, 102, 105
Cowan, Dr. 91, 105
Cowan, James W. 89
Cowan, Lew W. 49, 89-91
Cowan, Mrs. Lew W. 50, 52, 66, 77, 89-90
Cox, Perry G. 79
Cox, William W. 23, 49-50, 52, 56, 77, 79, 88, 92, 103
Craig, George 1
Crane, Miss Nellie P. 76, 108, 117-119
Crawford, Harry 141, 144-145, 148, 163
Cree, James E. 23, 32, 35, 37, 43, 48
Crosson, Dr. Francis 23, 34
Cruickshank, Dr. Charles Glanville 23, 73, 130-133, 136, 138-139, 145-147, 150, 154, 160-161
Cunningham, 119, 155
Curran, P. H. 41, 43

D

Daugherty, Harry M. 175
Davenport, Tom 120, 136, 156, 167
Davis, Dan 82, 121-122
Day, Scott 104
DeMier, J. R. 152
Devlin, 79
Dieter, Adam J.98
Dodd, 38-39
Doherty, J. M. 123-126, 129, 147-148, 154-156, 158-159, 162, 165-166, 168-169, 171
Domingue, Benseslado 77
Dow, Les 85

E

Eddy, C. B. 83, 89, 93
Ellis, 23, 44-45, 51, 54, 56, 65
Elly, 137
Ely, 143-146, 149, 160, 163
Evans, Aquillo L. "Doc" 1, 23

F

Fajardo, 41-42, 46-48, 56
Fall, Albert B. 13, 15-17, 21, 23, 25, 39, 42-45, 49-50, 52, 54, 56, 61, 63, 65, 67, 69-71, 77-83, 84, 86-87, 89-91, 102, 105, 115-116, 148, 173, 175-176
Ferguson, Harvey B. 75, 80, 85, 175
Fitchett, Dan 23, 50, 53, 63
Fountain, Albert, 80, 174
Fountain, Colonel Albert J. 1, 4, 7-13, 15, 19-23, 25, 27, 31-32, 34-35, 40-43, 45-51, 54, 56, 58-60, 62, 64-66, 68, 70-75, 77-78, 80-81, 84, 86-87, 90, 92-93, 96-100, 102, 104, 110-111, 113, 116, 119-120, 122-123, 126-128, 131, 134, 138, 140-143, 147-148, 150-151, 156-157, 159, 162-163, 165, 168-170, 173-176-178,
Fountain, Henry J. 1, 3-4, 7, 9-13, 21-22, 25, 27, 46, 173, 176
Fountain, Jack, 23, 46, 81, 89
Fountain, Mariana (Contreras Pérez de Onate) 2, 7
Fountain, Tom 46
Fraser, John Conklin 117-11912-15, 17, 23, 29-30, 33-34, 41, 48, 57, 68-69, 109, 111-112, 114, 118, 125, 173
Freeman, Judge Andreius A. 23, 25, 123, 147-148, 155
Freudenthal, Julius 23, 46-49
Frey, J. J. 30, 111

G

Gallegos, Jose Angel 68, 73, 124-125, 127, 146
Garcia, Alexandro 105, 113, 124-125, 165
Garcia, Antonio 177-178

Garrett, Patrick Floyd Jarvis 11-13, 17, 19, 21-24, 27, 33, 43, 48, 50, 52-57, 59-68, 70-71, 73-75, 77, 79, 83, 85-86, 88, 93, 104, 106, 110-112, 114-116, 119, 148, 150, 173-175
Gibson, A. M. 15
Gililland, James R. "Jim" 6, 15, 21, 23, 32, 37, 50-51, 54-55, 61, 64, 76, 82, 85, 95, 100, 104, 122, 173-176
Gillam, 43
Gleason, Owen 126
Gomez, Barnadillo 71, 97, 99, 170
Goode, Walter 51, 121
Graham, Buck 127
Graham, Frank 23, 25, 86, 91
Gray, Bob 35-37
Greago, Garcia 25, 120, 126-127, 129, 147, 164
Griego, Maximiano 123-125, 146, 148, 155, 164-166
Guerra, Alvino 23, 25, 59-60, 67, 96, 104

H

Haftey, F. J. 132
Hall, 112, 118, 122, 160
Hamilton, Judge 147-148, 168
Hanna, S. J. 132-134, 149, 160, 163
Hardin, John Wesley 79
Hatton, 53
Hawkins, A. W. 57, 82
Henley, Charles 126
Herrera, Luis 25, 119, 150
Hightower, Sandy 126
Hill, Frank 25, 84, 86, 89, 91-92, 102, 105, 107, 151-153
Hill, Oscar 126
Hilton, C. F. 22
Holmes, 151
Holt, Herbert H. 20

J

James, Emerald 25, 134-140, 142-145, 149, 151, 155-156, 160, 163, 166-167, 169
Jimmy the Tough, 126
Johnson, Charles 54, 67, 96-97, 138
Johnson, John 96
Jones, Charles 86, 89, 91-92, 102

K

Kearney, Perry 98, 100
Kearney, Phil 101
Kellum, Bill 51
Kuns, F. A. 20

L

Langhly, 123
Latham, John 126
Lee, Mrs. 175
Lee, Oliver Milton 4-5, 7, 11, 15, 21, 23, 25, 32-34, 38, 41-42, 44-45, 51, 54-55, 59-63, 65, 67, 69-71, 76, 79-84, 87, 93-94, 96, 100, 105, 115-116, 121-122, 139-141, 152, 157, 173-176
Lenoir, L. W. 43
Llewellyn, Major William Henry H. 24-25, 32-33, 41, 43-44, 49-52, 55-56, 58-59, 61-67, 69-70, 73, 75, 77, 81, 83, 85-88, 93, 101, 103, 105, 110, 114, 150, 178
Llewellyn, Morgan 25, 50, 102
Lohman, Harry 130
Lohman, Oscar 17, 25, 85, 114, 130
Luna, Florencia 25, 66, 71

M

Martin, Robert 150, 152, 155
Martin, William E. 20-21
Maxwell, G. W. 77
Maxwell, John "Jack" W. 24-25, 27, 34, 58, 61, 63, 68, 76, 95, 115, 122, 175-176
McComb, Dallas 163
McCowan, Duncan 25
McCowan, Mrs. Duncan 25, 49, 78-79, 91, 103
McDonald, Mrs. W. C. 98
McDonald, W. C. 35, 120-121, 168
McDougal, 50, 53
McFie, Judge John Robert 20, 24-25, 44, 64, 82, 152-154
McKee, 128
McNew, William "Bill" 7, 19, 21, 25, 32-36, 42, 45, 54-55, 60-62, 64, 76, 82, 87, 94, 96, 115, 121, 139-140, 157, 164, 173-175
McParland, James 13, 25, 29-31, 33, 57, 69, 76, 108-110, 112, 114, 117, 170
McSween, Alexander A. 21, 58
Meadows, John P. 25, 58, 66, 93-94, 100-101
Meana, 124
Merritt, Bud 38
Mestos, Marcus 97, 99, 102
Miles, George W. 38-39
Miller, Aberan (Abram) 1
Miller, Ely E. "Slick" 1, 18-19, 21, 23, 34-35, 38, 62, 82, 86, 112, 115, 117-122, 147, 158, 160-162, 164-166
Montgomery, 146
Morgan, Joe 25, 28, 38, 42, 44-45, 53-54, 78-79, 83, 86-88, 92-95, 102-103, 126
Mothersill, Colonel Phillip 22, 25, 105, 107, 140-142, 144, 149-154, 163
Mothersill, Mrs. Phillip 150
Murphy, Lawrence 27
Myers, Charles 100

N

Newcomb, Simon B. 20, 24-25, 32-33, 59-60, 64, 66, 69
Nicolas, 66
Niles, H. P. 91

O

O'Donnell, Tom 140-145, 163
O'Neill, Charles 83, 89
Olive, 87

P

Palen, Major R. J. 58, 69
Parker, H. K. 93, 95-96, 104
Parker, Mrs. H. K. 95, 97
Parrett, Charles 138
Parrett, Mrs. Charles 138
Pedro Luna, 11, 27
Pellman, Frank W. 27, 56, 93-94, 104, 110-112
Pellman, Mrs. Frank W. 94
Perry, Charles C. 24-27, 52-53, 55, 61, 64, 66-67, 70, 75-76, 83, 85, 88, 103-104, 111-112, 115-116, 131, 150, 175
Porter, H. M. 127
Powder Bill, 36
Prieto, Juan 25, 126
Pérez, Maria de Jesus 3
Pérez, Tomas 3

R

Railston, Cole 151, 153
Reese, William C. 126
Rey, Antonio 27, 66, 71, 92-93, 97, 99, 101-102, 177
Rey, Mrs. Antonio 93, 101-102
Rey, Santos 102
Reymond, Numa 17, 23, 27, 58, 62, 64-65, 75, 84-85, 105, 114
Reynolds, 101
Richards, Fred 145
Richardson, 54
Rico, Santa Rosa 86
Riley, John H. 27, 39, 75, 85-86, 91, 97, 105-106, 110, 116, 121
Roberts, Andrew "Buckshot" 7, 21
Roberts, Walter 126
Rose, W. M., see Ely E. "Slick" Miller
Rubio, Isidro 23
Runnels, Randolph 143
Russ, Emmet 100-101
Russell, Baldy 27, 145

S

Saiz, Arcadio 170-171
Saunders, Jeff 97, 150
Sayers, William C. 13, 22, 30, 109, 112-113, 116-117
Scott, C. R. 93, 95-97
Scott, Green 27, 74, 105-106, 120, 124, 126-127, 159
Selman, 167
Serna, Pedro 86
Sherfield, 126
Shields, William P. "Billy" 7, 27, 41, 97-99
Shutz, Max 87
Skidmore, 50, 52, 66, 77
Smith, 27
Smith, Bud 59, 62
Smith, Geo. 127
Smith, H. C. 65
Smith, J. T. 76
Smith, James 22
Smith, Judge 63-64
Sonnichsen, C. L. 13, 15
Spence Bros, 35
Spence, Charles 35-37, 126, 157
Spence, Fred, 126
Springs, Bob 126
Steen, William. 132-133, 135-137, 146, 155
Stevens, Mrs. 70
Stoes, Henry 8, 15
Stoes, Katherine D. 8, 14-16, 176
Summerford, 151
Sutherland, David M. 4, 27, 41, 96, 100-101
Sykes, Bill 36

T

Tabor, 79, 92
Taylor, 27, 32, 48, 54
Taylor, Mrs. Eva 59-61, 67, 96, 104
Tell, Major 39
Tewkesbury, 86, 91
Tewkesbury, James 27
Thergood, Eugene 142-143, 145, 148, 151, 163
Thompson, John 65
Thornton, Governor William T. 11, 13-14, 17-19, 27, 29-35, 41-43, 48, 51, 57-59, 62-64, 68-69, 71, 73, 76, 84, 107, 109, 111-114, 117-119, 122-123, 129, 132, 141, 146-148, 157, 159-162, 164-166, 168, 170
Truitt, James 27
Tucker, Jack, 27
Tucker, Thomas "Tom" 27, 32, 3-37, 44-45, 51, 54, 76, 82, 86-87, 91, 94, 98, 107, 112, 115, 118-119, 121, 123, 139-140, 152-153, 157, 164, 166

V

Van Cleve, 57
Van Patten, Major Eugene 9, 27-28, 33, 50-51, 53-54, 56, 66

W

Waddingham, 150, 152
Wait, William 59
Walker, Donaldson 127-131, 133, 137-139, 142, 145, 149, 154
Walters, Russell 86, 91
Warren, Judge 63-64, 75
Westervelt, E. J. 150
Williams, Ben 28, 37-39, 44-45, 69, 97
Williams, Lee, 28
Wilson, Dick 38-39
Wilson, Wain 126
Wilton, Mrs. William 136, 138, 163
Wilton, William 136, 138

Y

Yost, Hiram 84, 86, 89, 90-92, 102, 105, 107, 110, 151
Yost, John 151
Young, 33, 43-44, 52, 63, 83, 86-87, 90-91

Doc45 Publications

La Posta – From the Founding of Mesilla, to Corn Exchange Hotel, to Billy the Kid Museum, to Famous Landmark, David G. Thomas, paperback, 118 pages, 59 photos, e-book available.

"For someone who grew up in the area of Mesilla, it's nice to have a well-researched book about the area – and the giant photographs don't hurt either.... And the thing I was most excited to see is a photo of the hotel registry where the name of "William Bonney" is scrawled on the page.... There is some debate as to whether or not Billy the Kid really signed the book, which the author goes into, but what would Billy the Kid history be without a little controversy?" –Billy the Kid Outlaw Gang Newsletter, Winter, 2013.

Giovanni Maria de Agostini, Wonder of The Century – The Astonishing World Traveler Who Was A Hermit, David G. Thomas, paperback, 208 pages, 59 photos, 19 maps, e-book available.

"David G. Thomas has finally pulled back the veil of obscurity that long shrouded one of the most enduring mysteries in New Mexico's long history to reveal the true story of the Hermit, Giovanni Maria de Agostini. ...Thomas has once again proven himself a master history detective. Of particular interest is the information about the Hermit's life in Brazil, which closely parallels his remarkable experience in New Mexico, and required extensive research in Portuguese sources. Thomas's efforts make it possible to understand this deeply religious man." – Rick Hendricks, New Mexico State Historian

Screen With A Voice - A History of Moving Pictures in Las Cruces, New Mexico, David G. Thomas, paperback, 194 pages, 102 photos, e-book available.

The first projected moving pictures were shown in Las Cruces 110 years ago. Who exhibited those movies? What movies were shown? Since projected moving pictures were invented in 1896, why did it take ten years for the first movie exhibition to reach Las Cruces? Who opened the first theater in town? Where was it located? These questions began the history of moving pictures in Las Cruces, and they are answered in this book. But so are the events and stories that follow.

There have been 21 movie theaters in Las Cruces – all but three or four are forgotten. They are unremembered no longer. And one, especially, the Airdome Theater which opened in 1914, deserves to be known by all movie historians – it was an automobile drive-in theater, the invention of the concept, two decades before movie history declares the drive-in was invented.

Billy the Kid's Grave – A History of the Wild West's Most Famous Death Marker, David G. Thomas, paperback, 154 pages, 65 photos.

"Quien es?"

The answer to this incautious question – "Who is it?" – was a bullet to the heart.

That bullet – fired by Lincoln County Sheriff Patrick F. Garrett from a .40-44 caliber single action Colt pistol – ended the life of Billy the Kid, real name William Henry McCarty.

But death – ordinarily so final – only fueled the public's fascination with Billy the Kid. What events led to Billy's killing? Was it inevitable? Was a woman involved? If so, who was she? Why has Billy's gravestone become the most famous – and most visited – Western death marker? Is Billy really buried in his grave? Is the grave in the right location?

These questions – and many others – are answered in this book.

Killing Pat Garrett, The Wild West's Most Famous Lawman - Murder or Self-Defense?

Pat Garrett, the Wild West's most famous lawman – the man who killed Billy the Kid – was himself killed on leap day, February 29, 1908, on a barren stretch of road between his Home Ranch and Las Cruces, New Mexico.

> Who killed him?
> Was it murder?
> Was it self-defense?

No biographer of Garrett has been able to answer these questions. All have expressed opinions. None have presented evidence that would stand up in a court of law. Here, for the first time, drawing on newly discovered information, is the definitive answer to the Wild West's most famous unsolved killing.

Supplementing the text are 102 images, including six of Garrett and his family which have never been published before. It has been 50 years since a new photo of Garrett was published, and no photos of his children have ever been published.

Garrett's life has been extensively researched. Yet, the author was able to uncover an enormous amount of new information. He had access to over 80 letters that Garrett wrote to his wife. He discovered a multitude of new documents and details concerning Garrett's killing, the events surrounding it, and the personal life of the man who was placed on trial for killing Garrett.

- The true actions of "Deacon Jim" Miller, a professional killer, who was in Las Cruces the day Garrett was killed.
- The place on the now abandoned old road to Las Cruces where Garrett was killed.
- The coroner's jury report on Garrett's death, lost for over 100 years.
- Garrett's original burial location.
- The sworn courtroom testimony of the only witness to Garrett's killing.
- The policeman who provided the decisive evidence in the trial of the man accused of murdering Garrett.
- The location of Garrett's Rock House and Home Ranches.
- New family details: Garrett had a four-month-old daughter the day he killed Billy the Kid. She died tragically at 15. Another daughter was blinded by a well-intended eye treatment; a son was paralyzed by childhood polio; and Pat Garrett, Jr., named after his father, lost his right leg to amputation at age 12.

Garrett's life was a remarkable adventure. He met two United States presidents: President William McKinley, Jr. and President Theodore Roosevelt. President Roosevelt he met five times, three times in the White House. He brought the law to hardened gunmen. He oversaw hangings. His national fame was so extensive the day he died that newspapers from the East to the West Coast only had to write "Pat Garrett" for readers to know to whom they were referring.

2020 Will Rogers Medallion Award Finalist for Excellence in Western Media
2020 Independent Press Award Distinguished Favorite, Historical Biography
2019 Best Book Awards Finalist, United States History
2019 Best Indie Book Notable 100 Award Winner.

The Trial of Billy the Kid

This book is about Billy the Kid's trial for murder, and the events leading to that trial. The result of Billy's trial sealed his fate. And yet Billy's trial is the least written about, and until this book, the least known event of Billy's adult life.

Prior biographies have provided extensive — and fascinating — details on Billy's life, but they supply only a few paragraphs on Billy's trial. Just the bare facts: time, place, names, result.

Billy's trial the most important event in Billy's life. You may respond that his death is more important — it is in anyone's life! That is true, in an existential sense, but the events that lead to one's death at a particular place and time, the cause of one's death, override the importance of one's actual death. Those events are determinative. Without those events, one does not die then and there. If Billy had escaped death on July 14, 1881, and went on to live out more of his life, that escape and not his trial would probably be the most important event of Billy's life.

The information presented here has been unknown until now. This book makes it possible to answer these previously unanswerable questions:

- What were the governing Territorial laws?
- What were the charges against Billy?
- Was there a trial transcript and what happened to it?
- What kind of defense did Billy present?
- Did Billy testify in his own defense?
- Did Billy have witnesses standing for him?
- Who testified against him for the prosecution?
- What was the jury like?
- What action by the trial judge virtually guaranteed his conviction?
- What legal grounds did he have to appeal his verdict?
- Was the trial fair?

Supplementing the text are 132 photos, including many photos never published before.

www.ingramcontent.com/pod-product-compliance
Lightning Source LLC
Chambersburg PA
CBHW051945290426
44110CB00015B/2113